5/08

FROM
THE PRIMARIES
TO THE POLLS

FROM
THE PRIMARIES
TO THE POLLS

How to Repair America's Broken Presidential Nomination Process

THOMAS GANGALE

PRAEGER

Westport, Connecticut
London

Library of Congress Cataloging-in-Publication Data

Gangale, Thomas.
From the primaries to the polls : how to repair America's broken presidential nomination
process / Thomas Gangale.
    p. cm.
    Includes bibliographical references and index.
    ISBN 978–0–313–34835–8 (alk. paper)
    1. Primaries—United States.   2. Presidents—United States—Nomination.
[1. Political conventions.]   I. Title.
  JK522.G36   2008
   324.273'15–dc22   2007036436

British Library Cataloguing in Publication Data is available.

Library of Congress Catalog Card Number: 2007036436
ISBN: 978–0–313–34835–8

First published in 2008

Praeger Publishers, 88 Post Road West, Westport, CT 06881
An imprint of Greenwood Publishing Group, Inc.
www.praeger.com

Printed in the United States of America

The paper used in this book complies with the
Permanent Paper Standard issued by the National
Information Standards Organization (Z39.48–1984).

10 9 8 7 6 5 4 3 2 1

CONTENTS

FIGURES AND TABLES

FIGURES

TABLES

PREFACE

With luck, the 2012 presidential nomination races in the Democratic and Republican parties will be unlike any in recent history. Iowa and New Hampshire will not have the disproportional influence that they have had traditionally; rather that influence will be transferred to other low-population states where a low-budget campaign can engage in door-to-door, retail politicking without being swamped by advertising blitzes in mass media markets, it can get its message out to the voters, score some early wins, and attract more grassroots support and funding as the campaign moves on to more and larger states. With the power of early and massive campaign funding hobbled in small venues, shoestring campaigns will have a chance to grow strong enough to take on the Big Money in later states. The voters in these later primaries will have had several months to see and hear the candidates via the national media, and to decide. And, because so many of the states will hold their caucuses and primaries late in the season, they will have a real decision to make. The nominations in one or both major parties may not be locked up until the end of June. Indeed, the summer of 2012 may witness an event not seen in more than half a century: a nomination battle at a national convention.

In a way, it will be a return to a brief moment in the past, to the early years of the modern presidential primary era. In 1976, the first year in which both major political parties substantially implemented the McGovern-Fraser reforms, an obscure, former Georgia governor came out of nowhere with very little money, and at the end of the year he was the president-elect. It was also the year that a former California governor challenged the sitting president and waged a battle all the way to that summer's national convention. These great political dramas played out across a four-month period, during which every registered Democrat and Republican had an opportunity to cast a meaningful vote in a race that had no foregone conclusion. This was the way the modern presidential nomination process was meant to work.

Unfortunately, reform often brings unintended consequences. The reforms recommended by the Democratic Party's 1969–1972 McGovern-Fraser Commission were intended to take the nomination process out of the smoke-filled rooms of political bosses and give it to the voters at the ballot box. Yet, within a decade, the effective decision-making mechanism began to be taken out of the hands of the voters and to be placed into the hands of the check-writers, not because of a deliberate conspiracy, but due to a "tragedy of the commons" phenomenon; states are acting in their individual self-interest to the ruin of all. What we have now is the facade of a democratic process, in which the candidate who raises the most money before the first vote is cast is anointed by the media as the frontrunner, in which the earliest caucuses and primaries inevitably fulfill this prophesy, and in which as much as 80 percent of the American electorate is excluded from even the charade of participation.

How did we get here, and where can we go from here? This book briefly recounts the evolution of the presidential nomination process, from the eighteenth century congressional caucuses to the rise of national party conventions in the nineteenth century, to the advent of presidential primaries early in the twentieth century. It explains the McGovern-Fraser Commission in the context of the 1968 Robert F. Kennedy assassination and the riot outside Democratic National Convention in Chicago, and how the commission's recommendations for a more democratic process tragically led to a new, undemocratic process. Having described the problem and how we got to where we are now, I offer a solution to restore the environment in which the McGovern-Fraser reforms were intended to operate, and compares this solution to other proposed solutions. Finally, this work tells the still developing story of the quest to implement a new reform, to energize the grassroots, to gather support within both the Republican and Democratic parties' organizational structures, to work with members of Congress and state election officials, and to build consensus in the political science community.

PART I

THE PROBLEM

ANY GIVEN TUESDAY

TO LIVE AND DIE IN LA

There was a time when presidential nomination races largely occurred out of the public view. In most of the states, decisions were made in "smoke-filled rooms," where party fat cats were imagined to chomp on cigars and dicker with each other for hours, as to who would represent the state at each party's national convention, and which presidential candidate each state delegation would support. A few states held presidential primaries, which were certainly more public events; however, often these primaries were nonbinding, and the state parties remained free to support whomever they pleased, although it can be inferred that such "beauty contests" influenced their decisions. Even among the states that held binding primaries, the rules governing the awarding of delegates committed to specific candidates varied; some were "winner take all," while others were proportional in their allocation of the fruits of victory. But since only about a third of the states held any sort of presidential primary at all, most of the decision making was in the hands of state party elites, with little or no input from the electorate.

Then came 1968. There weren't any more primaries that year than there had been in 1960 or 1964; actually there were slightly fewer. Yet, the few that were held mattered more. Certainly television coverage played its part. The same miniaturization of electronics, which at the end of the year would transmit images of humans orbiting the Moon, had made it easier for TV crews to transmit live from remote locations on the campaign trail. Surely the growing unpopularity of the Vietnam War was another factor in the heightened visibility of the presidential nomination race, and just as certainly television's ability to bring the war into the living room played its part in that.

One would think that these factors would have had equal impact on the Democratic and Republican nomination races, bringing both into stark focus in the electorate's eye, yet the events of the 1968 campaign that history best remembers were all on the Democratic side, rather than the process by which Richard Nixon became the Republican nominee . . . and president. On March 12, in the New Hampshire primary, traditionally the first one of the campaign, Senator Eugene McCarthy (D-MN), campaigning on an antiwar platform, stunned the Democratic Party establishment by scoring a near-upset over President Lyndon Johnson. Four days later, Senator Robert F. Kennedy (D-NY) declared his candidacy, and just like that, Johnson was in real political trouble. At the end of March, Johnson announced that he would not seek and would not accept the nomination of the Democratic Party to serve another term as president. In the next two months, as Kennedy scored one primary victory after another, eclipsing both McCarthy and Lyndon Johnson's handpicked successor, Vice President Hubert Humphrey, Bobby appeared to be cruising to the Democratic nomination.

Then, in the early hours of June 5, shortly after declaring victory in the binding, winner-take-all California primary, the biggest prize of the nomination race, shots split the night in the confines of a kitchen in Los Angeles' stately Ambassador Hotel on Wilshire Boulevard, shots fired into the heart of the American democratic process. And television was there.

Television was not there as Humphrey, in one smoke-filled room after another, without entering a single primary, patiently amassed delegates committed to voting for him at the Democratic National Convention in Chicago. But television was there in Chicago. The whole world was watching as antiwar demonstrators rioted against Humphrey's nomination, which he achieved without once facing the voters.

A war, an assassination, and a riot. By three acts of violence, one national, one individual, and one civil, presidential electoral politics were changed forever. A chain of events was set in motion, which for a time made presidential nomination races more democratic than they had ever been, but subsequently have made them as undemocratic as they ever were, with the dangerous difference that the trappings of democracy have been preserved to deceive us.

THE CONGRESSIONAL KINGMAKERS

During the first decades of the United States, it had no political parties; there was simply the Revolution. George Washington was elected to two terms as president by the acclamation of the Electors. However, despite the fact that political parties were viewed as something to be avoided, their emergence was inevitable. Thoughtful men had differing visions of how the Revolution should evolve.

No one agrees with everyone all the time, and when people disagree in deliberative bodies such as the House of Representatives and the Senate, they naturally cultivate as many votes as they can for their position. It doesn't take long to recognize that some people are voting with you fairly regularly and others are voting against you. Political factions formed. The presidency didn't have nearly the power that it has today; however, the president did have the power to veto legislation. Thus, as congressional factions formed, the presidency became an office coveted by them, and the senators and representatives of each party caucused to choose their faction's presidential candidate.

THE STATE CONVENTIONS

Eventually, the Congressional factions became institutionalized as political parties, transforming themselves from being merely Capitol Hill phenomena by sinking their roots into the politics of the individual states. As state party organizations grew in size and power, they began to demand a role in the presidential nomination process, a role that the Congressional caucuses had become accustomed to acting out alone and one they were reluctant to share. In 1824, the "Era of Good Feeling" that had been marked by the disintegration of the Federalist Party, leaving the United States a single-party regime under the Democratic-Republicans, came to an end as several state legislatures nominated outspoken critics of the established presidential nomination process in opposition to the Congressional caucus' choice of William C. Crawford (DR-PA): John Quincy Adams (DR-MA), Andrew Jackson (DR-TN), and Henry Clay (DR-KY). Because of the multiplicity of candidates, this was the first presidential election in which no one had a majority of the electors. Although Jackson had a plurality, in the political wheeling and dealing that led up to the contingent election in the House of Representatives pursuant to the Twelfth Amendment, House Speaker Clay, who had come in fourth in the electoral vote and was therefore left out of the contingent election, threw his support to Adams, who won the election. This "corrupt bargain," as Jacksonians called it, had several consequences. Four years later, Jackson, who had won a plurality of both the popular vote and the Electoral College, was back, stronger than ever, and trounced Adams. Jackson's faction of the Democratic-Republican Party emerged as the new Democratic Party. Furthermore, how badly the Congressional caucus had miscalculated in snubbing the demands of the states to share in the decision-making became evident from the fact that Crawford finished ahead of only Clay in electoral votes. "King Caucus" had been deposed.

THE NATIONAL CONVENTIONS

After a few presidential cycles, during which state legislatures and state party conventions nominated presidential candidates, the Democratic Party (formed by Jackson) and the Whig Party (formed by Clay) established national conventions, to which the states sent delegations. The Democratic Party held the first of these national conventions for the 1832 presidential cycle. Methods of choosing delegates varied from autocratic to oligarchic to democratic. In some states, the governor made the selection; in others, the party central committee. In such states, of course, there was little room for campaigning of maneuvering; either a candidate had an "in" with the governor or the party bosses, or he did not. If not, political concessions might be traded for political support. In many states, the process would begin with local party caucuses, which would select delegates to county caucuses, which in turn would select delegates to state party convention, where delegates to the national party convention would be chosen. These methods still prevailed in 1968, and when Hubert Humphrey captured the presidential nomination of the Democratic Party.

THE PRESIDENTIAL PRIMARIES

To outward appearances, the caucus/convention process was open and democratic, and in comparison to the other delegate selection methods of the time, it was certainly an improvement. In practice, however, the party leadership still exercised a great deal of control over the outcome of the process, and they saw to it that "their man" came out on top. During the Progressive movement at the turn of the twentieth century, party activists pushed for more open processes that would wrest some power from the party bosses and include more of the rank-and-file party members.

Delegates to the national convention from states with caucus or convention systems are not selected on the initial voting day. Most caucus states select national convention delegates at congressional district conventions or state conventions, which are held weeks or months after the initial precinct caucuses. . . .

When a voter participates in a primary, the election process takes just a few minutes as the voter marks the ballot with his or her choices. However, the time commitment for a caucus is much greater: a precinct caucus can last several hours as the voters attending debate the selection of delegates to the next level caucus or convention, and also debate party issue positions. Because of the larger time commitment, caucus participants tend to be more active party members.[1]

So there is a tradeoff: the more inclusive process has the potential to be dominated by the "casual voter" who is not particularly well versed in the issues or the candidates.

A 1901 law made Florida the first state to allow the parties to choose delegates to the national conventions via a primary election, which was subsequently held in 1904. In 1905, Wisconsin passed a law requiring the state political parties to do so, the first of these being held in 1908. Still, in neither of these cases did the names of the presidential candidates themselves appear on the ballots; rather the delegates were elected as free agents, able to vote their conscience at the national conventions. The first primary that legally bound delegates to presidential candidates was instituted in Oregon in 1910 and held in 1912. By the 1916 presidential cycle the primary bandwagon was in full swing, with no less than twenty-five presidential primaries being held around the country.

It was not long, however, before enthusiasm for presidential primaries began to wane. After experimenting for a few presidential cycles, some states concluded, with some arguing by party leaders who had never embraced the idea, which the low voter turnout wasn't worth the expense of holding the primary, and one by one, states reverted to less-inclusive processes. Among the few states to hold on was New Hampshire. The Granite State was not the first one to institute a presidential primary (it was part of the 1916 wave), nor in that year was the New Hampshire primary the first one held (the Indiana primary preceded it, and the Minnesota primary was held on the same day); however, in the 1920 cycle, due to states either moving the dates of their primaries or abandoning them entirely, the New Hampshire primary found itself in the post position, and over the years it acquired the iconic "first in the nation" status.

Presidential primaries began to make a slow comeback during the prosperous years following the Second World War, and by the 1960s the number of primary states had leveled off, fluctuating between fifteen and eighteen, depending on the year and the party.

WON'T YOU PLEASE COME TO CHICAGO

This left the presidential nomination process in two-thirds of the states ostensibly in the hands of the party regulars but often actually in the hands of party leaders in the case of caucus/convention states, and in other cases in the hands of party central committees or governors outright. In the summer of 1968, with the antiwar movement in disarray following the Robert Kennedy assassination, it became apparent that Vice President Humphrey, who was committed to continuing President Johnson's policies, would be the Democratic Party nominee. It really wasn't even a contest, with Humphrey easily defeating Gene McCarthy by 1,760 votes to 601. McCarthy and Kennedy had taken their cases to the people; Humphrey had wooed the party elites. It was an inside job, but the outsiders were in Chicago, too. The anger of demonstrators outside the convention site, combined with rough handling by the police, proved to be a volatile mixture, which exploded spectacularly in full view of the national television networks.

But this far from tells the whole story of Humphrey's path to victory. McCarthy supporters ran into so many roadblocks that were contrived by the party establishment to diminish their numbers and influence that they formed an informal commission in the weeks leading up to the convention. They catalogued the procedural abuses they had suffered and presented them to the Democratic Party's Rules and Bylaws Committee and its Credential Committee.

Their efforts resulted in resolutions at the national convention calling for state parties to institute procedures that would afford all Democrats "a full, meaningful, and timely opportunity to participate in the selection of delegates," and calling for the Democratic Party to form a commission to recommend procedures to achieve these goals for implementation in time for the 1972 presidential cycle.[2] Although the delegates seated at the Chicago convention were overwhelmingly Humphrey supporters, perhaps the chanting of the mob and the sirens of the police echoed in the convention hall, for the resolutions passed. In light of the tumult in the streets and the confusing procedure by which the resolutions came to the convention floor for a vote, one analyst questions whether the delegates fully comprehended their import.[3]

THE McGOVERN-FRASER COMMISSION

In any case, in accordance with the resolutions, Democratic National Committee chair Lawrence O'Brien empanelled the Commission on Party

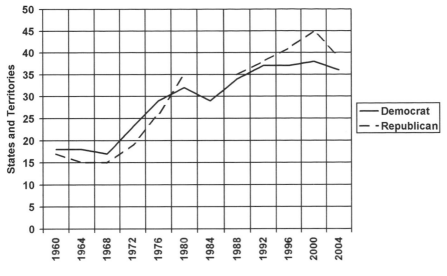

Figure 1.1: Growth of primaries since 1960.

Structure and Delegate Selection in 1969, naming Senator George McGovern (D-SD) as its chair. After two years, McGovern resigned from the commission to seek the Democratic Party's presidential nomination for 1972, and Representative Donald Fraser (D-MN) succeeded him as chair of the commission. The commission had as its goals the opening up of the delegate selection process, and creating a process that would better ensure that the demography of the delegates would reflect that of the registered party members. Among the recommendations that the commission reported were that:

- All delegates be selected during the election year.
- 75 percent of the delegates be selected at the congressional district level.
- Only a limited number of delegates be selected by state committees.
- The "unit rule," according to which some states required all their delegates to vote as a bloc, be prohibited.
- Demographic quotas be instituted to ensure equitable representation of minorities.[4,5]

The consequences were substantial, and in the short-term, positive. By 1980, the number of primary states doubled (see Figure 1.1), and both the delegate selection process and the presidential nomination process were indeed opened up. In 1972, Sen. McGovern, having gained from his tenure on the commission an understanding that the new party rules favored a more populist campaign, triumphed over party insider Hubert Humphrey as well as Humphrey's 1968 running mate, Sen. Edmund Muskie (D-ME). Four years later, Jimmy Carter, a little-known, one-term, former Georgia governor, came out of nowhere, and starting with a shoestring campaign, captured the Democratic nomination and the White House. That same year, with the Republican Party having instituted many of the same reforms, former California governor Ronald Reagan waged a seesaw campaign in one primary after another that nearly unhorsed the sitting president from his own party, Gerald Ford. The McGovern Fraser reforms appeared to have delivered what they promised: a level playing field on which any presidential candidate might beat another on any given Tuesday.

What happened next was totally unexpected.

NOTES

1. Republican National Committee, Advisory Commission on the Presidential Nominating Process. 2000. *Nominating Future Presidents*, 33–34. Washington, DC: Republican National Committee. Available from http://www.rnc.org/media/pdfs/brockreport.pdf; accessed February 13, 2003.

2. Democratic National Committee, Commission on Party Structure and Selection. 1970. *Mandate for Reform.* Washington, DC: Democratic National Committee.

3. Shafer, Byron. 1983. *Quiet Revolution: The Struggle for the Democratic Party and the Shaping of Post-Reform Politics*, 33–36. New York: Russell Sage Foundation.

4. DiClerico and Davis, 2000. "Evolution of the Presidential Nominating Process." In *Choosing Our Choices: Debating the Presidential Nomination Process*, ed. Robert DiClerico and James W. Davis, 8–13. Lanham, MD: Rowman and Littlefield Publishers, Inc.

5. Democratic National Committee. 1982. *Nominating Presidential Candidates: Our Self-Inflicted Wound.* Washington, DC: Democratic National Committee. Available from http://www.campbell.edu/faculty/schroeder/Presidential%20Nominations.htm; accessed February 10, 2005.

HELL-BENT FOR ELECTION

SUPER TUESDAY

The traditional schedule of presidential primaries, caucuses, and conventions is one that evolved piecemeal over a period of decades, without any systematic architecture. Iowa and New Hampshire always go first because . . . they are Iowa and New Hampshire. Originally, the other states' primaries and conventions were spread fairly evenly throughout the spring season, leading up to the nominating conventions in the summer. Whereas now there are only a handful of states that do not hold presidential primaries, prior to the McGovern-Fraser reforms in the early 1970s, only a third of the states held such primaries. In those prereform days, instead of the delegates of a state being chosen in one day as in a primary election, they were usually selected in the course of a long process beginning with precinct caucuses, running through district or county caucuses, and culminating in state conventions. The process of selecting a party's presidential candidate was the aggregation of decisions made in thousands of smoke-filled rooms. Such a process did not lend itself to as much media attention nor to a sense of a candidacy building momentum. Rather, there was more the sense that the delegate selection processes in each state were relatively isolated, with little influence on each other. In such an environment, there was little perceived advantage in a state choosing its delegates early.

The McGovern-Fraser reforms changed this process. More states switched to primaries, which attracted more media attention. The concept of campaign momentum took shape; with increasing frequency, candidates without sufficient momentum dropped out of the race before the national conventions. Eventually, states realized that they could exert more influence over the process and the candidates as well as attract more campaign spending and media coverage if they moved their primaries to the beginning of the season. The more the system shifted from caucuses to primaries, the more incentive it created for "front-loading." the presidential nomination calendar. This was the unintended and adverse consequence of the McGovern-Fraser reforms.

The first break significant with tradition came in 1988, when a bloc of southern states decided to hold their primaries on the second Tuesday in March, calling it "Super Tuesday." But any state or region of the country can play that game, and in the years since, most of them have. In 1996, California (a region in its own right) moved its presidential primary from the first Tuesday in June to the second Tuesday in March; still content with that, the most populous state in the union moved its primary to the first Tuesday in March four years later. California was joined by eleven other states, creating a "Mega Tuesday" in which a third of all conventional delegates were awarded on the same day. Also in 2000, a bloc of western states moved their primaries to the Saturday between Mega Tuesday and the South's Super Tuesday.

Front-loaded extravaganzas such as Super Tuesday and Mega Tuesday are the weapons of mass destruction in presidential politics. They destroy candidacies by the score. In the last three contested Republican presidential nominations—1988, 1996, and 2000—the campaign season began with six, ten, and twelve candidates respectively. In each case, the race was conceded to the front-runner by the Ides of March.[1] Both Bill Bradley (D-NJ) and John McCain (R-AZ) conceded their parties' nomination on March 8, 2000, the day after Mega Tuesday, before the Western Regional Primary and Super Tuesday even took place. Until 1976, New Hampshire held the first primary of the season on the first Tuesday in March, an event that began the campaign in earnest. In 2000, however, the first Tuesday in March marked not the beginning of the campaign, but the end.

Even so, we had yet to see the worst of it. As I wrote in an opinion editorial in the *Philadelphia Inquirer* on April 13, 1999:

> Don't for a moment believe that it will stop there. New Hampshire already has had to move its primary to February to stay ahead of the pack. Clearly, March Madness will eventually give way to February Frenzy, and I invite you to come up with your own alliteration for January. In this brave new world of the 21st century, the word *campaign* will be obsolete in the political lexicon, to be replaced by *blitzkrieg*.[2]

My prediction came true. Iowa held its 2004 caucus on January 19, and the New Hampshire primary occurred on January 27. The "February Frenzy" was so furious that Howard Dean threw in the towel on the nineteenth of

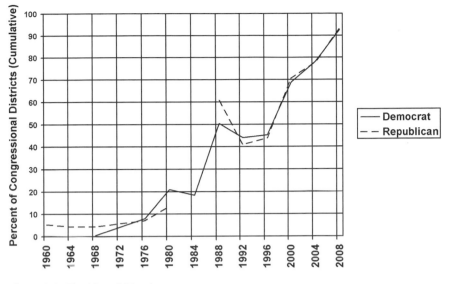

Figure 2.1: The Ides of March.

that month. Only 20 percent of the delegates to the Democratic National Convention had been selected, but the other 80 percent of the American electorate didn't matter. The nomination had been decided.

Figure 2.1 shows the progression of front-loading over the past four decades in terms of the percentage of congressional districts represented in state party conventions and presidential primaries held on or before March 15. It can be seen that throughout the 1960s and 1970s, less than 10 percent of presidential contest occurred on this date. By 1988, this number had risen above 50 percent, and while it dropped a bit in the 1990s, it surged to 70 percent in 2000 and to 78 percent in 2004. By March 15, 2008, 93 percent of the delegates will have been chosen.

Political scientists Lisa K. Parshall and Franco Mattei attempt to explain the motivations of the various villains in the collapse of the presidential nomination process, and how their combined actions result in the disenfranchisement of an entire class of voters, those whose states have refrained from joining the stampede to the front of the calendar:

Candidates gain "momentum" by winning or by beating the expectations set by pundits or pre-election polls; success in doing so will enhance the perceived viability of some candidates at the expense of other contenders who either fail to live up to expectations or lose a primary (caucus). Facing longer odds, negative media coverage and reluctance among potential contributors, some of these contenders choose to withdraw from the race well before the finish line.[3]

Although true, candidates can generate momentum over either a long or short campaign, and during a long campaign, momentum can pass between them. The questions to be asked are, which candidates stand to gain from a short season, and how do they game the system to this end? Obviously a short race to the finish line advantages the runner who starts ahead of the others. Since a president who chooses to face reelection is usually the frontrunner, there is an incentive for him to influence the party rules to his advantage. However, there is little to suggest that sitting presidents have materially contributed to the shortening of the nomination calendar.

> National parties, as institutions, seek to achieve unity in support of their standard bearer; this goal requires a rapid conclusion of the selection process affording the party greater time to coalesce and rally behind the winner in preparation of the Fall campaign.[4]

Again, although true, this is relevant to the political parties only in relation to each other. How long does a party need to coalesce and rally behind its standard-bearer? This healing of rifts after a battle for the nomination is relative rather than absolute. In times past, the lull between the summer national conventions and Labor Day was deemed sufficient. So long as both parties play by the same rules (i.e., operate under substantially the same schedule of primaries and caucuses) there is no advantage to either party. Thus neither party is currently advantaged by having the nomination decided in the first week of March, since both parties do so, and they would be just as well served by returning to a longer, more graduated primary schedule. Still, Parshall and Mattei raise a valid point, in that political parties may perceive an opportunity to gain an advantage over the other party in this way. What constrains the achievement of any significant advantage, however, is that although the caucus of one political party might be scheduled ahead of the other party's, the overwhelming majority of states are now primary states, and most states hold their Democratic and Republican primaries on the same day; if one moves, so does the other.

> States seek to maximize their media exposure, reap the economic advantages related to widespread coverage and hard-fought campaigns waged by all potential nominees, and increase influence on the outcome of the candidate selection process. These rewards are bestowed disproportionately to the states at the

forefront of the schedule. Thus, Iowa and New Hampshire have been adamant about the preservation and protection of their unique lead-off spot in the calendar. In addition, as soon as it became clear that the first caucus and primary were much more than isolated local events, and that both deeply affected the development and/or result of the campaigns, other states have moved up the date of their primaries (caucuses) in an effort to retain or increase their leverage on the process.[5]

Exactly so. The states have had the motive, method, and opportunity for perpetrating this crime. At best, the political parties have been accessories. And as for the candidates, they have always played the game with whatever rules have been in place, and they always will.

THE BEST THAT MONEY CAN BUY

Not only does front-loading disenfranchise millions of voters by presenting them with a nomination that is already a *fait accompli* by the time they get the opportunity to vote, but it also cheapens the value of the votes that are cast by the fortunate few at the front of the process, because many of the starting candidates are forced out of the race before the first vote is even cast. In 1996, two Republican candidates bowed out of the race before the first delegate was selected.

In practical terms, the field of serious contenders has actually contracted . . . largely as a result of the dramatically increased costs of campaigning for the nomination, and the consequent need for extraordinary sums of money to wage effective campaigns. . . . The vast majority of nomination contenders have been able to raise only enough money to seriously compete in the first few delegate selection contests, counting on strong showings in the early contests to generate momentum and much-needed financial support to replenish depleted campaign coffers.

In a sense, the ability to raise the sums necessary to compete effectively has become the first primary for both parties—what some analysts call "the money primary." Because it is widely believed that political donations flow to candidates already perceived as having a good chance of winning, those who enter the race with strong national name identification—or the ability to self-finance a national campaign—have a clear advantage over other, lesser-known candidates.

One GOP strategist observed the front-loading phenomenon greatly exacerbates this problem: lesser-known candidates without the financial resources effectively to plan and wage a national campaign, reduced as they are to betting on strong showings in the early contests, are handicapped when contest after contest comes rushing at them, leaving no time in-between contests to raise the necessary funds to continue an effective campaign.[6]

A few weeks after Senators McCain and Bradley ended their candidacies in 2000, Senator Joseph Lieberman (D-CT) gave the following testimony before a Senate committee:

> Instead of a system that tests a candidate's character and his ability to offer reasoned opinions over the long haul, we have an increasingly compressed schedule, one in which States whose primaries once were spread out over months now compete to see who can hold their contests the earliest. Instead of allowing the broadest electorate to winnow the field of potential nominees, we have a situation in which those willing to give money to candidates have enormous say over who ends up with the nomination or even competing with it. Indeed, this year's so-called money primary eliminated a significant portion of the Republican primary field even before the first primary voters ever stepped foot into an election booth.[7]

In fact, six Republican candidates—half of the total field of twelve—dropped out of the race during the money primary, "more than three months before the first voter cast a ballot that counted for purposes of delegate selection."[8] The Brock Commission report summed up the overriding importance of the money primary in the starkest terms:

> It is an indisputable fact that in every nomination campaign since 1980, in both parties, the eventual party nominee was the candidate who had raised the most money by December 31 of the year before the general election.[9]

In other words, since 1980, the American people have had the best presidential candidates—and the best presidents—that money can buy. The choice has been taken out of their hands and placed in the hands of those who carry suitcases full of cash.

WHY IOWA AND NEW HAMPSHIRE?

One defect of the traditional presidential primary schedule was that the states voted in much the same order from one quadrennial cycle to the next. Traditionally, Iowa held the first caucuses and New Hampshire held the first

Table 2.1: Ethnic Demographics of Iowa and New Hampshire

State	Black or African-American	American-Indian and Alaska Native	Asian	Pacific Islander	Hispanic or Latino (of any race)
Iowa	2.1	0.3	1.3	0.0	2.8
New Hampshire	0.7	0.2	1.3	0.0	1.7
United States	**12.3**	**0.9**	**3.6**	**0.1**	**12.5**

Source: U.S. Census Bureau 2002.

primary. One of the rationales for Iowa and New Hampshire always going first, aside from historical precedent, is that being such small states, relatively obscure candidates running shoestring campaigns can get out their messages almost as effectively as the well-known and well-heeled "front-runners." In Iowa and New Hampshire, where candidates can literally campaign door-to-door, everyone has a fighting chance. It is probably as close to a level playing field as American politics ever gets.

A level playing field, yes... but it is analogous to a football game in which the opposing teams don't switch goals every quarter, so one team enjoys the advantage of always having the wind at its back. In 1984, would Jesse Jackson have gotten off to a better start if South Carolina had been first instead of Iowa, or Mississippi instead of New Hampshire? The percentages of African-Americans in Iowa and New Hampshire (2.1 percent and 0.7 percent, respectively) fall far short of the national average (12.3 percent). In fact, every race enumerated by the U.S. Census is significantly underrepresented in these two states (see Table 2.1). But it's not just about ethnicity; it's about economic class. The percentages of families below the poverty level (Iowa, 6.0 percent; New Hampshire, 4.3 percent) also fall significantly short of the national average (9.2 percent).[10] Since the demographics of Iowa and New Hampshire are nowhere near representative of the entire nation, some candidates play these first primary games with the wind at their back, while others have the wind in their face. It is also inherently unfair to the voters of other states to always have to wait for Iowa and New Hampshire to go first.

In proposing his plan for primary reform, Senator Robert Smith (R-NH) raised a number of points in favor of his state's privileged status:

> From the candidate's perspective, I would attest that the most important reason is the historical certainty it offers for candidates. Parties in states like Louisiana or Alaska or Delaware will pop up now and then and threaten to conduct a caucus or primary before New Hampshire and Iowa. This distracts and confuses

the campaigns and the result is wasted effort by candidates and ultimately a disorganized poorly planned caucus or primary that offers little to the Party.[11]

Perhaps a candidate who is easily distracted and confused by having to campaign in states other than New Hampshire and Iowa ought not to be the next leader of the global superpower. The job of the president is to lead this nation into the future, which is by definition uncertain. An inflexible primary system rooted in "historical certainty" does little to illuminate a candidate's ability to adapt to fluid situations. Looking at this issue another way, no professional sports team plays the same schedule year after year. Shouldn't the next president of the United States be at least as competent as a football coach?

Senator Smith pointed to several advantages of the current position of Iowa and New Hampshire. First of all:

Historically, they are first. Campaigns understand this and, as early as possible, can begin assembling a grass roots organization and scheduling candidate tours. Without that clarity, the candidates will be forced to waste lots of energy and time in states that may or may not go early.[12]

Essentially, this is an argument in favor of homesteading, the practice of campaigning in certain states for years prior to the election. Candidates spend years building organizations and appealing to tiny constituencies that are unrepresentative of the nation as a whole. As Senator Robert Packwood (R-OR) said of this practice, "Given enough time, any candidate with 10,000 zealots can win a state. Garibaldi took Italy with 10,000 redshirts. You shouldn't confuse that with mass appeal."[13]

Next, Senator Smith contended:

The Media understand Iowa and New Hampshire. They understand the processes and they are ready for them. They are fully prepared to cover televised debates, and they normally have substantial on-the-ground coverage to ensure that the local activities are televised on a national scale. The media have the ability to gauge the support candidates are receiving at the local level, allowing a lesser known candidate to gain momentum by having his local success broadcasted to a national audience.[14]

The media are fully prepared to go anywhere any time news is being made. They have the ability to develop a working knowledge of the issues quite rapidly and report them to the public, anything from hanging chads to debonded space shuttle tiles.

Senator Smith's third point was that:

> The two parties have traditionally supported Iowa and New Hampshire's early status. The Democrats are committed to keeping them first. While, of course, it is our prerogative as Republicans to choose whatever primary dates we want, it is useful to maintain the kind of media focus as well as voter participation if both parties have their early primaries on the same date.[15]

If blackmail can be called support, then the two parties do indeed support Iowa and New Hampshire's early status. If a party said otherwise, those two states would be highly offended and the other party would be quick to take political advantage. In an era when presidential elections are decided by a handful of electoral votes, which party can afford to write off Iowa and New Hampshire? Beneath the surface of the public fawning over these two prima donnas, there is secret indignation over their pretensions.

Next, Senator Smith pointed out:

> The states of Iowa and New Hampshire are fully committed to the early dates. In fact, New Hampshire's state law requires it to be first. State sponsorship provides an organized, professionally conducted, adequately funded primary, as well as a more unbiased vote count. This is essential in the early primaries because it lends credibility to the result in the eyes of the media and the national public.[16]

The argument that New Hampshire's state law requires it to be first is the intellectual equivalent of, "Because I said so." As a matter of constitutional principle, the laws of one state cannot preempt those of another. California has as much right to legislate that its presidential primary be first, for instance. Furthermore, states other than New Hampshire are capable of organized and professionally conducted elections.

Senator Smith concluded his argument in favor of the current privilege of his state with a tribute to his fellow citizens:

> What other state parties ignore is that with this privilege comes a unique responsibility and a unique burden. New Hampshire citizens are fully aware of their responsibilities in the area of picking presidential nominees. They take this responsibility seriously. . . . We have survived and refined this process over the past several decades, and I believe we provide America with an extraordinary service in reviewing and assessing the candidates without interference by big money and slick media campaigns.[17]

Although this is all very nice for the people of these two states, it hardly seems appropriate to defend the current privileged position of Iowa and New Hampshire as an exclusive civics lesson for their populations. The citizens of other small states should be given the opportunity to sit in the front row of the classroom of democracy. Should the citizens of the nation's capital, for instance, be any less expert practitioners of the democratic process than the citizens of New Hampshire? In this day and age, a more smugly patronizing position in American politics is scarcely imaginable. There, there, the good people of Iowa and New Hampshire have all that is necessary to make the best decisions for the rest of us.

Parshall and Mattei, in constructing their constitutional argument against the current system based on the First and Fourteenth Amendments, observe:

> Nor can the early states assert that long-standing first-in-the-nation status has created a tradition or political culture of informed participation which gives entitlement to their voters. The mere fact that a handful of states have enjoyed the privilege of hosting the first nominating contests of the election year is not sufficient justification for diluting the First and Fourteenth Amendment rights of late-state voters. "Historic accident, without more, cannot constitute a compelling state interest."[18] An argument that the first states play a special role in the winnowing process, have a more informed electorate, or just plain "do it better" than other states is based on circular logic, is debatable, and utterly lacking in constitutional foundation.[19]

Parshall and Mattei also present a compelling argument against the "first in the nation" privilege of Iowa and New Hampshire on the basis of Congress' authority to regulate interstate commerce (Article I, Section 8, Clause 3).

> Nor may a state seek to extend the effect of its laws beyond its own borders or in a manner which destroys or impairs the rights of citizens in other states. To ensure the protection of national interests, commerce principles therefore authorize federal regulation of in-state activities where such activities have an impact outside the state.[20]

A commerce analogy is appropriate for two reasons. First...among the benefits that states gain in securing a date early in the presidential nomination process are the economic rewards generated by the campaigns and the national media attention which the first contests receive. "Candidates do more than just visit Iowa and New Hampshire. They also rent office space, hotel rooms and cars, eat at local restaurants and buy millions of dollars of advertising."[21] Hosting the nation's first primaries thus provides first status states with a "cyclical economic boom."[22] In the commerce jurisprudence,

state laws which similarly "hoard" interstate resources or enact protective legislation designed to economically advantage in-state interest at the expense
of out-of-state citizens, are forbidden. The Constitution would seem no less
offended when the fundamental freedoms of association and voting are at
stake.[23]

Indeed, Iowa and New Hampshire have a booming "political tourism"
industry, functioning on the quadrennial presidential election cycle, which
brings not mere millions, but billions into those states. These huge sums come
from cash cow states where candidates ride in with great fanfare to raise money
and never come back to campaign. According to California Democratic Party
chair Art Torres, in the 2004 election, "over $181 million dollars left our
state, never to come back."[24] The current system operates as something of a
racket, bleeding wealth from the "ATM states" to the great benefit of Iowa
and New Hampshire, with the presidential candidates acting as the bag men,
while the political parties look the other way under the threat of incurring the
ire of those two states. Forget about the highfalutin constitutional questions;
it sounds like a RICO (Racketeer Influenced and Corrupt Organizations) Act
case waiting to be filed.

TINKERING AROUND THE EDGES

On the heels of George McGovern's humiliating loss to Richard Nixon in
1972, the Democratic Party empanelled a new commission, chaired by Representative Barbara Mikulski (D-MD). Perhaps the McGovern-Fraser reforms
had gone too far and had generated a nomination process that strengthened
the left wing of the party at the expense of its center, making it less competitive in the general election. Certainly McGovern had turned out to be an
extraordinarily weak candidate in the contest against Nixon. The Watergate
break-in and other dirty tricks aside, many of the Democrats' wounds in the
1972 campaign were self-inflicted. Was it possible that the party had made
itself too inclusive?

In any case, the Mikulski Commission had only limited success in reversing
the McGovern-Fraser reforms. Demographic quotas were relaxed into "affirmative action." Additionally, only registered Democrats would be allowed
participate in Democratic primaries; open primaries were prohibited. The
commission reaffirmed the proportional allocation of delegates to candidates
according to their vote percentages in the primaries, but recommended a
15 percent threshold, below which, a candidate would receive no delegates

at all. This latter measure would freeze out fringe candidates and allow more mainstream contenders to battle for their share of the delegates.[25,26]

Even before the next presidential election, the Democratic Party empanelled still another commission, this time chaired by Michigan party chair Morley Winograd. Working from 1974 to 1978, the Winograd Commission's goals were to limit or reverse the spread of presidential primaries and provide for a more closed nomination process that would return influence to party regulars. It was an attempt to turn back the clock from the disaster of 1972 to the party's triumphs in 1960 and 1964. But, while this quiet counterrevolution was being worked by the party leaders, Jimmy Carter came off his peanut farm to lead the Democratic Party to victory in 1976. The McGovern-Fraser process had worked. It had produced a strong Democratic nominee, and the Republican Party's establishment candidate, the sitting president, barely held off a challenger who was arguably the stronger candidate. Nevertheless, among the Winograd Commission's recommendations were to:

- Institutionalize Iowa and New Hampshire as the first-in-the-nation contests.
- Permit caucus states to raise their thresholds to 20 percent, and primary states to 25 percent (which would favor incumbent Carter over any challengers).
- Create "super delegates" chosen by party leaders rather than by caucuses or primaries, comprising 10 percent of the total number of national convention delegates.
- Make the result of primaries binding on the delegates; they must vote at the convention accordingly.

The Winograd Commission also called for a shorten the primary season, running from the second Tuesday in March to the second Tuesday in June; however, it granted four states special exemptions, scheduling the 1980 Iowa caucuses on January 21, the New Hampshire primary on February 26, and the Massachusetts and Vermont primaries on March 4. In reality, therefore, the 1980 nomination season was to be about as long as it had ever been.[27,28]

Although Jimmy Carter defeated Gerald Ford in 1976, Ronald Reagan's strong challenge to Ford in the nomination battle put him in position to capture the Republican nomination in 1980, and he defeated Carter in the general election. It was yet another occasion for Democratic introspection. Working from 1980 to 1982, a new commission chaired by North Carolina governor James Hunt reaffirmed many of the Winograd Commission's recommendations, including closed primaries, affirmative action, and slowing or reversing the transition from caucuses to primaries. It increased the number of superdelegates to 14 percent, and repealed the "bound delegates" rule in favor of a more permissive "good conscience" rule.

Another factor in the Hunt Commission's deliberations was the hopeless but protracted nomination battle that Edward Kennedy had waged against Jimmy Carter in 1980. Many felt that the lack of winner-take-all primaries had allowed Kennedy to dog Carter's heels all the way to the national convention, whereas Carter could have squashed the insurgency with some early winner-take-all victories. To make outcomes more decisive, the commission recommended that the winner-take-all system be allowed in states that selected their delegates by congressional districts; that proportional allocation states be allowed to award a bonus delegate to the winner of each congressional district ("winner-take-more"); and that in proportional allocation states, the 20 percent threshold be a hard and fast rule.

Like its predecessor, the Hunt Commission attempted to shorten the nomination calendar, recommending that delegate selection begin on March 13, 1984, without exception; however, Iowa and New Hampshire pressured the Democratic National Committee into granting exemptions. Meanwhile, Massachusetts and Vermont lost their exemptions. Again, the attempt to shorten the season by having it begin later failed.[29,30]

During this period, the Democratic Party achieved its goal regarding the growth of presidential primaries. After zooming from seventeen to twenty-nine primary states between 1968 and 1976, the number tapered off at thirty-one in 1980, and dropped back to twenty-nine in 1984. However, something else was happening: the date by which the first 50 percent of national convention delegates were chosen was moving earlier in the calendar year. In 1968, the median delegate selection date for the Democratic Party had been June 4; by 1980 it had moved forward six weeks to April 22. In large part, this could be explained by the shift from caucuses to primaries. Caucuses were only the beginning of a multistage delegate selection process spread over several months that culminated with state conventions; thus the state conventions, where the actual delegate selection occurred, tended to be held in the later part of the nomination season. Primaries, on the other hand, were single-day delegate selection events, and as such could be moved around the calendar with much greater flexibility. As a default, there was a tendency for primaries to be scheduled earlier than the conventions, and the shift from the caucus/convention process to the primaries caused the median delegate selection date to drift forward. Also, the Winograd Commission had given four states formal exemptions to go ahead of all others. In any case, although a trend toward an earlier delegate selection process was developing, this did not appear to raise any alarms at the time.

Following the 1984 nomination season, two outsider candidates, Senator Gary Hart (D-CO) and Reverend Jesse Jackson (D-IL), complained that the 20 percent threshold and the 14 percent superdelegate level were too high. After all, together they had amassed 55 percent of the vote, and had their delegate counts been proportional to that number, establishment candidate Walter Mondale (D-MN) would not have won the nomination on the first ballot. The Democratic Party called upon South Carolina party chair Don Fowler to head a commission to look into these issues, which abolished both the winner-take-all and bonus delegate options and rolled back the delegate threshold to 15 percent. However, the commission increased slightly the number of superdelegates to 15.5 percent.[31]

Thus, after twenty years of tinkering, the Fowler Commission brought Democratic Party rules nearly back to those instituted under the McGovern-Fraser reforms. In fact, the most substantial change in place since the Mikulski Commission's institution of the 15 percent threshold was the superdelegates. At this point, the Democratic Party appeared satisfied with the status quo, and it would not empanel another commission on the presidential nomination process until 2004.

REFORM EFFORTS

Citing a "growing interest in the presidential nominating process,"[32] the White Burkett Miller Center of Public Affairs at the University of Virginia established a bipartisan commission in the summer of 1981 to examine the ways in which the two major political parties selected their candidates for president. This commission was cochaired by former Secretary of Defense Melvin Laird and former Senator Adlai E. Stevenson III. The first paragraph of the commission's 1982 report hardly could have been more dramatic:

No political process in the United States is more important than our method of nominating presidential candidates, yet none has given rise to so much dissatisfaction. From both ends of the political spectrum come demands for change. A growing resolve on the part of concerned Americans to find a solution to this problem unites Democrats and Republicans, liberals and conservatives, and advocates and opponents of recent reforms. This new movement knows no partisan cast, nor does it seek to benefit any one candidate or faction. It is motivated solely by the belief that the public interest is ill served by the current nominating system. Its conviction is as simple as it is significant: there must be reform.[33]

The Laird-Stevenson Commission noted several drawbacks of primaries:

> One of the most frequently heard complaints was that both parties have too
> many primaries, placing unnecessary burdens on the candidates and detracting
> from the deliberative process that should determine the nomination results.
> Primaries do, of course, serve as one valuable method of judging rank and file
> preferences. But a nearly total reliance on primaries not only conflicts with other
> objectives of the nominating process, but also provides an imperfect and unre-
> liable way of determining the popular will. . . . The primary electorate . . . does
> not always represent the views of either party's traditional supporters or the
> views of the electorate as a whole. Participation in primaries is low and has
> generally been decreasing, and primary voters tend to be wealthier, more highly
> educated, and more ideologically motivated than the electorate at large.[34]

To the degree that primary voters tended to reflect the wings of the parties
rather than their centers, the commission observed that "there are too many
incentives for candidates to create factional divisions within parties and not
enough to promote consensus." The commission also expressed concern that
the shift to more primaries was creating a more money-driven process: "the
rules of campaign finance produce unnecessary burdens for the candidates
and interfere with the expression of natural political forces." Accordingly,
the commission recommended that the number of presidential primaries be
reduced to sixteen. It also called for the caucus/convention process to produce more formally uncommitted delegates, and that all committed delegates
be given greater flexibility to exercise individual judgment at the national
conventions. The commission expressed its approval of ex officio delegates,
similar to the Democratic Party's superdelegates, which represented the party
leadership; thus a balance would be struck between the activists and the
hierarchy.[35]

The commission also noted testimony that "the democratic appearance of
the decision-making process is often specious . . . with many voting after the
nomination decision has already been made."[36]

> The current sequential arrangement of primaries tends artificially to narrow
> the choice of candidates and to reduce the options not only for the delegates
> but for those who vote in primaries during the latter stages. In addition, it gives
> an unjustifiable degree of influence to those states (Iowa and New Hampshire)
> that hold their delegate selection contests well in advance of the others. In
> 1980, for example, the nomination decision had effectively been made before
> nearly one-fifth of the population went to the polls to choose their delegates in
> the June 3 primaries.

> ... [C]hanges in the scheduling of primaries would help to reduce the un-
> desirable effects of the current arrangement. The objective is not to eliminate
> completely the existence of a sequence, for the sequence has the positive ef-
> fects of allowing lesser-known candidates a reasonable chance and permitting
> the people and delegates to observe the candidates over a series of different
> contests.[37]

To address these issues, the commission recommended that the national parties
enforce a strict time frame within which the primaries, caucuses, and other
nominating events might be held, and:

> ... that national parties or Congress fix regional primary dates within this
> period, and define the regions according to time zones. For each election year
> the order of these primaries would be established by lottery.[38]

Although there had been earlier proposals for a system that would either rotate the schedule or determine it by lottery, the Laird-Stevenson
Commission may have been the first one to call for a comprehensive reform of the presidential nomination calendar to end the schedule advantage that some states enjoyed perennially over others. Nearly two decades
would pass before another commission made a recommendation of similar
scope.

The Republican Party remained officially silent on the presidential nomination process for a very long time, yet to some extent it was carried along by
the same forces that were at work in the Democratic Party. It is true that many
changes to the Democratic rules have had little effect on the Republican Party;
states can choose to be winner-take-all or proportional, and for the latter there
is no mandated threshold. Also, there are no GOP superdelegates. Perhaps
the most significant effect of the McGovern-Fraser reforms on the GOP was
the rapid shift from caucuses to primaries; in most primary states, the government bore the expense of conducting the election, therefore, it made little
sense for one party to foot the bill for a separate caucus/convention process
where the state was picking up the tab for a primary. Accordingly, the growth
of presidential primaries occurred in the two parties simultaneously, and the
calendar of nominating events in the two parties became more closely coupled
in time.

The advent of Super Tuesday in 1988 represented the first effort by a
group of states to grab disproportional power over the nomination process by
leaping ahead in the calendar. By 1992, the median delegate selection date

had moved forward to April 7. In 1996, it was March 19. In a March 3, 1996 opinion editorial aptly titled "Primary Madness," David S. Broder decried "the most absurdly foreshortened primary process the nation has ever seen."[39] Of course, 2000 promised to be even worse, and the Republican Party decided to step up to the plate.

Even before the 1996 nominating process began, then (Republican National Committee) RNC Chairman Haley Barbour recognized the problems inherent in such a front-loaded system. He appointed a RNC taskforce in February 1996 to examine the delegate selection rules and to make recommendations on how best to ease the front-loading situation. Chairman Barbour appointed Colorado National Committeeman and then RNC Rules Committee Chairman Jim Nicholson to chair the Presidential Primary Task Force.

... The task force suggested that states holding their delegate selection events later in the process be given extra delegates. The 1996 national convention delegates ultimately approved new rules for a delegate allocation system that included date bonus delegates. Therefore, in the 2000 presidential election cycle, states were awarded a five percent delegate bonus if they held their primary or caucus between March 15 and April 14; a 7.5 percent bonus if their event was between April 15 and May 14; and a 10 percent bonus if they held their primary or caucus between May 15 and June 20. These bonus percentages were half of what the task force had originally recommended.

So, as Republican state party leaders set about planning their delegate selection procedures for the 2000 Republican presidential nominating process, they did so with the knowledge that they could have a larger delegate presence at the national convention if they held their primary or caucus later in the season. However, the date bonus delegate inducements were not strong enough to hold back the rush to the front of the selection calendar. As the 2000 selection calendar demonstrated, a number of states pushed their event to earlier in the process.

The result was the most front-loaded delegate selection process in the history of the Republican Party. Whereas in 1996, 59 percent of the delegates were chosen by the second week of March, in 2000, fully 63 percent of the delegates would be chosen by March 14.[40]

The first national party attempt to arrest front-loading had been a spectacular failure. State didn't want to send more delegates to the national convention if it meant holding their nomination event later in the season; what really mattered to them was getting in the game early to attract the time, money, and political attention of the presidential campaigns.

The GOP would make another grand attempt to address the problem a few years later, and the next commission would propose another, much bolder plan to the party. At about the same time, the National Association of Secretaries of State would form a group to study the problem and would come up with a different idea. Still another solution—an outsider, a dark horse—would come out of nowhere.

NOTES

1. Republican National Committee, Advisory Commission on the Presidential Nominating Process. 2000. *Nominating Future Presidents*, 9 10, 14. Washington, DC: Republican National Committee. Available from http://www.rnc.org/media/pdfs/brockreport.pdf; accessed February 13, 2003.

2. Gangale, Thomas. 1999. "Realign Presidential Primaries to Dilute Power of Region, Money." *Philadelphia Inquirer*, April 13. Available from http://www.ops-alaska.com/ps/gang13.html; accessed February 1, 2003.

3. Parshall, Lisa K., and Franco Mattei. 2002. "Parties and the Presidential Nomination Process: Political and Constitutional Implications of 'Front-Loading,'" 9. Presented at the 2002 Conference of the Southern Political Science Association, Savannah, Georgia, November 7–9.

4. Ibid., 5.

5. Ibid., 7.

6. Republican National Committee 2000. *Nominating Future Presidents*, 15.

7. Lieberman, Joseph. 2000. "Testimony on Regional Presidential Selection Act of 1999." Washington, DC: U.S. Government Printing Office. Available from http://www.senate.gov/member/ct/lieberman/general/r032900a.html; accessed January 25, 2003.

8. Republican National Committee 2000. *Nominating Future Presidents*, 13.

9. Ibid., 14.

10. U.S. Census Bureau. 2002. Available from http://www.census.gov/census2000/states/; accessed February 5, 2003.

11. Smith, Robert. 2000. "Senator Bob Smith's 'Fairness in Primaries' Plan." Memorandum to the Republican National Committee Members and Delegates. Available from http://www.gwu.edu/~action/smithplan.htm; accessed December 24, 2002.

12. Ibid.

13. *Congressional Quarterly Weekly Report*. 1972. "Presidential Primaries: Proposals for a New System." July 8, 1650–1654.

14. Smith 2000. "Senator Bob Smith's 'Fairness in Primaries' Plan."

15. Ibid.

16. Ibid.

17. Ibid.

18. *Illinois vs. Socialist Workers Party*. 1979. 440 US 173. Quoted in Lisa K. Parshall and Franco Mattei, 2002. "Parties and the Presidential Nomination Process: Political and Constitutional Implications of 'Front-Loading.'"

19. Ibid., 25–26.

20. Ibid., 27.

21. Stark, Leonard P. 1996. "The Presidential Primary and Caucus Schedule: A role for Federal Regulation?" 15. *Yale Law and Policy Review*, 331. Quoted in Parshall and Mattei 2002. "Parties and the Presidential Nomination Process."

22. Udall, Morris K. 1981. "A Proposal for Presidential Primary Reform," 10. New York University Review of Law and Social Change, 19. Quoted in Parshall and Mattei 2002. "Parties and the Presidential Nomination Process."

23. Parshall and Mattei 2002. "Parties and the Presidential Nomination Process," 27–28.

24. Democratic National Committee 2005. Commission on Presidential Nomination Timing and Scheduling. Transcript, 6. October 1. Available from http://a9.g.akamai.net/7/9/8082/v001/democratic1.download.akamai.com/8082/pdfs/20051001_commissiontranscript.pdf; accessed December 27, 2005.

25. DiClerico and Davis, 2000. "Evolution of the Presidential Nominating Process." In *Choosing Our Choices: Debating the Presidential Nomination Process*, ed. Robert DiClerico and James W. Davis, 14–16. Lanham, MD: Rowman and Littlefield Publishers, Inc.

26. Democratic National Committee. 1982. *Nominating Presidential Candidates: Our Self-Inflicted Wound.* Washington, DC: Democratic National Committee. Available from http://www.campbell.edu/faculty/schroeder/Presidential%20Nominations.htm; accessed 10 February 2005.

27. DiClerico and Davis 2000. "Evolution of the Presidential Nominating Process," 17–19

28. Democratic National Committee 1982. *Nominating Presidential Candidates*.

29. DiClerico and Davis 2000. "Evolution of the Presidential Nominating Process," 19–20

30. Democratic National Committee 1982. *Nominating Presidential Candidates*.

31. DiClerico and Davis 2000. "Evolution of the Presidential Nominating Process," 20–21

32. University of Virginia, White Burkett Miller Center of Public Affairs, Commission on the Presidential Nominating Process. 1982. *Report of the Commission on the Presidential Nominating Process*, 1. Charlottesville: University of Virginia. Available from http://www.campbell.edu/faculty/schroeder/Presidential%20Nominations.htm; accessed December 24, 2002.

33. University of Virginia 1982. *Report of the Commission on the Presidential Nominating Process*, 2.

34. Ibid., 4–5.

35. Ibid., 4.

36. Ibid., 5.

37. Ibid., 6.

38. Ibid., 6–7.

39. Broder, David S. 1996. "Primary Madness." *Washington Post*, March 3.

40. Republican National Committee 2000. *Nominating Presidential Candidates*, 11.

PART II

THE SOLUTION

A GRADUAL PROCESS,
A RANDOM SELECTION

THE BASELINE DESIGN

In a truly fair primary system, states other than Iowa and New Hampshire would have an opportunity to hold the first presidential caucus or primary. But if a large state such as California or Texas went first, a low-budget campaign would never get off the ground. It takes Big Money to win in a big state. The advantage of having small states hold the first few contests is that Big Money has less of an impact in the early going. Early victories in small venues by less moneyed candidates enable them to attract the contributions that in turn allow them to advance to and be competitive in the later rounds of larger and more numerous caucuses and primaries. Such a process favors the candidate with the best message, rather than the loudest bullhorn. In the interest of encouraging a larger and more diverse field of candidates at the beginning of the process of choosing the next president of the United States, the idea of having the smaller states hold the early primaries should be preserved.

An ideal presidential primary system, therefore, would meld the best feature of the traditional schedule—smaller early, bigger later—with the idea of moving the date of each state's primary from year to year. The Graduated Random Presidential Primary System is such a plan.

The conceptual basis of the Graduated Random System, which has become known popularly as the American Plan, includes both types of geopolitical entities in the federal system of government—the state and the congressional district—which incidentally is also the basis of the Electoral College, the constitutional body that actually elects the president. Thus the Graduated

Random System is analytically consistent with the theoretical underpinnings of the Constitution, which balances the interests of the permanent arbitrary geopolitical units (the states) and the transitory, population-based political units (the congressional districts) through the clockwork-like, interlocking mechanism of the bicameral legislature. No other proposed system of presidential primary reform utilizes both units of analysis and reflects the duality of the federal system; rather, they focus solely on the states.

The schedule is weighted as an ascending scale based on the number of congressional districts in each state. The actual number of delegates for each state would be set by the political parties themselves, as they always have been, on the basis of party strength in each state. American Samoa, the District of Columbia, Guam, Puerto Rico, and the Virgin Islands, which also send delegates to both national conventions, are each counted as one district in this system, although they in fact have no voting representatives in Congress. When these five territories are added to the 435 congressional districts, the American Plan comprises a total of 440 districts. It happens that this number is equal to:

$$\sum_{n=1}^{10} 8n$$

which is the short way of writing:

$$8 + 16 + 24 + 32 + 40 + 48 + 56 + 64 + 72 + 80$$

Thus the Graduated Random System is structured as a schedule consisting of ten two-week intervals, during which the number of congressional districts contested gradually increases from one interval to the next, and in each interval, randomly selected states may hold their primaries or caucuses. This twenty-week schedule is the approximate length of the traditional presidential primary season.

In the first interval, a randomly determined combination of states with a combined total of eight congressional districts would hold their primaries or caucuses. This is approximately equal to the total number of congressional districts in Iowa (five) and New Hampshire (two), thus preserving the door-to-door "retail politicking." However, these two particular states would not necessarily comprise the first round. Any state or combination of states amounting to a total of eight congressional districts could be in the first round of primaries and caucuses. This could include such ethnically diverse jurisdictions as Alaska, the District of Columbia, Hawaii, New Mexico, Arkansas, Mississippi, Oklahoma, South Carolina, Alabama, Louisiana, Arizona, and

Table 3.1: First Round Eligibility in the Graduated Random System

State or Territory	Congressional Districts	State or Territory	Congressional Districts
American Samoa		New Mexico	3
District of Columbia	(each counted as	Utah	3
Guam	one district)	West Virginia	3
Puerto Rico		Arkansas	4
Virgin Islands		Kansas	4
Alaska	1	Mississippi	4
Delaware	1	Connecticut	5
Montana	1	Iowa	5
North Dakota	1	Oklahoma	5
South Dakota	1	Oregon	5
Vermont	1	Kentucky	6
Wyoming	1	South Carolina	6
Hawaii	2	Alabama	7
Idaho	2	Colorado	7
Maine	2	Louisiana	7
New Hampshire	2	Arizona	8
Rhode Island	2	Maryland	8
Nebraska	3	Minnesota	8
Nevada	3	Wisconsin	8

Source: U.S. Census Bureau 2002.

Maryland (see Table 3.1). These jurisdictions have large proportions of people of color such as Asians, Pacific Islanders, Hispanics, Native Americans, and African-Americans, and seventeen of thirty-eight of the first-round eligible jurisdictions have poverty rates above the national average (see Table 3.2). Opening the first contests to this field of jurisdictions would empower demographic groups that the current system marginalizes, yet, in the aggregate, the pool from which the first-round states is chosen closely reflects America as a whole.

In the second period—two weeks later—the eligibility number would increase to sixteen (8 × 2). Every two weeks, the combined size of the contests would grow by eight congressional districts, until a combination of states totaling eighty congressional seats (8 × 10)—nearly one-fifth of the total—would be up for grabs in the tenth and last round toward the end of June. As the political stakes increased every two weeks, a steady weeding-out process would occur, as less successful campaigns reached the point at which they were no longer competitive in these larger contests. This system would foster the widest possible political debate, commensurate with the need to resolve the debate to one or two viable candidacies at the end of the delegate selection process.

Table 3.2: Demographics of First-Round Eligible Jurisdictions

State or Territory	Black or African-American	American-Indian and Alaska Native	Asian	Pacific Islander	Hispanic or Latino (of any race)	Families Below Poverty Level (percent)
Alabama	**26.0**	0.5	0.7	0	1.7	6.7
Alaska	3.5	**15.6**	**4.0**	0.5	4.1	**12.5**
Arkansas	**15.7**	0.7	0.8	**0.1**	3.2	12.0
American Samoa			2.8	**91.6**		61.9
Arizona	3.1	5.0	1.8	**0.1**	25.3	9.9
Colorado	3.8	**1.0**	2.2	**0.1**	17.1	6.2
Connecticut	9.1	0.3	2.4	0	9.4	5.6
Delaware	**19.2**	0.3	2.1	0	4.8	**16.7**
District of Columbia	**60.0**	0.3	2.7	**0.1**	7.9	6.5
Guam	1.0		32.5	44.6		38.7
Hawaii	1.8	0.3	41.6	9.4	7.2	7.6
Idaho	0.4	**1.4**	0.9	**0.1**	7.9	6.0
Iowa	2.1	0.3	1.3	0	2.8	8.3
Kansas	5.7	**0.9**	1.7	0	7.7	6.7
Kentucky	7.3	0.2	0.7	0	1.5	**12.7**
Louisiana	**32.5**	0.6	1.2	0	2.4	**15.8**
Maine	0.5	0.6	0.7	0	0.7	6.1
Maryland	**27.9**	0.3	**4.0**	0	4.3	7.8
Minnesota	3.5	**1.1**	2.9	0	2.9	5.1
Mississippi	**36.3**	0.4	0.7	0	1.4	**16.0**
Montana	0.3	**6.2**	0.5	**0.1**	2.0	10.5
Nebraska	4.0	0.9	1.3	0	5.5	8.3
Nevada	6.8	**1.3**	**4.5**	0.4	19.7	6.7
New Hampshire	0.7	0.2	1.3	0	1.7	4.3
New Mexico	1.9	**9.5**	1.1	**0.1**	42.1	14.5
North Dakota	0.6	**4.9**	0.6	0	1.2	7.5
Oklahoma	7.6	**7.9**	1.4	**0.1**	5.2	**11.2**
Oregon	1.6	**1.3**	3.0	**0.2**	8.8	7.9
Puerto Rico	8	0.4	0.2	0	98.8	55.3
Rhode Island	4.5	0.5	2.3	**0.1**	8.7	8.9
South Carolina	**29.5**	0.3	0.9	0	2.4	**10.7**
South Dakota	0.6	8.3	0.6	0	1.4	**9.3**
Utah	0.8	**1.3**	1.7	**0.7**	9.0	6.5
Vermont	0.5	0.4	0.9	0	0.9	**44.6**
Virgin Islands	**76.2**				14.0	6.3
West Virginia	3.2	0.2	0.5	0	0.7	5.6
Wisconsin	5.7	**0.9**	1.7	0	3.6	**13.9**

(continued)

Wyoming	0.8	**2.3**	0.6	**0.1**	6.4	8.0
1st-Round-Eligible Avg	**11.2**	**1.6**	**2.2**	**0.3**	**11.1**	**11.2**
U.S. Avg	**12.3**	**0.9**	**3.6**	**0.1**	**12.5**	**9.2**

Note: Values in boldface are above the national average.
Source: U.S. Census Bureau 2002.

The random process for generating the schedule every four years could be administered by the Federal Election Commission. The system would be reformulated every ten years as congressional districts were reapportioned among the states based on the report of the U.S. Census Bureau.

A handy way to conceptualize how the Graduated Random Presidential Primary System would operate is to compare it to the Parker Brothers' board game Risk, a strategy game that lets a player conquer the world. In Risk, each player starts out with a small number of armies, so no one gets blown out of the game early. However, every time a player turns in cards, she gets more armies than the previous player did when he turned in his. Also the more territories one occupies, the more armies one is allocated at the beginning of a turn. The winners get stronger, the losers get weaker, and one by one, players are swept from the board. The game cannot go on forever, though, because as increasingly massive forces scythe across the continents, it eventually becomes mathematically improbable for two players to remain on the board. The game is designed to produce a winner in about three hours of play. The Graduated Random System would work in much the same way; every two weeks the delegate prize would get larger and larger, until nearly one-fifth of the delegate total would be at stake in the final two weeks of the campaign.

Small states like Iowa and New Hampshire would be eligible for the entire primary season. They might get lucky and be first, get stuck with the last interval, or end up somewhere in the middle. Not every state would have a chance to go first (population would be a limitation), but every state would have an opportunity to be last. No one region of the country would consistently have an advantage over all the others, while there would be fairly equal advantage in being a large, small, or medium-size state.

THE CARE AND FEEDING OF THE FIFTY-THREE-DISTRICT GORILLA

Having fifty-three congressional districts, California could hold its primary no earlier than the seventh interval, since at this point the eligibility number

Table 3.3: Earliest Eligibility for Larger States

State	Districts	State	Districts
Round 2		Round 3	
Indiana	9	Ohio	18
Missouri	9	Illinois	19
Tennessee	9	Pennsylvania	19
Washington	9	Round 4	
Massachusetts	10	Florida	25
Virginia	11	New York	29
Georgia	13	Texas	32
New Jersey	13	Round 7	
North Carolina	13	California	53
Michigan	15		

would be fifty-six (8 × 7). For this reason, the initial impulse of California and other big states might be to object to this system, but this reaction would be based on the old way of thinking in the front-loaded system that has existed for two decades. Until California moved its primary from June to March, its voters were frustrated by the reality that presidential nominations were already locked up before they got the opportunity to cast their ballots. They would be understandably reluctant to return to that scenario. At the same time, it must be pointed out that because of California's much larger population in comparison with other states, its eligibility no earlier than the seventh round stands in stark contrast to the Graduated Random System's treatment of other states (see Table 3.3). Texas, the second most populous state, is eligible in the fourth round, as are New York and Florida.

Table 3.4 shows the percentage of the U.S. population that votes in each round of the baseline Graduated Random System, and cumulatively, the percentage of the U.S. population that votes before each round. Averaging these cumulative numbers (to account for random selection) over the intervals for which each state is eligible provides a measure of the relative schedule advantage that small states enjoy over large states. In the baseline system, an average of 30 percent of the U.S. population votes prior to a first-round eligible state, since such a state could be scheduled to vote in any of the ten rounds. For the fourth-round eligible states of Florida, New York, and Texas, this figure is 41.8 percent, a spread of 11.8 points from the first-round eligible states. For California, whose earliest eligibility is the seventh round, this figure is 59.1 percent, a spread of 17.3 points from the fourth-round eligible states and 29.1 points from the first-round eligible states.

Table 3.4: Baseline Percent of Population Voting in Previous Rounds

Interval	Congressional Districts		Percent of Population Voting in Previous Rounds	
	(total)	(percent)	Earliest Eligibility	Average Eligibility
1	8	1.8	0	30
2	16	3.6	1.8	33.3
3	24	5.5	5.5	37.3
4	32	7.3	10.9	41.8
5	40	9.1	23.6	
6	48	10.9	30.9	
7	**56**	12.7	**45.5**	**59.1**
8	**64**	14.5	54.5	
9	**72**	16.4	70.9	
10	**80**	18.2	81.8	

Note: California's eligibility is in boldface.

It would be politically desirable for California to be eligible in the fourth interval, despite its huge population, so that it would be treated like Texas, New York, and Florida. This would entail changing the eligibility number of the fourth round in order to accommodate California. The most straightforward solution would be to shuffle the eligibility numbers of the fourth through seventh rounds. In the baseline Graduated Random System, the eligibility number for each round is a simple arithmetic progression. The simplest modification would essentially insert the seventh interval before the fourth interval (a Mod 1 schedule). This idea of reshuffling the order of voting intervals can be carried further in consideration of California. Not only could Interval 7 precede Interval 4, but Interval 8 could precede Interval 5, and Interval 9 could precede Interval 6 (a Mod 2 schedule). Figure 3.1 shows that the deviation from the baseline curve could be lessened by extending the interval between the third and fourth rounds from two weeks to three, then shortening the interval between the ninth and tenth rounds from two weeks to one (a Mod 2A schedule). Referring to Table 3.5, the Mod 2A schedule would bring the treatment of California in line with the position of the other three large population states. Note that in this schedule the relative advantage of the smallest states over the largest states would be only 13 points. Thus, in spite of its highly stratified structure, it is possible for the Graduated Random System to treat all states great and small with a surprising evenhandedness.

In view of some of the issues raised by Parshall and Mattei,[1] another point in favor of the Mod 2A schedule is that it substantially reduces the merits of a possible legal challenge on the basis of the Fourteenth Amendment's equal

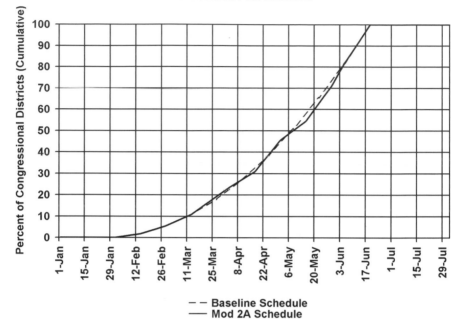

Figure 3.1: 2012 Baseline and Mod 2A graduated random system schedules.

Table 3.5: (Mod 2A) Percent of Population Voting in Previous Rounds

Interval	Congressional Districts		Percent of Population Voting in Previous Rounds	
	(total)	(percent)	Earliest Eligibility	Average Eligibility
1	8	1.8	0	32.5
2	16	3.6	1.8	36.2
3	24	5.5	5.5	40.5
4	56	12.7	10.9	45.5
5	32	7.3	23.6	
6	64	14.5	30.9	
7	40	9.1	40.0	
8	72	16.4	50.9	
9	48	10.9	65.5	
10	80	18.2	81.8	
	California		10.9	44.5

Note: California's eligibility is in boldface.

protection clause, given that on average the most favored (small population) states vote after 34 percent of the total U.S. population has voted, the least favored (large population) states after 45 percent of the entire country has voted, and that due to the graduated schedule, the presidential nomination race is likely to be competitive going into the ninth or tenth rounds, prior to which 65 percent and 82 percent of the United States, respectively, will have voted. Thus the lost opportunity of a citizen of a populous state to cast a meaningful vote, relative to that of a citizen of a small population state, is minor, and is substantially outweighed by the compelling national interest in having a presidential selection process in which a wide field of candidates, and by extension their supporting electorate, can meaningfully participate. A sample Mod 2A schedule for 2012 is shown in Table 3.6. It is this form of the Graduated Random Presidential Primary System that was first published in the scholarly literature in 2004 as the California Plan,[2] and popularized beginning in 2005 as the American Plan.

If California is allocated more than fifty-six congressional districts as a result of future censuses, further adjustments will be necessary. The size of Round 4 will need to grow to accommodate California, and to compensate, as Round 4 increments by one, the adjacent Rounds 3 and 5 will alternately decrement by one.

THE LOTTERY DATE

In the historical system, in which Iowa and New Hampshire always led off the presidential nomination season, candidates spent years building organizations and appealing to targeted constituencies in these two states that were unrepresentative of the nation as a whole, a phenomenon known as homesteading. Now that the Democratic Party has allowed Nevada and South Carolina to move into the pre-window period with Iowa and New Hampshire, homesteading can be anticipated to occur in the new states as well. Although there are a few who see nothing wrong with homesteading, most commentators see it as distorting the nomination process. To preclude homesteading, the American Plan schedule for each presidential election cycle should be announced shortly before the beginning of the campaign season, commensurate with the lead times state election officials need to properly organize their presidential primaries. Possibly, the campaign schedule lottery could be held on the first Tuesday in November of the preceding year, which would allow about a hundred days for officials to organize the earliest primaries.

Table 3.6: 2012 Graduated Random System Sample Schedule (Mod 2A)

Interval	Date Range	Districts	State	Count
Interval 1	February 12–February 25, 2012	8 Districts		
			Maryland	8
Interval 2	February 26–March 10, 2012	16 Districts		
			Virginia	11
			Connecticut	5
Interval 3	March 11–March 31, 2012	24 Districts		
			Georgia	13
			Tennessee	9
			Hawaii	2
Interval 4	April 1–April 14, 2012	56 Districts		
			California	53
			Nebraska	3
Interval 5	April 15–April 28, 2012	32 Districts		
			Texas	32
Interval 6	April 29–May 12, 2012	64 Districts		
			Michigan	15
			Indiana	9
			Arizona	8
			Iowa	5
			Mississippi	4
			Oregon	5
			New Mexico	3
			Nevada	3
			Rhode Island	2
			Alaska	1
			American Samoa	1
			District of Columbia	1
			Delaware	1
			Guam	1
			Montana	1
Interval 7	May 13–May 26, 2012	40 Districts		
			Pennsylvania	19
			Illinois	19
			Maine	2
Interval 8	May 27–June 9, 2012	72 Districts		
			Florida	25
			Wisconsin	8
			Colorado	7
			Kentucky	6
			Oklahoma	5
			South Carolina	6
			Arkansas	4
			Utah	3
			West Virginia	3
			Idaho	2
			New Hampshire	2
			Puerto Rico	1
Interval 9	June 10–June 16, 2012	48 Districts		
			New Jersey	13
			Washington	9
			Minnesota	8
			Alabama	7
			Louisiana	7
			Kansas	4
Interval 10	June 17–June 30, 2012	80 Districts		
			New York	29
			Ohio	18
			North Carolina	13
			Massachusetts	10
			Missouri	9

OPTIONS

As the American Plan gained a wider audience in 2004 through 2006, a number of options were suggested to me, and I developed others by following posed questions to their conclusions. Sometimes these came from the blogosphere, sometimes in face-to-face conversations. These options, which demonstrate the flexibility of the American Plan, and by no means exhaust the possibilities, are representative of some of the tailoring that might result from negotiations as the political parties work toward a consensus on implementing the plan.

CONUS Option

The CONUS Option would restrict Round 1 to the contiguous United States, including the District of Columbia. This would reduce campaign travel expenses early in the nomination process.

Date-Bonus Delegate Option

The date-bonus delegate concept was recommended by the Republican National Committee's (RNC) 1996 Nicholson Task Force. As an incentive to arrest or reverse front-loading, it was a dismal failure, which was why the RNC's Brock Commission came fast on the heels of the Nicholson Task Force. Thus, it was predictable that the date-bonus delegate formula recommended by the Democratic National Committee's (DNC) 2005 Herman-Price Commission would meet with no greater success. However, incorporating the date-bonus delegate concept into the American Plan could take the sting out of a state's drawing a late round in the lottery. The bonus makes better sense as compensation for a state's involuntarily being scheduled for a late round than as a stand-alone incentive to voluntarily move a state's primary or caucus to a later date. It would also compensate populous states for the 11 percent systemic bias in favor of low-population states that preserves retail politicking in the early rounds. A cumulative 2 percent per round might be a good number (see Table 3.7).

One-Time no Replacement Option

The One-Time No Replacement Option ensures that no state would be selected for the same interval in two consecutive quadrennial cycles. This can be thought of as an insurance policy against two consecutive bad outcomes.

Table 3.7: Date Bonus Delegates

Interval	Date Bonus Delegates
1	0%
2	2%
3	4%
4	6%
5	8%
6	10%
7	12%
8	14%
9	16%
10	18%

Whatever the first throw of the dice is, a state is stuck with it; that is the deductible. But if the second throw is the same, the state is indemnified; it gets to roll again. This option also decreases the chance of two good throws in a row, reducing the possibility that a state would have a disproportional influence over two consecutive nomination races. Overall, it levels the cumulative outcomes for all states in a shorter period of time.

Peer-Review Option

A criticism of the reforms that have taken the presidential nomination process away from the smoke-filled rooms of the party elites and placed it in the hands of the rank-and-file is that personal knowledge of the candidates no longer influences the selection process. One positive aspect of the old boy system was that the people who knew the candidates the best decided which of them would make the best president. Instead, the decision is now made by people who at best know the candidates from brief campaign appearances and speeches, and at worst only from campaign advertisements and sound bites. The Democratic Party attempted to compensate for this when it created superdelegates in 1984, as recommended by the Hunt Commission.[3] Superdelegates are those senators, governors, members of the House of Representatives, and national committee members who are granted automatic delegate status outside of the primary/caucus system; however, William G. Mayer questions whether the number of superdelegates is "large enough to alter the system's fundamental dynamics."[4]

In the absence of radically expanding the number of superdelegates, thereby making the nomination process less democratic, the issue becomes how to communicate effectively the party elites' personal assessments of the character of the candidates to the rank and file. A Round 0 could be added to the

American Plan to answer this criticism of the primary-driven process. Round 0 would be a national peer-review caucus in which only party elites would participate. Such a Round 0 would select no national convention delegates, but it would enable party elites to strongly communicate their judgment of the field of candidates to the rank and file. These peer-review caucuses might be conducted under the auspices of the National Association of Secretaries of State (NASS), and in deference to their historical early placement in the presidential nomination process, the caucuses might be held in conference centers in Iowa and New Hampshire, with the two major parties alternating between the two states every four years. Thus, some echoes of tradition would survive under the new system.

Swing States Option

Another consideration is how competitive a given state is likely to be in the next general election. Rather than randomly choosing among states stratified only by size, why not stratify first by competitiveness, then by size within categories of competitiveness? For example, say there were twelve states in which the vote split in the last presidential election was in the 45 to 55 percent range. Therefore, start the primary season with those twelve states, since they would provide a good test of "fitness," sequencing them by size over the first two or three intervals of the process, with the smallest states going first. The next batch might be states that scored in the 35–45 and 55–65 range, then (appropriate for this triage approach) the no-chance and sure-thing states last. Would not such a two-stage stratification improve the scheme by adding greater informational value to voters, contributors, media, and party kingmakers?

A Swing States Option has been suggested that would reserve one half of the districts in each of Rounds 1 through 3 to "swing" states, where the general election is expected to be competitive. This option would give an advantage to the candidate who appeals to broadest spectrum of the electorate, better ensuring the party's victory in the general election. There are several drawbacks to this idea. First, it would give a calendrical advantage in the American Plan to the swing states, which already command so much attention from the presidential nominees, and disadvantage the noncompetitive states, which are far too much ignored as it is. Secondly, by what criterion would "swing state" be defined? Presumably this would be decided based on the margin of victory in a given state in the previous presidential election; however, this criterion would need to be adjusted from one quadrennial cycle to the next, based on the national margin of victory. For example, in contrast to the Bush versus Gore cliffhanger of 2000, there were fewer states that were close calls in Ronald Reagan's 1984 landslide victory over Walter Mondale.

Although an interesting idea, this approach is problematic for several reasons. First of all, how well one can predict the competitiveness of a state based on the previous election? In 1960 and 1968, would California have gone to a Republican nominee other than Richard Nixon, or would it have gone to the Democrat instead? In 1980, would California have gone to a Republican nominee other than Ronald Reagan, or would it have gone to Jimmy Carter instead? Also, competitiveness is relative, not absolute. In landslide elections such as 1964, 1972, and 1984, competitiveness might have to be judged by a lower standard. In each of these cases, however, how relevant was the outcome to the next election? Electoral outcomes are determined by the individuality of the candidates as well by the demographics of the electorate.

Cherry-picking battleground states over safe states would tend to favor middle-of-the-road candidates over those appealing to the extreme wings of their parties. However, would this necessarily result in the nomination of the candidate most fit to represent the party in the general election? In 1980, Ronald Reagan, who was well to the right of George Bush, won the Republican nomination and went on to handily unseat Jimmy Carter, the Democratic incumbent. It is impossible to say whether Bush would have done even better against Carter, but it is a reasonable proposition that he would not have.

The finally objection is, would it be fair to the people of Utah to force them to vote last because they heavily favor Republicans, or to penalize the District of Columbia for always voting for Democrats? Not only that, but given that the most likely avenue to adoption of a presidential primary system is through the national party conventions, the idea of penalizing the states with the strongest party organizations is probably a political poison pill.

Two-State Maximum Start Option

The American Plan algorithm typically selects two small states or one larger state (a total of eight congressional districts) for the first interval, but can occasionally select more and smaller venues. If desirable, the algorithm could be modified to ensure that are no more than two states in the first round.

NOTES

1. Parshall, Lisa K., and Franco Mattei. 2002. "Parties and the Presidential Nomination Process: Political and Constitutional Implications of 'Front-Loading,'" 17–19,

24–25. Presented at the 2002 Conference of the Southern Political Science Association, Savannah, Georgia, November 7–9.

2. Gangale, Thomas. 2004. "The California Plan: A 21st Century Method for Nominating Presidential Candidates." *PS: Political Science and Politics*, January.

3. Democratic National Committee. 1982. *Nominating Presidential Candidates: Our Self-Inflicted Wound.* Washington, DC: Democratic National Committee. Available from http://www.campbell.edu/faculty/schroeder/Presidential%20Nominations.htm; accessed February 10, 2005.

4. Mayer, William G. 2003. "In Search of Reform: Race for the Nomination." *National Voter*, September–October. Available from http://www.lwv.org/AM/Template.cfm?Section=Home&section=2004&template=/CM/ContentDisplay.cfm&ContentFileID=40; accessed February 24, 2007.

POSSIBLE CONSEQUENCES

Former Senator Bill Brock remarked to me in September 2005, "Every reform has unintended consequences. In a few decades, someone will have to come along and fix problems that you created." While a bit discouraging, Brock's observation is no doubt wise. As an engineer, I learned the value of a rigorous systems engineering process by which a new design is evaluated for its potential affects on the existing components of the whole system. Clearly, more work needs to be done on the American Plan in this regard, and certainly it will be done as more elements of the American political scene become engaged in the debate. This chapter discusses some of the issues that have been raised to date.

TOO MUCH COMPETITIVENESS?

Since the American Plan delays the need for candidates to raise and spend money, possibly many more candidates would toss their hats in the ring than under the current system. This would hopefully include candidates, having talent but only modest means, who would otherwise be discouraged by the high entry costs of the current system. Conceivably, this might mean that voters would be confused by a huge flood of candidates, a cacophony of disparate political messages.

There were twelve Republicans who started out to seek the 2000 nomination. Half of them dropped out before the Iowa caucuses because they did not raise enough money in the preseason (also referred to as the money primary). Without big bucks, they knew they were going to get blown out by the second week of March, so there was no point in going on. There were about the same number of major Democratic candidates for 2004, and again, about half of them dropped out of the running before a single vote was cast. Historically, this is not an unusually large number to start out with. While it is likely that a system less driven by money would encourage a somewhat larger initial field of candidates, perhaps as many as eighteen, only a half-dozen or so will win, place, or show in a sufficient number of the first month's contests. The rest will have demonstrated their nonviability and will drop out of the race. Over the next couple of months of caucuses and primaries, this half-dozen should slowly dwindle, until perhaps two to four candidates remain viable going into the ninth round.

Is it more or less likely under American Plan versus the current system that a candidate who might be highly competitive in a later large-state primary and the national general election would be prematurely discouraged and eliminated by the outcomes of early small-state primaries? At first blush, one might regard it as somewhat more likely due to the "smaller-earlier" structure of the American Plan; however, how does one define "small" versus "large?" Virginia is the twelfth most populous state, and under the Delaware Plan it always would vote in the last of four rounds. On the other hand, in the American Plan, Virginia would be eligible to vote in the second of ten rounds. If a candidate expected to win Virginia in the second round, he or she should not be so discouraged by outcomes in the first round as to drop out of the race. So faint a heart ought not become president.

The current system demands that a candidate prove his or her viability in Iowa or New Hampshire, because shortly after these come Tsunami Tuesday. However, because of the gradually increasing size of primary contests under the American Plan, the first round of caucuses and primaries would not be "do or die" states. A candidate need only make a respectable showing to survive to the second round.

Competitiveness in the later rounds would be a function of several factors. First of all is the quality of the campaigning. If a candidate were successful in early rounds, this would be likely due in part to his or her message resonating with the voters, together with a well-organized campaign that was effective in getting that message out. A successful campaigner would change message but little; he or she would keep going with what works, expecting that it would keep working. Similarly, a competent campaign organization would be unlikely to "unlearn" from its early successes and be less competent in later stages of the campaign. Rather, a successful organization would learn lessons from wins and losses alike and transmit the benefit of those experiences to the later contests.

Independent of this is the "bandwagon effect," in which the herd mentality uncritically votes for the front-runner. This is a drawback of any sequential process; however, it is balanced by the opportunity that voters around the nation have to learn about the candidates via the national media over an extended period of time.[1]

Last, but not least, of course, is what Jesse Unruh, former Speaker of the California Assembly, called "the mother's milk of politics:" money. The time-structure of the American Plan gives candidates time to collect contributions and arrange loans for the big, final push at the end of the primary season. The intrinsic qualities of the successful campaign organization, together with the uncritical "bandwagon effect" and critical voter learning, increase the likelihood that early successes at the polls will translate into money to fight the final, large battles. Thus, candidates are less dependent on raising huge sums of money during the year before the primary season. Currently, it is this so-called "money primary" that determines who will actually face the voters. The American Plan greatly reduces the power of this money-driven, down-selection process, and allows candidates to "earn as they go."

The elegant American Plan curve is based on a straightforward mathematical hypothesis that such a curve should provide the healthiest growth medium for a broad spectrum of candidates, the perfect political Petri dish. However, simple mathematical models rarely reflect the complexity and inelegance of the real world. Thus one might be led to ask, would some lumpy, discontinuous, step-function alternative, although mathematically ugly, be more optimally adapted to the objective of producing a party candidate most fit to compete in the general election? Why not require at least one large-population state early in the process to achieve a shake-out of the David Dukes and Pat Buchanans before resuming the smooth, monotonic sweep up the American Plan's electoral curve; in essence, why not put at least one speed bump in the system early on?

The counterargument is that, is an early speed bump necessary? The Dukes and Buchanans are like hardy weeds that occasionally grow in the cracks of the pavement, but never spread out to cover the landscape of presidential politics, for the politics of fear and anger often stunt their own growth. But a big speed bump in 1968 or 1976 might have prevented a Gene McCarthy or a Jimmy Carter from flowering. The current system, with its huge speed bumps at the beginning of the process, no longer produces the McCarthys or Carters anymore, but the Dukes and Buchanans still come and go. This seems like the worst of both worlds. We don't need to erect new barriers to candidacies; we need to tear down existing ones. In any case, while many find the Dukes and Buchanans objectionable, some do not, and they have as much right to access the democratic process as anyone else.

Of course, the test of any hypothesis is data. As will be discussed later in this book, it turns out that the graduated curve of the American Plan corresponds to a surprising high degree to historical data from an era when competitive campaigns were much more common than they are today.

Could marginal candidates with narrow appeal, who might otherwise be weeded out in an early large-state primary, instead win blocks of votes and gain momentum in small states that are unrepresentative of the national electorate, making him or her hard to stop at a later stage? If one looks at the American Plan's process as a type of stratified sequential sampling, and if the first stage small-state samples are grossly unrepresentative of the U.S. electorate that will decide the final outcome in the general election, is it possible that the American Plan would select out more wheat and select in more chaff in the early primaries, resulting in a higher likelihood of survival of the unfit for combat in the general election?

How credible is this scenario? Patrick Buchanan is sometimes cited as an example of a marginal candidate with narrow appeal who in 1996 won New Hampshire, a small, unrepresentative state. Yet Robert Dole had little problem stopping him in later primaries. If Buchanan had turned out to be hard to stop, wouldn't this mean that he wasn't a marginal candidate with narrow appeal? In the final analysis, it is (or ought to be) the electorate that determines who is marginal and who is not, rather than the pundits.

In 2000, the Democratic Party took the position that too much competition for the presidential nomination would put it at a disadvantage. Having won the two most recent presidential elections under an increasingly front-loaded system, and confidently looking forward to a third victory, this time behind Al Gore, the Democratic National Convention (DNC) Rules and By-laws Committee attitude was, "Don't fix it if it ain't broken," in utter denial of the inconvenient truth that the system was indeed broken. Subliminally, the Democratic Party's position was, "If it's broken, at least it's breaking our way, but if we fix it, it may not." Its report to the DNC chair Ed Rendell in April 2000 stated that "criticism about a front-loaded schedule has to be weighed against a process that seems to be working well. In the last few cycles, the current system has allowed the Democratic Party to identify its presumptive nominee early. As a result, the process has helped the Party unify behind its nominee and focus its resources on the general election. . . . Therefore, at this point, there is little incentive to change the system."[2]

Al Gore started out as the heir-apparent and easily captured the 2000 nomination. However, he went on to run an abysmal campaign against George

W. Bush, squandering the advantage of being the sitting vice president during the longest economic boom in memory. In retrospect, Democrats have to wonder whether Bill Bradley, whose challenge to Gore was blown out early due to front-loading, might have been a better choice for the party. A more deliberative process would have better ensured that the party was represented by the best candidate, rather than the best fund-raiser, or the heir-apparent, or the pundit-anointed front-runner. At the very least, a challenging preliminary bout with Bradley would have better prepared Gore for the main event with Bush.

This disappointing experience in 2000 with the front-loaded system did not change the Democratic Party's mind, however. Looking forward to 2004, its overriding political concern was the sky-high popular approval that President George W. Bush had enjoyed since the Al Qaeda attacks of September 11, 2001, and throughout the early war years in Afghanistan and Iraq. "[Democratic] Party leaders anticipated an uncontested nomination on the Republican side and did not want to grant the opposition an additional competitive advantage by prolonging the search of their candidate."[3] However, the economy had been sluggish, there had been corporate scandals in the energy industry to which both the president and vice president had business and campaign contribution ties, and there was also a controversy over whether intelligence on Iraqi weapons of mass destruction was politicized and distorted to justify the war. Despite these political liabilities, Bush had no opposition for the 2004 Republican presidential nomination. The front-loaded schedule was a major reason why. It squeezed what otherwise could have been a legitimate and well-reasoned dissent within the Republican Party into an untenable blip in time. It gave an insurmountable advantage to the front-runner, and the sitting president was the ultimate front-runner. Were both parties to adopt a schedule more permissive of competition, challenges to an incumbent would be more likely.

The anticipation of "no contest" in one party incentivizes the other party to consciously craft (or leave be) a system designed to end the process as early as possible. But what evidence is there for the idea that parties are best served by narrowing the field of candidates and restricting political debate? After all, it took Franklin Roosevelt four ballots at the 1932 Democratic National Convention to win the nomination, yet he went on to defeat Herbert Hoover in one of the biggest landslides in American history. In the nine most recent presidential elections, shown in Table 4.1, it can be seen that in all four cases in which a party nomination was uncontested, the general election was won by that party. However, of the five elections in which the nomination was contested on both sides, in all four cases in which the nomination in one

Table 4.1: Competitiveness of Presidential Nomination Campaigns, 1972–2000

Year	Democratic Party Start	Democratic Party End[a]	Republican Party Start	Republican Party End[a]	General Election Winner
	Number of Candidates				
1972	13	9	uncontested		Republican
1976	18	10	2	2	Democrat
1980	4	3	13	6	Republican
1984	13	8	uncontested		Republican
1988	12	7	11	6	Republican
1992	8	5	2	2	Democrat
1996	uncontested		10	6	Democrat
2000	3	1	10	6	Republican
2004	10	1	uncontested		Republican

[a]Candidates remaining in the race at the time of the national convention.
Source: Parshall and Mattei 2002, "Parties and the Presidential Nomination Process," 41.

party was clearly the more contested in terms of the number of candidates, the general election was won by that party (the 1988 nominations were roughly evenly contested in both parties). Thus the historical data suggests that the next best thing to an uncontested nomination, which can only occur in the case of a popular incumbent (and would be less likely to occur in a nonfront-loaded schedule more permissive of competition), is a highly contested nomination. Such a contest generates more media attention, more interest in the party's candidates, more diversity of issues, and hopefully in the end, a more fully vetted political platform. Since a contested nomination is statistically more likely than an uncontested one, it behooves the parties to have a more competitive system to better ensure the nomination of the most electable presidential candidate.

One can draw an analogy between the current strategy in presidential politics and nuclear strategy during the Cold War. Essentially, front-loading has collapsed the strategic space in political planning into first-strike and launch-on-warning scenarios. It is the American electorate that gets nuked every four years.

EMPOWERING ETHNIC DIVERSITY

The possibility of anomalous demographics in early contests should be examined. In the traditional system, the first stage small-state sample (namely

Table 4.2: Ethnic Demographics of Pre-Window States

State	Black or African-American	American-Indian and Alaska Native	Asian	Pacific Islander	Hispanic or Latino (of any race)
Iowa	2.1	0.3	1.3	0.0	2.8
Nevada	6.8	**1.3**	**4.5**	**0.4**	**19.7**
New Hampshire	0.7	0.2	1.3	0.0	1.7
South Carolina	**29.5**	0.3	0.9	0	2.4
Pre-Window Avg	**13.7**	0.5	1.8	0.1	5.8
American Plan 1st-Round-Eligible Avg	11.2	**1.6**	2.2	**0.3**	11.1
U.S. Avg	12.3	0.9	3.6	0.1	12.5

Note: Values in boldface are above the national average.
Source: U.S. Census Bureau 2002.

Iowa and New Hampshire) is already grossly unrepresentative of the U.S. electorate . . . disproportionately white, rural, and middle-class (see Table 4.2). Even adding Nevada and South Carolina to the pre-window in 2008 leaves all but one ethnic minority group severely underrepresented. We can do far better than this. Consider the thirty-eight jurisdictions that would be eligible for the first round of the American Plan (see Table 3.2 in Chapter 3). The first-round eligibility pool has a population of 88.5 million people, or 31.5 percent of the total population. Clearly, this is a far more representative pool from which to select the first states.

Although it is certainly possible that in a given year, the first round of the American Plan might comprise a predominately African-American population, and in another year a predominately Hispanic population, etc., it is unlikely that the initial round would be skewed to favor the same ethnic group, cycle after cycle, as it is now and as it historically has been—in favor of whites. Over several cycles, the potential for anomalous ethnic distributions averages out.

Considering a single election year, not only is the eligibility pool for the second round even larger than for the first, it is twice as large a sample, thus the probability of anomalous ethnic distributions in the second round is much less than in the first round. Also, any anomalous ethnic distribution in the second round would most likely be something other than whatever anomalous ethnic distribution occurred in the first round. The first round might include a disproportionately large number of Asians, for instance, while the second round might be skewed toward African-Americans. The potential for ethnic skewing of the sample diminishes in each successive round and tends to counter any ethnic skewing in the previous round, and each successive round

Table 4.3: Asian and Hispanic Populations of Large States

State	Asian	Hispanic or Latino (of any race)
California	**10.9**	**32.4**
Florida	1.7	**16.8**
New York	**5.5**	**15.1**
Texas	2.7	**32.0**
United States	3.6	12.5

Note: Values in boldface are above the national average.
Source: U.S. Census Bureau 2002.

carries more weight than the previous one. The combination of these effects should dampen ethnic (and any other type of demographic, such as household income) skewing down to the noise level by the third or fourth round.

Twenty simulations of the graduated random algorithm were analyzed for anomalous ethnic distributions in the early rounds of the baseline design. As expected, the anomalous distributions tended to balance each other from one round to the next, and to diminish with each successive round. By the third interval (at which time only 11 percent of the country has voted) the cumulative deviation from the total U.S. population for any ethnic group was generally less than 5 percent. The standard deviations for the major ethnic groups fell off rapidly from the first interval to the third interval, and for all but one of them the decline continued into the fifth interval. The surprise was that the standard deviation for the Hispanic population increased from the third round to the fourth round; however, this is easily explained. It is in the fourth that Texas becomes eligible in the baseline design, and the second largest state in the union has nearly triple the percentage of Hispanics as the national average (see Table 4.3). Because of this, the representation of Hispanics can vary more widely in the fourth round, depending on whether or not Texas is selected to vote in that round. The standard deviation for Hispanics declined from the fourth interval to the fifth interval, and it could be expected that it would further diminish in the sixth round, rise in the seventh round as California (which has the same percentage of Hispanics as Texas) becomes eligible, then steadily decline in the remaining intervals.

However, it was noticeable in the twenty baseline-schedule simulations that Hispanics and Asians were generally underrepresented in Rounds 1 through 3. This was due to the fact that the four largest states, none of which are eligible in the first three intervals, all have large Hispanic populations, and two of them have large Asian populations. This underrepresentation was not as consistent in Round 1, in which the random process might select a few states favoring these ethnic groups, and it was somewhat alleviated in Round 4, in which Florida, New York, and Texas become eligible. Overall, however, this bias could not be completely eliminated until California became eligible in the seventh interval in the baseline design. Accounting for one-eighth of the population of the United States, California has triple the percentage of both Hispanics and Asians compared to the national average. There was no way to balance the ethnic books in the early voting rounds without advancing California's eligibility. The ethnic biases were zeroed out in any round in which California was eligible, which brought the average representation of all ethnic groups to within 1 percent of the national average in the fourth round, whereas in the baseline scheme, whites were cumulatively overrepresented by an average of 2.6 percent in the fourth interval, and Hispanics were cumulatively under-represented by 3.3 percent.

Although it cannot be denied that the current demographics result in Asians and Hispanics being underrepresented by a few percent in the first three rounds of the American Plan, this phenomenon may diminish as these ethnic groups diffuse from their current concentrations in the four most populous states into other parts of the nation.

In the American Plan, the initial overrepresentation or underrepresentation of any ethnic group is short-lived, and the initial advantage or disadvantage of each ethnic group changes from schedule to schedule. These transitory advantages are unlikely to have a dominating effect on a campaign. Rather, this constitutes a healthy variation in the starting conditions of a presidential campaign within a system that inexorably converges toward consensus and solution. However, for the sake of argument, let us consider the possibility that an initial anomalous ethnic distribution could materially affect the outcome of a campaign. For instance, when whites had the initial advantage, as they currently do in Iowa and New Hampshire, a white candidate might end up winning the presidential nomination. To point out that this is not an uncommon occurrence under the current system may seem rather fatuous. On the other hand, in the event that the American Plan produced a schedule that offered some other ethnic group a significant and persistent initial advantage . . . might we see the first Hispanic, African-American, or Asian nominated for national office by a major party?

It might be argued that such an outcome might not produce a party candidate most fit to compete in the general election. Naturally, this is always the objective of a political party, but is the absolute assurance of such an outcome in every presidential cycle imperative to the health of the republic? Can it not be argued that democracy gains from the occasional glorious failure that sets an important precedent for a future victory? Alfred E. Smith, the first Catholic to be nominated for president by a major political party,

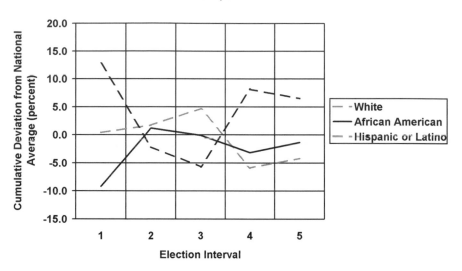

Figure 4.1: Anomalous ethnic distributions, simulation 17

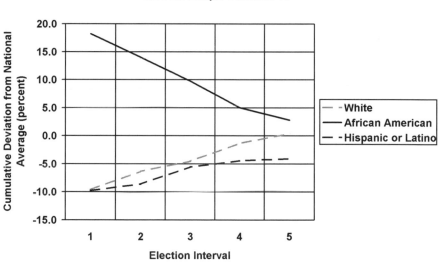

Figure 4.2: Anomalous ethnic distributions, simulation 18

lost spectacularly in the general election of 1928, but surely that precedent mitigated the issue of John F. Kennedy's religion in 1960. In the long run, what is more important: that Representative Geraldine Ferraro (D-NY) lost by a landslide along with Walter Mondale in 1984, or that she was the first woman to receive the vice-presidential nomination of a major political party?

The best measure of the system is whether it opens the future to such possibilities, over whether it guarantees the most competitive candidate every single time. This is not to suggest that the two concerns are always mutually exclusive, rather I suggest that the political parties—and American polity as a whole—are best served by a judicious regard for both. An economic analogy may serve to illustrate the distinction. The political parties compete in the marketplace of ideas. As self-interested entities, they naturally seek to maximize the outcome of each transaction. However, specifically who gains the maximum advantage from each outcome is not the concern of the market system. The broader issue is whether the marketplace is maximally open to participation and competition. The political parties should not operate in an environment in which they play it safe within narrow limits by erecting, as they have, barriers to political competition; rather they should operate in an environment in which they are equally empowered to take risks, and to more openly and efficiently appeal to constituencies that have historically been marginalized. The "invisible hand" is prevented from evolving such a political market because the major parties constitute an oligopoly. Therefore the objective should be to engineer a more open marketplace on their behalf, and implement it via their simultaneous assent.

WILL STATES RESIST MOVABLE PRIMARIES?

An objection to the American Plan that is sometimes raised is that changing the primary dates every four years will be a hardship on states' electoral systems. But, what is the actual history? Have primary dates been set in stone? Table 4.4 shows that since 1988, the percentage of states in either party changing their dates from one cycle to the next has averaged 42 percent. In no party's cycle has the rate of date shifting been less than 30 percent, and in both 1988 and 2008, roughly 60 percent of Republican primaries and caucuses were shifted from their previous dates. States have changed the dates of their primaries and caucuses for either party quite frequently. The mean number of changes for a single state is about five per six cycles. In fact, Kansas and Minnesota have had a date shift in at least one of the parties in all six

Table 4.4: Changes in Primary and Caucus Dates, 1988–2008

Year	1988	1992	1996	2000	2004	2008
Democrats	44.0%	31.7%	30.0%	30.0%	46.0%	58.0%
Republicans	59.5%	35.0%	44.7%	44.0%	36.7%	62.0%

cycles studied. Finally, not only are these changes frequent, but they also tend to be large schedule shifts. The median change in a primary or caucus date is thirty-four days. In other words, in any cycle and in any party, any given state can be expected to change its primary or caucus date by five weeks—of its own volition!

All told, the data disprove the idea that states, and more importantly voters, would not respond well to a system that mandates the movement of primary and caucus dates. This is quite simply a myth. States do it all the time, and voters are already acclimated to it. Indeed, California has scored a first by moving its presidential primary twice within a single quadrennial cycle. After experiencing the letdown of having its early March 2004 primary rendered irrelevant by Howard Dean's collapse a month earlier, California decided to move its primary back to its historical place on the first Tuesday in June; however, in 2007 it reversed itself and scheduled a stand-alone presidential primary on February 5, 2008, while leaving its primary for state and local elections in June.

Finally, and perhaps most importantly, the National Association of Secretaries of State's favored plan for systematic reform of the nomination calendar is the Rotating Regional Presidential Primary Plan. This national organization of state election officials has endorsed quadrennial shuffling of the calendar.

FLEXIBLE CAMPAIGN STRATEGIES

How would the altered structure of rules and political opportunities under the American Plan likely change the strategies and tactics of candidates in terms of timing their entry, choosing their issues, etc.? For instance, would a candidate with big-state appeal risk coming up a loser by competing in the early small-state primaries? Given the small numbers of votes at stake, might such a candidate opt out until Rounds 3 or 4 or even later under the American Plan? If a number of candidates stayed out of those early races, what kind of meaningful test of electoral fitness would those primaries provide absent the tougher competition that the abstaining candidate might represent?

If anything, this hypothetical scenario reinforces the virtues of the Graduated Random model, removing some of the big trees early to allow the sprigs to grow under more favorable conditions. However, this scenario is extremely unlikely. It is a dangerous—possibly even a foolhardy—strategy to allow one's opponent to seize the initiative and gather momentum. It is true that candidates have occasionally opted not to contest Iowa; however, it is almost unheard of for someone to sit out both Iowa and New Hampshire. Similarly, it is improbable that one candidate—much less several—would avoid competing in the first several rounds of the American Plan.

Another concern that has been raised is that the American Plan's ten time slices (fourteen days each) seem very tiny. In rapid sequence, they do not seem to allow much time to pull down the campaign tents and put them up again, moving from state to state. However, any way one slices it, there are fifty states. Which is better, to spread out the campaign out over three or four months, as it once was, or to implode it into a couple of weeks, the situation toward which the current system is rushing? The system has degenerated into two really huge slices sandwiched on top of each other: the pre-window states, immediately followed by the early window states. Essentially, candidates have to campaign in several dozen states in parallel. Ten time slices allows campaign strategists more latitude to choose the most effective mixture of parallel and serial efforts.

MAXIMIZING VOTER TURNOUT

In addition to maximizing the pool of candidates competing in the primaries, minimizing the influence of money, and giving talent a chance to be demonstrated and rewarded, another legitimate objective of any election system is to maximize voter turnout. If one accepts that the Graduated Random model will make races more competitive, this in itself should increase voter turnout. Voters tend not to turn out when a nomination has already been locked up. This was one of the virtues touted for the Delaware Plan, so it is not unreasonable to make the same claim for the American Plan.

SYNCHRONIZATION WITH STATE ELECTIONS

For purposes of sequencing and maximizing voter interest and turnout, would it be useful to know which states are holding primaries for the U.S. Senate and for governor in a given presidential year?

Consider that some states elect their governors every two years, others every four years, some in synch with the presidential cycle, others out of synch with it. The upshot is that a few states elect their governors in presidential years, but the majority does not. This may well be a deliberate strategy to prevent state gubernatorial politics from being overshadowed by national presidential politics. Would it be fair to reward or punish states based on whether they elected their governors in synch with presidential elections? What would be the effect of this? Would it not incentivize states to synch up with the presidential cycle, and would this not distract more voters from focusing on gubernatorial races?

On the other hand, the senatorial cycle is determined by the Constitution and would be almost impossible to manipulate. One-third of the senate is elected every two years, and this includes presidential years (each state holds two senatorial elections in three presidential years). Conceivably, the Graduated Random System's scheduling algorithm could be modified to give preference to states holding a senatorial election, placing those states in the earliest interval for which they are eligible based on their number of congressional districts. The simplest change to the algorithm would apply only to regular senatorial elections. It would be more complex to alter the scheduling system to apply to special elections for filling a vacancy. Another consideration is that even when senatorial elections occur in a presidential year, the state may not hold its presidential and senatorial primaries on the same date. When important races are decoupled in this way, does this reduce voter turnout, and if so, should the primary scheduling system withhold preferential treatment to such states? In view of the above discussion as to why so many gubernatorial elections may be decoupled from presidential elections, it should be considered whether it is more desirable to maximize voter turnout for a consolidated primary versus decoupling the presidential and senatorial primaries so that the electorate can focus on each separately.

NOTES

1 Ridout, Travis N. 2002. "The Effects of a Front-Loaded Presidential Primary Calendar on Voter Learning." Political Behavior Research Group, University of Wisconsin, Madison, November 11. Available from http://www.polisci.wisc.edu/~behavior/papers/Ridout2002.pdf; accessed January 25, 2003.

2 Democratic National Committee. 2000. *Beyond 2000: The Scheduling of Future Democratic Presidential Primaries and Caucuses*, 11, 16. Washington, DC: Democratic National Committee.

3 Parshall, Lisa K., and Franco Mattei. 2002. "Parties and the Presidential Nomination process: Political and Constitutional Implications of 'Front-Loading,'" 9. Presented at the 2002 Conference of the Southern Political Science Association, Savannah, Georgia, November 7–9.

PATHS TO IMPLEMENTATION

The nomination of presidential candidates is an issue that straddles the gaps in our federal system of government. It cuts across party lines and jurisdictional boundaries. No single political institution, either partisan or governmental, either state or federal, has sole ownership of this issue; there are many competing interests. Because of this, a number of mechanisms have been proposed for implementing a national solution to the problem of presidential primaries.

COORDINATED STATE LEGISLATION

The National Association of Secretaries of State (NASS) has considered the problem for several years. In February 1999 the NASS endorsed a system of rotating regional primaries.[1] However, NASS is a voluntary, consultative body rather than a formal institution, thus it lacks the legal authority to construct and operate a national primary system. Moreover, while state departments have the authority to administer primary elections in most states, many states have election boards that are independent of the secretary of state. Also, a number of states elect delegates to national political conventions via caucuses or state party conventions, entirely removing state governments from the process.

The coordinated implementation of a national primary system by fifty states and five territories, commonwealths, and districts constitutes a formidable collective action problem. This approach would require the unanimous adoption of the system by these fifty-five entities. Since nearly all of these jurisdictions have bicameral legislatures, this implementation approach entails the passage of the same bill by over one hundred legislative chambers and the signatures of chief executives. A few holdouts would be sufficient to scuttle the project, or in the unlikely event of initial unanimity, a small number of defectors would threaten the integrity of the entire system, just as the breakdown of the traditional system began with the independent actions of a few states advancing their primary schedules.

However, in the event that an effort is mounted via this mechanism, a model state bill for implementing the American Plan is provided in Appendix 1, based on model legislation adopted by NASS.[2]

FEDERAL STATUTE

A number of bills have been introduced in Congress over the years to implement a national primary system. In 1972 alone, bills were introduced by Senators Mike Mansfield (D-MT) and George Aiken (R-VT), Senator Robert Packwood (R-OR), Senator Thomas Eagleton (D-MO), Representative Gerald Ford (R-MI), Representative Morris Udall (D-AZ), and Representative Silvio Conte (R-MA).[3] More recently, bills were introduced in the Senate by Slade Gorton (R-WA) and Joseph Lieberman (D-CT) in March 1996 and again in October 1999.[4,5,6] Representative Sander Levin (D-MI 12th) introduced another bill (HR 4014) in March 2000,[7] and revived essentially the same idea in 2007.[8]

In testifying on behalf of his bill before the Senate Committee on Rules and Administration, Senator Gorton stated:

> As a former state attorney general, I am absolutely confident that Congress has the constitutional prerogative to direct the presidential election process. The Constitution clearly grants Congress the authority to regulate the time, place and manner of federal elections.[9]

The source of congressional authority over elections is Article I, Section 4, Clause 1:

> The Times, Places and Manner of holding Elections for Senators and Representatives, shall be prescribed in each State by the Legislature thereof; but the Congress may at any time by Law make or alter such Regulations, except as to the Places of chusing Senators.

However, this paragraph specifically pertains to the election of senators and representatives, and is in no way relevant to the election of the president.

Article II, Section 1, Paragraph 4 gives Congress the power to determine the date of "chusing the Electors" for president and vice president, but this applies to the general election, rather than to state primaries that choose delegates to each national party convention. Finally, the Twenty-Fourth Amendment states:

> The right of citizens of the United States to vote in any primary or other election for President or Vice President, for electors for President or Vice President, or for Senator or Representative in Congress, shall not be denied or abridged by the United States or any state by reason of failure to pay any poll tax or other tax.

The Twenty-Fourth Amendment does not explicitly give Congress the authority to regulate the timing of such primaries. Thus any Congressional authority over the timing of presidential primaries is not to be found directly in the Constitution.

Nevertheless, Parshall and Mattei cite a body of case law in which the Supreme Court has asserted federal authority over elections:

> According to the Court, "[i]f [the national] government is anything more than the mere aggregation of delegated agents of other states and governments, each of which is superior to the general government, it must have the power to protect the elections on which its existence depends...."[10] "In presidential elections [where] no parochial interests of the State, county or city are involved,"[11] these national interest are "greater than that of any individual state."[12, 13]

Parshall and Mattei also observe that:

> Supreme Court doctrine has recognized the interdependency of state and party regulations in the creation of a unified structure of voter choice. Thus, the Court has ruled primary contests to be an integral aspect of the general election. In practical terms, the primaries are critical to shaping general election results.[14]

Since the Constitution gives clear authority to Congress in regulating federal general elections, by extension it has authority over primary federal elections as well.

> With the "[Classic] decision the doubt as to whether or not such primaries were part of 'elections' subject to federal control...was erased." The Court wrote, "[i]t may now be taken as a postulate that the right to vote in such a primary

for the nomination of candidates without discrimination by the State, like the right to vote in a general election, is a right secured by the Constitution"[15] Indeed, the Twenty Fourth Amendment's protection of the "right of citizens of the United States to vote in any primary or other election for President" constitutionally established the nomination process as integral to presidential elections.[16]

Therefore it is not inconceivable that the Supreme Court would find such authority for Congress should the national legislature choose to regulate the timing of presidential primaries, and should such a regulatory law ever be subjected to legal challenge. In the event that an effort is mounted via this mechanism, a federal bill (adapted from SB 1789 and HR 4014) for implementing the American Plan is provided in Appendix 2.

However, history holds little promise of federal legislation being the road to reform. Roughly a hundred bills have been introduced in the course of the past three decades, and every single one has died in committee. Also, federal legislation to regulate party processes would go against the grain of the Republican Party's philosophy; thus bipartisan support for such a bill remains an open question.

CONSTITUTIONAL AMENDMENT AND IMPLEMENTING FEDERAL STATUTE

The one remaining legislative remedy would appear to be an amendment to the Constitution giving the Congress the power to enact implementing legislation. The Twenty-Fourth Amendment sets a precedent for some federal regulation of the conduct of primaries. This approach has historically received little attention because of the difficulty of amending the Constitution of the United States. While the procedure is certainly arduous, it presents less of a collective action problem than the coordinated state legislation approach. The constitutional amendment route would require passage by two-thirds of the Senate and the House of Representatives, then ratification by three-fourths of the state legislatures (approximately seventy-five chambers).

In the event that an effort is mounted via this mechanism, a constitutional amendment giving Congress explicit authority to regulate the timing of the presidential nomination process would read something like this:

The Congress shall have power to determine the time of choosing delegates to national conventions of political parties, convened for the purpose of choosing candidates for President and Vice President, by each of the several States and the district constituting the seat of Government of the United States, and by citizens of the United States residing outside of the States and the said district.

SUPREME COURT CHALLENGE

Parshall and Mattei suggest that case law based on the First and Fourteenth Amendments might constitute a basis for judicial intervention to reform the presidential nomination process.

Parshall and Mattei set the stage for their legal arguments by observing that a front-loaded nomination calendar inflicts two distinct injuries on voters in late states:

- The winnowing of candidates leaves late-state voters with a diminished field from which to select, thereby depriving them of the opportunity to associate with like-minded voters in support of a shared candidate.
- Party nominations are determined before late-state voters have cast their ballots, thus rendering their votes ineffective in this integral stage in the presidential election process.[17]

From here, the authors explore First Amendment implications. Although the Supreme Court has not found a direct right to vote in the First Amendment, it has ruled that it protects "two different, although overlapping kinds of rights— the right of individuals to associate for the advancement of political beliefs, and the right of qualified voters, regardless of their political persuasions, to cast their votes effectively."[18]

Front-loading virtually ensures a winnowing of candidates so that voters in the late states have a more limited range of choices. Although the Court has "never defined candidacy as a fundamental right, [it has] clearly recognize[d] that restrictions on candidacy impinge on the First Amendment rights of candidates and voters."[19] Thus, if "[a] candidate serves as a rallying point for like-minded citizens,"[20] front-loading impedes associative freedom by precluding affiliated voters from effectively associating in support of a candidate and/or political beliefs. Constituents for the same office are presented with disparate slates of candidates, with the discrepancies largely attributable to the arbitrary factor of scheduling. A candidate's viability is determined in a limited number of contests in which only a fraction of the nation's voters had the opportunity to cast their preferences. When candidates are forced to withdraw because of early losses, worse-than-expected performance and the related financial pressures, late voters are denied the chance to effectively combine their expressions of support with those of the early voters. The viability of a particular candidate, therefore, is not so much the product of all voters' preferences as it is a function of which voters get to speak first and, given the dynamic nature of nominating campaigns, when. A front-loaded nominating process does not transmit the voice of all voters but rather amplifies the voices of a select few. The voters' "voice" in the nominating process is the casting of a ballot in support of one's candidate of choice. When the parties' nominations are mathematically determined before late voters have had the opportunity to express their preferences, those voters have been silenced.[21]

Parshall and Mattei's argument on the basis of the Fourteenth Amendment is more complex, tying together disparate bits of case law regarding the Due Process and Equal Protection clauses:

> Since electoral participation involves "rights so vital to the maintenance of democratic institutions,"[22] the Court has long ruled that state electoral regulations must conform to Equal Protection standards. Indeed, the Court has gone so far as to invalidate state exclusion of voters in state and local elections as a violation of federal Equal Protection.[23]

A legal argument against front-loading based on the Equal Protection Clause might also be that front-loading creates a "class" of voters—those in late-voting states—to whom the equal protection of First Amendment rights has been denied.

> In decision after decision, the Court has made clear that a citizen has a constitutionally protected right to participate in elections on an equal basis with other citizens in the jurisdiction.[24]

Court rulings on reapportionment that have required the drawing of legislative districts of approximately equal population are founded on this interpretation of the Equal Protection Clause.[25,26,27,28]

> Since voters are served by the president as a shared national office, extension of the one-person-one-vote doctrine would suggest that the denial of an effective vote in the nomination process based on the primary date of one's state of residency is unconstitutional.[29]

Political parties might claim a need to reduce internal debate, promote party unity, and determine the presidential nominee early to prepare for the general election. Indeed, these were the motivations of Democratic National Committee chair Terry McAuliffe in pushing for a more-front-loaded schedule in 2004. Parshall and Mattei assert that such claims would not withstand legal challenge:

> The Court, however, has held that interest in a strong and stable two-party system does not justify a party, acting through the state legislature, insulating itself from the competition created by third parties or minor/fringe candidates.[30] And even where the Court upheld state interests in two-party stability it "did not suggest that a political party could invoke the powers of the state to assure monolithic control over its own members and supporters."[31] As such, states may not "enact election law to mitigate intraparty factionalism during a primary campaign" and "preserving party unity during a primary is not a compelling state interest. . . ."[32, 33]

The authors propose a judicial remedy to a political problem.

> Congress' regulatory authority over both congressional and presidential elections is essential to the preservation of national sovereignty.[34] This federal authority is not exclusive to Congress and no precedent precludes the courts from intervening in presidential election issues. On the contrary, there are prominent examples of judicial intervention in presidential election issues.[35, 36, 37, 38, 39]

This approach is fraught with dangers. With the "presidential selection" of 2000 still fresh in the memory of the republic, the last thing anyone should want is for the Supreme Court to intervene once again in the nation's political process. Were the Supreme Court to mandate a specific solution, such an intervention would only bear the imprimatur of a few unelected magistrates rather than the mandate of the people, and thus would be unpopular and divisive. On the other hand, were the Court to restrain itself to ruling the present system unconstitutional, and refer the development of a specific solution to the political process, even then that process might face such time constraints that a solution would be hastily crafted and rushed through to implementation. The nightmare scenario would be that a legal case were initiated immediately after a presidential campaign, wended its way through the federal court system for several years, and culminated in a Supreme Court decision a few months before the beginning of the next presidential primary season. In this event, whatever replacement system were quickly concocted, the next president chosen by such a system would be widely viewed as illegitimate, especially if the new system were in turn the subject of a legal challenge.

Faced with the prospect of the Supreme Court finding a role—any role—in reforming the presidential primary process, it behooves the nation that either Congress or the major political parties solve the problem to forestall the threat of judicial intervention.

NATIONAL PARTY RULES

Parshall and Mattei began their argument for judicial intervention by observing:

> As our survey of the problem reveals, there is little incentive for Congress or national party organizations to redress the issue through the political process. The most productive venue for addressing the constitutional infirmities of front-loading may therefore be the Supreme Court.[40]

This premise is disputable. Although the many federal bills on reforming the presidential primary calendar have died in committee, the Republican Party very nearly adopted the Delaware Plan in 2000. The example of the Delaware Plan is cause for hope rather than despair, and suggests that a subsequent effort, given a more widely vetted plan with buy-in from various party levels and from within both parties, might succeed. It is the political parties that nominate presidential candidates for the general election; therefore, the primary responsibility for the nomination system—primaries, caucuses, state committee meetings, and conventions—should rest with them. The political parties determine the rules for how their own nomination processes work.

The Delaware Plan, developed by Delaware Republican Committee member Richard A. Forsten and state chairman Basil Battaglia, was adopted on May 4, 2000, by the Advisory Commission on the Presidential Nominating Process, headed by former Republican National Committee chairman Bill Brock.[41,42] In contrast to the arguments, presented by Parshall and Mattei, the commission pointed out that the Supreme Court has given political parties considerable discretion to organize themselves and regulate their internal processes under the freedom of association principle in the First Amendment:

> It is significant that the courts have consistently upheld the political parties' fundamental constitutional rights to determine their own associations, to regulate their internal affairs, and to select a standard bearer who best represents the parties' ideologies. Therefore, it is indisputable that the national party itself may institute rules that govern the allocation and selection of its delegates to

the national nominating convention. The Republican Party has traditionally provided the general structure and minimum standards of the delegate allocation and selection process, leaving the states with a fair degree of flexibility in determining their own specific date and method.[43]

Moreover, the commission invoked philosophical objections to congressional meddling in party processes:

Federal legislation was presented as an option, but the Advisory Commission feels that such an approach to this issue would be contrary to the Republican Party's philosophy. The Commission strongly opposes allowing Congress to regulate in any area of protected political party authority.[44]

This places the ball firmly in the commission's court:

It is the Commission's view that the preferred approach is to implement the adopted reform model through the national and state political parties, and the state legislatures. Ideally, the Republican and Democratic Parties can unite on a general reform plan, and members of each party can work with members of their respective state legislatures to pass the appropriate legislation. State parties, of course, would be required to formulate rules to be in compliance as well.[45]

A general session of the Republican National Committee approved the Delaware Plan on July 23, 2000. At the time, it was reported that:

The biggest likely sticking point is the fear of doing the right thing without a similar commitment from the Democrats. If the Dems continue to pick their candidate by mid-March, they'll have a couple more months to run nationally before a Republican candidate is designated.

Bush advisor and former RNC Chairman [and Brock Commission member] Haley Barbour said, "Any solution has to be bipartisan. We and the Democrats have to agree."[46]

This was indeed a sticking point. In 2000, the Democratic Party showed no interest in arresting front-loading. Indeed, a month before the Brock Commission reported to the RNC, the Democratic National Committee's (DNC) Rules and Bylaws Committee reported that "the front-loaded schedule . . . seems to be working well," in that "the current system has allowed the Democratic Party to identify its presumptive nominee early,"[47] and the Democrats had won the last two presidential elections. Thus, the cooperation on reform that the Brock Commission hoped for was not forth-coming. The Delaware Plan had other political problems. The plan faced stiff opposition from populous states, which would always have been scheduled in the last round of primaries under the plan. For instance, Bill Jones, the California secretary of state and a member of the Brock Commission, wrote what was essentially a minority report appended to the Commission's report, which criticized the Delaware Plan and promoted the Rotating Regional Plan he had coauthored and which was the official position of the National Association of Secretaries of State.[48] Nor had Texans reason to love the Delaware Plan, although the principal concern of the presumptive presidential nominee, Governor George W. Bush (R-TX), was that bringing this far-reaching reform to the floor of the Republican National Convention would cause undue controversy and mar his coronation. Bush campaign aides rallied opposition to the Delaware Plan, and on July 28, 2000, the RNC Rules Committee rejected it in a 66–33 vote.[49]

No presidential primary reform plan has come as close to being implemented as the Delaware Plan. Its near-adoption by a major political party indicates that the national party approach is the most feasible one and should be tried again. There is every reason to believe that a plan that treated the populous states equitably would have succeeded with bipartisan support in 2000 and would succeed via this route if a future effort were made.

THE MOST LIKELY TO SUCCEED

A constitutional amendment constitutes a monumental collective action problem (two-thirds of each chamber of Congress, then passage by the legislatures of three-fourths of the states (passage in at least seventy-five chambers). Coordinated state legislation presents the even greater problem of the unanimous participation of fifty state and five territorial legislatures (106 chambers in all), plus the signatures of all fifty-five chief executives or the overriding of their vetoes. While roughly a hundred bills have been introduced in Congress, all have died in committee. Judicial intervention in a political process tends to be unpalatable, yet might provide the needed impetus for a political solution. Of the possible paths to implementation, the most likely would seem to be the one that nearly succeeded in 2000: national party rules.

The conventional wisdom (that such a sweeping reform of the political process is a leap of faith that the two major parties would have to take together) should be questioned. An equally tenable counterargument is that the substantial advantages of such a reform would accrue asymmetrically to the political party that had the vision to implement it first. The historical precedent for this is the McGovern-Fraser reforms of 1972. The Democratic Party leaped first, but as more states implemented presidential primaries in response to the McGovern Fraser Commission's recommendations, the Republican Party acquiesced in having its nomination process mutate into one that was more primary-driven. Best of all, of course, would be for the two major parties to take the leap of faith together. In doing so, they would do much to restore the faith of the people in the political process. It would give people hope, seeing that the bipartisan divide, so bitter for too many years, can be bridged, and that the two parties can cooperate to serve the best interests of the people.

In any case, perhaps the proper role for federal legislation would be to codify a joint solution previously agreed upon and implemented by the two major parties. There would be two benefits to such legislation. First, enacting the established bipartisan practice into federal law would forestall a possible future unilateral withdrawal from the system. Secondly, the legislation could provide federal funding to cover any costs to the states in operating the systematic presidential primary structure. Certainly, whereas all previous presidential primary reform bills have died in committee, an already done deal between the two major parties, plus a provision for federal funding to the states, should give such a bill very broad support.

NOTES

1. Lester, Will. 1999. "Regional Primary Plan Approved." *Washington Post*, February 13. Available from http://www.washingtonpost.com/wp-srv/politics/campaigns/wh2000/stories/primary021399.htm; accessed December 10, 2003.

2. National Association of Secretaries of State. 1999. "Model Presidential Primary Legislation." Available from http://www.gwu.edu/~action/nass.html; accessed April 28, 2003.

3. *Congressional Quarterly Weekly Report.* 1972. "Presidential Primaries: Proposals for a New System." July 8, 1650–1654.

4. Gorton, Slade, and Joseph Lieberman. 1999. "Regional Presidential Selection Act of 1999." Available from http://thomas.loc.gov/cgi-bin/query/z?c106:s.1789; accessed April 8, 2003.

5. Lieberman, Joseph, 1999. "Gorton, Lieberman Call for Presidential Selection Overhaul." News release, October 26. Available from http://www.senate.gov/member/ct/lieberman/general/r102699a.html; accessed January 4, 2003.

6. Gorton, Slade. 2000. "Testimony of Senator Slade Gorton (WA) Before the Committee on Rules and Administration," United States Senate, March 29, 2000.

Available from http://rules.senate.gov/hearings/2000/032900gorton.htm; accessed January 25, 2003.

7. Levin, Sander. 2000. "Interregional Presidential Primary and Caucus Act of 2000." Available from http://thomas.loc.gov/cgi-bin/query/z?c106:h.r.4014; accessed April 8, 2003.

8. Levin, Sander. 2007. "'Rush to the Front' Spotlights Need for Comprehensive Reform of Presidential Nominating System." Available from http://www.house.gov/apps/list/press/mi12_levin/pr031407.html; accessed May 28, 2007.

9. Gorton 2000. "Testimony of Senator Slade Gorton."

10. Ex Parte Yarborough. 1884. 110 US 651. Quoted in Lisa K. Parshall and Franco Mattei. "Parties and the Presidential Nomination Process: Political and Constitutional Implications of 'Front-Loading.'" Presented at the 2002 Conference of the Southern Political Science Association, Savannah, Georgia, November 7–9.

11. *Oregon vs. Mitchell*. 1970. 400 US 112. Quoted in Parshall and Mattei 2002, "Parties and the Presidential Nomination Process."

12. *Anderson vs. Celebrezze*. 1983. 460 US 780. Quoted in Parshall and Mattei 2002, "Parties and the Presidential Nomination Process."

13. Parshall and Mattei 2002. "Parties and the Presidential Nomination Process," 26.

14. Ibid., 3.

15. *Smith vs. Allwright*. 1944. 321 US 649. Quoted in Parshall and Mattei, 2002, "Parties and the Presidential Nomination Process."

16. Parshall and Mattei 2002. "Parties and the Presidential Nomination Process," 33–34.

17. Ibid., 11.

18. Ibid., 11–12.

19. *Clements vs. Flashing*. 1982. 457 US 957. Quoted in Parshall and Mattei 2002, "Parties and the Presidential Nomination Process."

20. *Anderson vs. Celebrezze*. 1983. 460 US 780. Quoted in Parshall and Mattei 2002, "Parties and the Presidential Nomination Process."

21. Parshall and Mattei 2002. "Parties and the Presidential Nomination Process," 12–13.

22. *Schneider vs. State*. 1939. 308 US 147. Quoted in Parshall and Mattei 2002, "Parties and the Presidential Nomination Process."

23. Parshall and Mattei 2002. "Parties and the Presidential Nomination Process," 18.

24. *Dunn vs. Blumstein*. 1972. 405 US 330. Quoted in Parshall and Mattei 2002, "Parties and the Presidential Nomination Process."

25. *Gray vs. Sanders*. 1963. 372 US 368. Quoted in Parshall and Mattei 2002, "Parties and the Presidential Nomination Process."

26. *Reynolds vs. Simms*. 1964. 377 US 533. Quoted in Parshall and Mattei 2002, "Parties and the Presidential Nomination Process."

27. *Wesberry vs. Sanders*. 1964. 376 US 1. Quoted in Parshall and Mattei 2002, "Parties and the Presidential Nomination Process."

28. Parshall and Mattei 2002, "Parties and the Presidential Nomination Process," 18–19.

29. *Elrod vs. Burns*. 1976. 427 US 347. Quoted in Parshall and Mattei 2002, "Parties and the Presidential Nomination Process."

30. *Timmons vs. Twin Cities Area New Party*. 1997. 520 US 351. Quoted in Parshall and Mattei 2002, "Parties and the Presidential Nomination Process."

31. *Anderson vs. Celebrezze*. 1983. 460 US 780.Quoted in Parshall and Mattei 2002, "Parties and the Presidential Nomination Process."

32. *Eu vs. San Francisco County Democratic Central Committee*. 1989. 489 US 214. Quoted in Parshall and Mattei 2002, "Parties and the Presidential Nomination Process."

33. Parshall and Mattei 2002. "Parties and the Presidential Nomination Process," 24–25.

34. *US vs. Classic*. 1941. 313 US 299; *Oregon vs. Mitchell*. 1970. 400 US 112. Both quoted in Parshall and Mattei 2002, "Parties and the Presidential Nomination Process."

35. *Burroughs vs. US*. 1934. 290 US 545. Quoted in Parshall and Mattei 2002, "Parties and the Presidential Nomination Process."

36. *Oregon vs. Mitchell*. 1970. 400 US 112. Quoted in Parshall and Mattei 2002, "Parties and the Presidential Nomination Process."

37. *Buckley vs. Valeo*. 1976. 424 US 1. Quoted in Parshall and Mattei 2002, "Parties and the Presidential Nomination Process."

38. *Bush vs. Gore*. 2000. 531 US 98. Quoted in Parshall and Mattei 2002, "Parties and the Presidential Nomination Process."

39. Parshall and Mattei 2002. "Parties and the Presidential Nomination Process," 17.

40. Ibid., 1.

41. Walsh, Susan. 2000. "Primary Reform Clears GOP Hurdle." CBSNews.com, July 26. Available from http://www.cbsnews.com/stories/2000/07/27/politics/main219401.shtml; accessed February 13, 2003.

42. Klett Rooney Lieber & Schorling. 2003. "Richard A. Forsten." Biography. Available from http://www.klettrooney.com/attorneys/alpha/f/forstenra.html; accessed February 13, 2003.

43. Republican National Committee, Advisory Commission on the Presidential Nominating Process. 2000. *Nominating Future Presidents*, 30. Washington, DC: Republican National Committee. Available from http://www.rnc.org/media/pdfs/brockreport.pdf; accessed February 13, 2003.

44. Republican National Committee 2000. *Nominating Future Presidents*, 30.

45. Ibid., 30.

46. Walsh 2000. "Primary Reform Clears GOP Hurdle."

47. Democratic National Committee. 2000. *Beyond 2000: The Scheduling of Future Democratic Presidential Primaries and Caucuses*, 11, 16. Washington, DC: Democratic National Committee.

48. Republican National Committee 2000. *Nominating Future Presidents*, 43–44.

49. Lester, Will. 2000. "GOP Abandons Plan to Overhaul Primary Schedule." *Associated Press*, July 28. Available from http://archive.nandotimes.com/election2000/story/0,3977,500233467-500339806-501946106-0-nandotimes,00.html; accessed January 4, 2003.

PART III

THE COMPETITION

OTHER CONCEPTS

A number of plans for reforming the presidential primary system have been proposed in addition to the American Plan. This chapter will explore some of the lesser constellations in the presidential nomination reform universe, while three widely publicized concepts will be covered in the following chapter. Table 6.1 provides a basis for classifying the various proposals. First, a number of nonschedule-based solutions will be examined, and then a group of schedule incentive plans. Systems that specifically formulate a schedule of primaries and caucuses appear to comprise three categories: fixed schedules, rotating schedules, and random schedules. Some of these geographically differentiate by region, while others do not. Some systems distribute the voting of the population over time in proportional manner, others in a graduated manner, still others in a nonproportional manner, and one system schedules all of the primaries as a single event.

THE PRE-PRIMARY CONVENTION MODEL

Testifying at the Brock Commission's Academic Forum, Professor Stephen Wayne of Georgetown University suggested a pre-primary convention where delegates would meet for a two-day convention early in the year of the presidential election. This convention would take place before any state held a primary or caucus. The delegates would vote on all presidential candidates who agree with the general principles of the party. Any presidential candidate who received the votes of a minimum percentage of the delegates, possibly 20 percent or 25 percent would be eligible to run for the party's nomination. All candidates approved by the pre-primary convention would then appear

Table 6.1: Taxonomy of Primary Reform Proposals

System Name	Basic Solution Type	Geographic Differentiation	Time-Based Vote Distribution	Election Segments
Preprimary Convention Model	nonschedule			
All Caucuses/ Conventions Model	nonschedule			
Two-Tier Nomination Process Model	nonschedule			
Proportional Phasing into Winner-Take-All Allocation Model	schedule incentive			
Caucuses First Model	schedule incentive			
Date Bonus Delegates Model	schedule incentive			
National Primary Day	fixed schedule	national	single day	1
Delaware Plan	fixed schedule	national	graduated	4
Playoff System	fixed schedule	national	graduated	5
Packwood Plan	random schedule	regional	proportional	5
Regional Lottery System	random schedule + incentive	regional	proportional	$1 + 4 \times 2$
Rotating Regional Plan	rotating schedule	regional	proportional	$2 + 4$
Time Zone Model	rotating schedule	regional	nonproportional	3
Interregional Plan	rotating schedule	national	nonproportional	6×6
Smith Plan	random schedule	regional	nonproportional	$2 + 4 \times 4$
American Plan	random schedule	national	graduated	10

on the presidential primary ballot in every state. The approved candidates would each be given time at the pre-primary convention to give a speech to kickoff their national campaign. Any presidential candidate that did not receive enough votes in the pre-primary convention to appear on the primary ballot could gain a position on the ballot through obtaining signatures. Any candidate who collected the signatures of 1 percent of the registered party members in a state would be eligible to appear on the primary ballot in that state.[1]

Wayne's plan adds procedural complexity (two national conventions rather than one) and creates a caste system of candidates (those with the *imprimatur* of the party and those without). What purpose does this serve? It does not address the central problem in the current system, which is the front-loading of the schedule and the consequent increase in the importance of the money primary. It might, however, exacerbate an existing problem, which is the diminishing level of viable candidacies as the campaign approaches the period of caucusing and voting.

THE ALL CAUCUSES/CONVENTIONS MODEL

In 2000, 90 percent of the delegates to the two major party national conventions were selected via primaries. However, the presidential nominating process was not always dominated by primaries. The first presidential primary did not take place until 1912, and except for a brief spike in 1916, primaries were not used by a majority of states until 1976.[2] One reform idea is to abandon presidential primaries and return to a system of state caucuses and conventions to select delegates to the national party conventions. The caucus/convention process is spread out over several levels of events, beginning at some local level, and culminating with the state convention. Since the process delays the final selection of state delegates for what may be several months, it was asserted that returning to this system would reverse front-loading.

Because of the larger time commitment, fewer people are involved in the caucus/convention process. The trend of the twentieth century was to open the political system to participation by a greater number of citizens. This idea seeks to turn back the clock to the nineteenth century; however, some of the issues debated today regarding presidential primaries would have sounded familiar ninety years ago: they are expensive, voter turnout is low, and although it is a more inclusive process, the typical presidential primary voter isn't nearly as well-informed as the typical caucus participant. These criticisms of the presidential primaries are difficult to counter, for they raise troubling questions. How much democracy are Americans willing to shoulder in a dedicated and responsible manner? Would a process that was limited to the fewer but better-informed produce better candidates?

Answers depend on whether the root problem is viewed as being information or apathy. If information is the problem, then giving more people more time to assimilate more information from the candidates may be the answer. If apathy is the problem, then giving more people more opportunity to cast a vote in a competitive process that includes a diversity of the candidates may be the answer. Extending the period of competitive campaigning, as the American Plan does, would address both of these issues. California Republican Party chair Duf Sundheim was blunt in his opposition to the suggestion of abandoning the presidential primary in his state. "It's best when people vote. It puts the emphasis on what people want rather than political organizations."[3] The challenge, therefore, is for the parties and the legislatures to craft a process that makes it worth the voter's while.

THE TWO-TIER NOMINATION PROCESS MODEL

Chip Wagoner, Republican National Committee member from Alaska, suggested a two-tier nominating process at the Republican National Committee (RNC) 2000 Winter Meeting. Under this system, all states would have both a primary and a caucus/convention process. All of the national convention delegates would be selected through caucuses and conventions.

> Each state would also hold a primary that would not be used to select delegates, but rather to narrow the field of presidential candidates who could be nominated by the national convention delegates. In order to be eligible to be nominated by the delegates at the national convention, a presidential candidate would have to meet some minimum level of achievement. For example, he or she would have to win five state primaries, or be one of the top three finishers in total number of primary votes cast.
>
> Under this system, the national convention would become the determinative step in securing the nomination, which could serve to energize the party structure. If the nominee was not determined until the convention, the media coverage of the convention could also increase.[4]

To achieve the goal of determinative rather than foreordained national conventions, this idea adds the complexity of requiring each state to hold primaries, caucuses, and conventions. It is unclear how such a system would alleviate the front-loading of the primary schedule. Even if the primaries did not select delegates, but were used only to deselect candidates, the motivations of both states and candidates would remain essentially the same. States would still be motivated to maximize their influence over the nomination process and would therefore wish to hold their primaries as early as possible. Candidates would still be motivated to win primaries, both to avoid being deselected and because primary results would still heavily influence the selection of delegates in the caucuses and conventions.

Meanwhile, voter turnout, already far too low, would fall off dramatically if primaries were no longer binding on the selection of delegates and were diluted in importance. Candidates would campaign just as hard and spend just as much money to win primaries, for less certain results. Moreover, they would also spend money campaigning to win in the caucus/

convention process. This would be a source of enormous frustration to all sides.

THE PROPORTIONAL PHASING INTO WINNER-TAKE-ALL ALLOCATION MODEL

Testifying at the Brock Commission's Academic Forum were Professors Ronald Rapoport of the College of William and Mary and Walter Stone of the University of Colorado at Boulder. In the first month of the presidential nomination season, states would be required to allocate all of their delegates based strictly on the proportion of the presidential primary vote each candidate received. In each successive month, states would be permitted to allocate successive thirds of its delegates to the winner of the primary; thus one-third winner-take-all and two-thirds proportional allocation in the second month, two-thirds winner-take-all and one-third proportional allocation in the third month, and entirely winner-take-all in the fourth month.[5]

It was considered that this idea might extend the number of primaries before a presidential candidate clinched the nomination, since the early delegates would be allocated proportionally based on the primary vote. Thus candidates other than the front-runner would be likely to stay in the race for a longer period of time to continue picking up delegates. There was also the thought that states would be incentivized to hold later primaries, when more of their delegates would be awarded under the winner-take-all formula.[6] However, the underlying premise that front-loading would be alleviated because states would prefer holding late, winner-take-all primaries over holding early, proportional-allocation primaries is unproven, and is somewhat refuted by the historical record. The Republican Party instituted a date bonus delegate incentive plan for the 2000 campaign to reverse front-loading, and it failed. The Democratic Party instituted a date bonus delegate incentive plan for the 2008 campaign to reverse front-loading, and it failed as well. It is clear that states prefer to hold their presidential nomination events early, while there are meaningful choices available; it is not at all clear what inducements would succeed in luring them away from the front of the calendar.

Even if the premise of this system were valid, the logical consequence would be that the magnetic poles of the system simply would reverse themselves on the calendar. States would overwhelmingly choose to hold late, winner-take-all primaries in order to maximize their influence over a single candidate. The result would be "back-loading," the stacking up of most of the primaries at the end of the season. In no way would this be an improvement over front-loading, for in either case the lion's share of the delegates would be selected within a week or two.

Worse still is the idea of encouraging winner-take-all primaries. The Brock Commission agreed:

> During the 2000 presidential election cycle, nearly half the states have used some form of the winner-take-all system for allocating their delegates to the Republican presidential candidates.
>
> Some have expressed concern that this has in fact contributed significantly to the short season in which there is an actual contest for the party's nomination. The criticism is that such a system forces presidential candidates out of the field before voters are able to truly focus on each candidate's ideas and message. Another argument against winner-take-all is that it does not provide a sufficient voice to voters who selected a candidate receiving a minority percentage of the vote.
>
> The Advisory Commission feels there is merit in moving towards a fully proportional method of allocating delegates to the presidential candidates. A proportional system would serve to lengthen the actual election contest, and to provide many more voters with a voice in the process.[7]

At the very least, although the Republican Party does not prohibit winner-take-all primaries as does the Democratic Party, preferring instead to let states decide for themselves, the GOP has no desire to encourage them.

THE CAUCUSES FIRST MODEL

Under the "caucuses first" reform model, states could hold caucuses starting on March 1. However, a state could not hold a primary until after March 31. This concept only obliquely addresses what is essentially a scheduling problem that would be best dealt with in a straightforward manner. More troubling is that it treats two distinct classes of states—and therefore their voters—in separate and manifestly unequal ways, which raises constitutional issues in the vein argued by Parshall and Mattei. The caucus/convention method is more feasible in some states than in others; it is not necessarily an arbitrary choice. For instance, while reconsidering California's place in the presidential nomination calendar for 2008 (e.g., whether to move the consolidated primary from June to February, or hold a February presidential primary and a June state and local primary), political leaders also looked into the idea of dumping the state's sixty-year presidential primary tradition in favor of instituting a caucus/convention process. California Democratic Party chair Art Torres expressed the problem this way: "A lot of us have toyed with the caucus idea, but then we looked at the numbers and almost got heart attacks."[8] It may work well in Iowa, but in California the cost to the parties would be astronomical. Therefore, for a scheduling system to discriminate between caucus states and primary states would be profoundly unfair.

THE PLAYOFF SYSTEM

Another system presented at the Brock Commission's Academic Forum was one designed by Professor Robert Loevy of Colorado College. Under this system, states would be grouped by the relative size of their populations into five pods, with the least populous states voting first, and the most populous voting last. The five pods of primaries, all of them proportionally allocating delegates, would be held two weeks apart. In the first pod of primaries, an unlimited number of candidates would be eligible to be on the primary or caucus ballot. In the second pod, the number of candidates would be limited to eight. In each successive round, the number of candidates appearing on the ballot would decrement by two, ending with only two candidates participating in the fifth pod.[9]

The Brock Commission report noted no advantages to this idea. However, it has some of the merits of the Delaware Plan, which the commission recommended. By grouping states by population, it provides for a gradual increase in the sizes of the primary contests, and therefore in the cost of campaigning. This would tend to encourage more candidates to enter the race. At the same time, the Playoff System has the same defect as the Delaware Plan; it forces a permanent ordering of the states, with the largest states voting last. This is manifestly unjust in that it effectively disenfranchises millions of citizens who would be forever barred from casting a meaningful ballot, since nominations would already be decided by the time they had the opportunity to vote.

Moreover, Loevy's system offers unique disadvantages. Mandating the elimination of candidates at each stage seems terribly heavy-handed and needlessly restrictive of public discourse. It is one thing to down-select to two candidates for the purpose of a runoff election. In such a case, all of the candidates have previously faced all of the constituents for the office in contest. In presidential primaries, however, the candidates face the voters only once, a different set of voters in sequence. To deny people the right to vote for the candidates of their choice on the basis of a varying statutory limitation on the number of candidacies from one primary to another would probably constitute a violation of the Fourteenth Amendment's Equal Protection principle.

In any case, to imagine the need for such a forced elimination formula is the height of optimism. Would that there were so many candidates capable of waging effective and protracted campaigns! This forced down-selection mechanism is a solution to a nonexistent problem. On the other hand, if enough candidates were able to hang tough, the Playoff System might pique voter interest by giving presidential politics a certain "reality show" feel, and an audience-interactive one at that, in which the electorate would vote two candidates "off the island" at the end of every episode.

THE TIME ZONE MODEL

Professor Mark Siegel of The George Washington University (and former Democratic National Committee [DNC] executive director) proposed a system in which states would be grouped roughly along time zone lines into three blocs—Eastern, Central, and Mountain/Pacific. Each zone would hold its primaries and caucuses on the first Tuesday of April, May, or June. The voting order of the zones would rotate from one cycle to the next.[10] Presumably, Alaska and Hawaii would vote with the Pacific Time zone. Where Arizona might fit in is unclear; since it observes Mountain Standard Time year around, it is synchronized with the Pacific states when they are on Daylight Time.

This system improves on regional primary concepts in that there would be no Northeastern, Southern, or Midwestern regional winner. For example, Massachusetts, New York, Virginia, and Florida would all vote the same day; on another day, Illinois, Oklahoma, and Texas would all vote. As with any regional primary scheme, all other things being equal, campaign costs would be reduced, although to a lesser extent in this system, since the country would be divided into three, very large regions.[11]

A rotating regional primary system divided into only three segments would blow out candidates with small campaign chests in the first round, because such candidates could not possibly compete in so many states simultaneously. Also, the time zones vary greatly in population, and in the case where the Eastern Time zone voted first, candidates would begin the season by facing nearly half the voters in the entire country. The Eastern Time zone contains more than twice the population of Alaska, Hawaii, the Pacific Time zone, and the Mountain Time zone combined. Fundamentally, the Time Zone Model is a misapplication of geography with the thinnest of political rationale. No matter which time zone voted first, only the most well-funded candidates would be able to compete with reasonable success in the first regional primary, thus the field would be very quickly narrowed to two or possibly three candidates in each party. One can predict that such a system would result in fewer candidates even daring to throw their hats into the ring, thereby giving the people fewer choices. Another criticism of rotating regional plans in general is that they do not address the practice of homesteading, since the region that will rotate into the first position in any given cycle is known years in advance.

THE INTERREGIONAL PLAN

On March 16, 2000, Representative Sander Levin (D-MI) introduced federal legislation (HR 4014) to create an interregional primary system.[12] This was an idea he had recycled from a bill in 1986 (HR 4453).[13] Under this plan, the states would be split into six regions, designated by number, and each of those regions would be split into six subregions, designated by letter:

- Region 1: (A) Maine, New Hampshire, Vermont; (B) Massachusetts; (C) Connecticut, Rhode Island; (D) Delaware, New Jersey; (E) New York; (F) Pennsylvania.
- Region 2: (A) Maryland; (B) West Virginia; (C) Missouri; (D) Indiana; (E) Kentucky; (F) Tennessee.
- Region 3: (A) Ohio; (B) Illinois; (C) Michigan; (D) Wisconsin; (E) Iowa; (F) Minnesota.
- Region 4: (A) Texas; (B) Louisiana; (C) Arkansas, Oklahoma; (D) Colorado; (E) Kansas, Nebraska; (F) Arizona, New Mexico.
- Region 5: (A) Virginia; (B) North Carolina; (C) South Carolina; (D) Florida; (E) Georgia; (F) Mississippi, Alabama.
- Region 6: (A) California; (B) Washington; (C) Oregon; (D) Idaho, Nevada, Utah; (E) Montana, North Dakota, South Dakota, Wyoming; (F) Hawaii, Alaska.

One subregion from each region would vote on each of six election days. The six election days would be the second Tuesday in March, the first Tuesday in April, the fourth Tuesday in April, the second Tuesday in May, the fourth Tuesday in May, and the second Tuesday in June. Every four years, the order in which the states vote would rotate.[14]

Since, in this system, the states vote as an aggregate of subregions from each region, it avoids the problem of giving advantage to a particular region. It treats states equally, rotating their positions in the schedule from one quadrennial cycle to the next. Problematic, however, is the fact that although

Representative Levin's plan divides the nation into six primaries, the aggregated subregions range from six to ten states, comprising anywhere from 51 to 127 congressional districts. In the case where the "A" subregions voted first, candidates would begin the campaign by having to face nearly one-third of the entire electorate of the United States. By eliminating small, early primaries this plan obliterates any possibility of grassroots campaigning.

THE PACKWOOD PLAN

Senator Robert Packwood (R-OR) was an early proponent of regional primaries, and the plan that the National Association of Secretaries of State adopted in 1999 is a direct descendant of Packwood's plan. He introduced a bill (S 3566) in 1972 that would have organized the country into five regions, roughly equal in population. The five regional primaries would be held once per month between March and July. The order of the primaries would be determined by lottery (rather than by rotation as in the National Association of Secretaries of State (NASS) plan). The regional ballots would contain the names of candidates judged to be serious contenders by a federal elections commission (the Federal Election Commission did not yet exist, but Packwood foresaw a need for one); however, other candidates could petition to be included on the ballot. Delegates would be awarded to candidates in proportion to the vote in each state provided they polled above a threshold of 5 percent.[15]

This plan treats the regions of the country equally, randomly placing them in the schedule from one quadrennial cycle to the next. Senator Packwood believed that breaking the primaries into five parts and spreading them over four months would allow a candidate with limited resources to enter the first primary to test his support. "In short, regional primaries would allow a candidate to gracefully withdraw if his campaign failed to catch fire. They would also allow a smoldering ember to be built into a blazing bonfire."[16]

In each of the regional primaries, candidates would have to have the money and organization to reach one-fifth of the nation's electorate. When Senator Packwood proposed his plan in 1972, only one-third of the states held primaries, so there might be only three primary states in which to campaign in a given round. Now, nearly all of the states hold presidential primaries, and this has greatly increased the cost of campaigning. Only the best-funded candidates would be able to compete with reasonable success in the first regional primary, thus the field would be very quickly narrowed to two or possibly three candidates in each party.

In any given presidential election year, one region of the country is favored over all others by being placed first in the schedule. This raises the specter of the presidency devolving upon a succession of regional favorite sons rather than on the best choice for the nation as a whole. This may delegitimate the office of president, as incumbents are by turns viewed by the people as "the South's president" or "the West's president."

THE REGIONAL LOTTERY SYSTEM

At the National Symposium on Presidential Selection in the spring of 2001, Center for Governmental Studies founder and director Larry Sabato proposed a regional lottery system:

> This plan divides the United States into four regions (identical to those in the Rotating Presidential Primary Plan). States in each region hold their nominating events in successive months, beginning in March and running through June. It is similar to the Presidential Primary Plan proposed by the NASS, but there are two key differences: the order of regions holding nominating events is determined by a lottery, and there are no lead-off states.
>
> Because it is a state-based system, each state will have the *right* to choose between a primary election and a caucus. To encourage the caucus system, which is cheaper to organize and assists in party-building, Sabato proposes that caucus states be first out of the gate—on the first of the month, followed by primaries on the fifteenth.
>
> The Regional Lottery System also enjoys many of the same advantages as the Rotating Presidential Primary Plan, but the key to this plan is the lottery used to determine the order each region will participate in the nominating process. Because candidates are unable to know more than a few months in advance which region will lead off the calendar, homesteading is eliminated and candidates are forced to focus equally on all areas.[17]

During the symposium, Craig Smith, campaign manager for Al Gore's 2000 presidential campaign, "recommended creating a second lottery to pick two small states to begin the contest, as Iowa and New Hampshire do now. . . . This lottery would include all states and the District of Columbia with electoral votes no greater than a predetermined number—for example, seven—but it would not include island territories." The Regional Lottery Primary System has subsequently been endorsed by the Center for Governmental Studies.

This plan treats the regions of the country equally, randomly placing them in the schedule from one quadrennial cycle to the next. For those who object to the historic prerogatives enjoyed by Iowa and New Hampshire, this plan substitutes two other small states at the front of the process by random selection. Outweighing these positive points, however, is that except in the first two states selected, this plan obliterates any possibility of grassroots campaigning by dividing the country into four regions of roughly equal population. In each of these stages, candidates would have to have the money and organization to reach one-quarter of the nation's electorate. And, as with all other regional primaries concept, in any given presidential election year, one region of the country is favored over all others, giving rise to the favorite son phenomenon.

THE SMITH PLAN

In June 2000, Senator Robert Smith (R-NH) proposed an alternative to the NASS-endorsed Rotating Regional Primary Plan and the Delaware Plan backed by the Republican Party's Brock Commission. Like the Rotating Regional Plan, it maintains the historic prerogatives enjoyed by Iowa and New Hampshire, and like both the Rotating Regional Plan and the Regional Lottery System proposed by Larry Sabato In 2001, it divides the nation into four regions of nearly equal population. However, Smith's plan contains two lotteries. The first determines the order of voting for the regions, as in the Regional Lottery System. A second lottery provides a mechanism for spreading out the timing of the primaries within each region.[18, 19]

With the exception of maintaining preferential treatment for Iowa and New Hampshire (in the vein of Orwellian doublethink, Smith dubbed it the "Fairness in Primaries Plan"), the plan treats states and regions equally in a random manner from one quadrennial cycle to the next. This plan makes more of an effort to smooth out the campaign season into a continuous process rather than a handful of blockbuster regional primaries. The problem is that the ability of this plan to enhance grassroots campaigning and increase "competitiveness by fostering a system where lesser-known and lesser-funded candidates can compete" is marginal. While it goes some way toward achieving these goals, it does not do all that might be done. The overall pace of the campaign under the Smith Plan remains the same as the Rotating Regional Plan and the Regional Lottery System.

Any system of regional primaries, whether random as in the case of the Smith Plan and Larry Sabato's Regional Lottery System, or rotating as in the case of the NASS plan, would mean that a regional favorite son would be likely to move into the White House every four years, not necessarily the best candidate in the country. One also wonders whether such a system might not lead to an ever-increasing sense of regionalism that would prove divisive to the nation as a whole.

NOTES

1. Republican National Committee, Advisory Commission on the Presidential Nominating Process. 2000. *Nominating Future Presidents*, 31. Washington, DC: Republican National Committee. Available from http://www.rnc.org/media/pdfs/brockreport.pdf; accessed February 13, 2003.

2. Kendall, Kathleen E. 1998. "Communication Patterns in Presidential Primaries 1912–2000: Knowing the Rules of the Game." Harvard University. Available from http://www.ksg.harvard.edu/presspol/publications/pdfs/R19.pdf; accessed April 9, 2003.

3. Skelton, George. 2006. "Giving California a Voice in Presidential Contests." Los Angeles Times, December 11. Available from http://www.latimes.com/news/columnists/la-me-cap11dec11,0,6144493,full.column?coll=la news-columns; accessed May 27, 2007.

4. Republican National Committee 2000. *Nominating Future Presidents*, 35 36.

5. Ibid., 32.

6. Ibid., 32.

7. Ibid., 22.

8. Skelton 2006, "Giving California a Voice in Presidential Contests."

9. Republican National Committee 2000. *Nominating Future Presidents*, 32–33.

10. Ibid., 34.

11. Schram, Martin. 2000. "There's Got to Be a Better Way," *Nando Times*, March 15. Available from http://archive.nandotimes.com/election2000/story/0,3977,500180639-500238280-501180129-0-nandotimes,00.html; accessed April 9, 2003.

12. Levin, Sander. 2000. Interregional Presidential Primary and Caucus Act of 2000. Available from http://thomas.loc.gov/cgi-bin/query/z?c106:h.r.4014; accessed April 8, 2003.

13. North Carolina State University [n.d.]. U.S. Congressional Bibliographies, 99th Congress. Available from http://www.lib.ncsu.edu/congbibs/house/099hdgst2.html; accessed May 30, 2007.

14. Republican National Committee 2000. *Nominating Future Presidents*, 34.

15. *Congressional Quarterly Weekly Report*. 1972. "Presidential Primaries: Proposals for a New System," July 8, 1650–1654.

16. Ibid.

17. University of Virginia, Center for Governmental Studies. 2001. *Report of the National Symposium on Presidential Selection*, 22. Charlottesville: University of Virginia. Available from http://www.centerforpolitics.org/reform/nssreport_entire.pdf; accessed January 4, 2003.

18. Smith, Robert. 2000. "Senator Bob Smith's 'Fairness in Primaries' Plan." Memorandum to the Republican National Committee Members and Delegates. Available from http://www.gwu.edu/~action/smithplan.htm; accessed December 24, 2002.

19. Hirsch, J.M. 2000. "Smith Releases Plan to Keep New Hampshire's Primary First," July 6. Available from http://smith.senate.gov/Releases/Releases/07062000.HTM; accessed January 4, 2003; Smith 2000, "Senator Bob Smith's 'Fairness in Primaries' Plan."

MAJOR LEAGUE

This chapter discusses the three most well-known reform ideas other than the American Plan.

THE NATIONAL PRIMARY DAY

Under this plan, all states would hold their primary or caucus on the same day. The idea dates back to Woodrow Wilson in 1913, but it has gained little support. It has not been seriously considered by either major party since 1970.[1] It is the simplest possible nominating process, and since it is so easily understandable, the national primary consistently scores high on public opinion polls. A Gallup Poll taken in May 1972, at the height of the primary season, found that 72 percent of voters favored a national primary, 18 percent opposed, and 10 percent had no opinion.[2] A New York Times/CBS poll in May 2000 found that 75 percent of voters would prefer a national primary to the current system.[3,4] It is quite likely, however, that voters would prefer other alternatives to the current hodgepodge, and perhaps even to the national primary, if offered the choice, and more importantly, if the implications of the available choices were given full discussion.

The obvious advantage of the single-day national primary is that since the vote would occur simultaneously in all states, it would eliminate the bandwagon effect, the tendency for a candidate to parlay a victory in one state into more victories (or stronger than expected showings) in the immediately following contests.[5] Another argument is that a national primary would shorten the prenomination season, and would thus expose candidates to less physical strain and the electorate to less media saturation. At the end of their article exploring the basis for a legal challenge to the current presidential primary system, Parshall and Mattei advocate a same-day national primary:

> Our arguments rest on the assertion that the current nominating schedule is arbitrary and violative of basic First and Fourteenth Amendment principles. As such, a remedy to protect the rights of qualified voters in late-voting states cannot be guaranteed by replacing one arbitrary method for scheduling nominating contests with another. While proposed schemes for clustering primaries and rotating their temporal order may address inequities created by states consistently located at the top or bottom of the calendar, there is no sound constitutional basis for preferring one arrangement over another. Under any sequencing of primaries, late states lose influence in the nominating process; indeed, front-loading is produced by the states' attempt to escape a diminished or irrelevant role in that process.
>
> The only alternative, therefore, is to set a single date for all states. A national primary day would leave administration and control of the election machinery to the states, dictating only that the time of the parties' preferred selection procedures be uniform. Such a specific constraint is justified in order to grant to the qualified voters of all fifty states equal opportunities of expression and association, and the right to cast an effective vote, irrespective of the state of residency.[6]

H. L. Mencken wrote, "For every complex problem, there is a solution that is simple, neat, and wrong." The national primary day is among the foremost of them. It is the worst-case front-loading scenario. If Super Tuesday and Mega Tuesday are weapons of mass destruction, the national primary day is a doomsday device. In the opinion of the Center for Governmental Studies at the University of Virginia:

> . . . it would almost certainly minimize direct contact between candidates and voters. Campaigns would be waged on the national level, primarily through paid and free media, making it virtually impossible for candidates without personal fortune or establishment backing to compete.[7]

As a member of the Brock Commission, then Senator Spencer Abraham (R-MI) commented:

> To have the selection process essentially come down to a single day of dozens of primaries ensures little to no deliberation on this extremely important decision.

It would result in minimal give-and-take on issues such that the succeeding candidate would not be the product of a thoughtful issue discussion.[8]

Advocates of a national primary day prescribe a course of treatment for the body politic that is not simply worse than the disease, but actually accelerates the progression of the disease to its terminal conclusion. For instance, Parshall and Mattei do not address the fact that the front-loaded schedule injures not just late-state voters, but early-state voters as well, because a substantial winnowing process occurs before the first vote is even cast. A candidate must raise enormous sums of money to have a hope of winning on Super Tuesday, Mega Tuesday, or whatever the next disaster may be dubbed by the media. Many candidates who do not raise enough funds in the "money primary" drop out of the race before facing the first voters. A national primary day would exacerbate this problem, not solve it. The arguments of Parshall and Mattei focus on the injury done to voters as individuals than to the exclusion of any consideration of compelling state and national interests. America is not simply an aggregation of 300 million individuals, but a carefully crafted federal system in which the interests of individuals, the states, and the nation are constantly seeking and redefining the appropriate balance. To level the playing field into perfectly leveled rubble does not serve the common good. The logic of Parshall and Mattei's argument is that the Constitution should permit all voters to be equally restricted to choosing from a narrow field of candidates. This is nonsense. The letter of the Constitution cannot be construed in such a manner as to violate its spirit; the principle of equality cannot be taken to the extreme result that we are all equally disenfranchised. A national primary day would greatly restrict the number of candidates entering the race, thus the First Amendment rights of all voters would be injured grievously by such a system, in that they would not be able to "voice" their support for candidates who could not raise enough money to wage a national campaign at the outset. Thus there is a compelling national interest in a primary system that is sufficiently spread out in time, so that it lowers the barriers to candidates entering the race, and results in more voices in the great political debate of the day.

The National Primary Day and the American Plan represent opposite poles in the presidential primary reform universe. The former collapses the entire process into a single, cataclysmic event, while the latter allows a measured pace of campaigning. This opens the process to the widest field of candidates, and gives the American voter more choices and a longer time to deliberate.

THE ROTATING REGIONAL PLAN

In February 1999, National Association of Secretaries of State (NASS) endorsed a system of rotating regional primaries.[9] Its main supporters were Secretary of State Bill Jones (R-CA) and Secretary of the Commonwealth Bill Galvin (D-MA). Additionally, bills were introduced in the Senate by Slade Gorton (R-WA) and Joseph Lieberman (D-CT) in March 1996 and again in October 1999 (SB 1789).[10, 11, 12] The Brock Commission recommended that the Rotating Regional Primary Plan be given consideration as an alternative reform in case the Delaware Plan was not adopted.[13]

In this system, each region of the country would form a bloc, and the states within each bloc would hold their primaries on the same date. There would be four such blocs, approximately equal in population, with primaries occurring on the first Tuesday in March, April, May, and June (see Table 7.1). The date on which a specific region voted would rotate every four years, so that each region would have an equal opportunity to be first, last, or somewhere in the middle. Iowa and New Hampshire would be exempted from the blocs, however, and would be allowed to choose their delegates ahead of the first regional primary.[14]

This plan certainly treats the regions equally (excepting Iowa and New Hampshire), rotating their positions in the schedule from one quadrennial cycle to the next. As stated in the Brock Commission report:

Unlike the current system in which many of the same states vote early every election, the rotating regional system would allow a different region to go first every four years. Each region would be eligible to vote in the opening month of the nominating schedule once every fourth presidential election. Since each state would be eligible to vote during the initial month only once every four elections and would be required to rotate to later in the process, no state under this plan would repeatedly hold a preeminent position in the nominating process.[15]

A clear advantage of any regional primary scheme is that, all other things being equal, campaign costs would be reduced:

Because many media markets serve more than one state, the cost of campaigning in a region could be less than the total cost of campaigning in each state individually. Also, states that are geographically close would have their primaries or caucuses during the same time period, thereby potentially reducing the cost of transportation for candidates and their staff.[16]

Table 7.1: 2012 Rotating Regional Plan Schedule

State or Territory	Date	Congressional Districts	State or Territory	Date	Congressional Districts
Iowa	21 Jan 12	5	Illinois	1 May 12	19
New Hampshire	31 Jan 12	2	Indiana	1 May 12	9
Connecticut	6 Mar 12	5	Kansas	1 May 12	4
Delaware	6 Mar 12	1	Michigan	1 May 12	15
Maine	6 Mar 12	2	Minnesota	1 May 12	8
Maryland	6 Mar 12	8	Missouri	1 May 12	9
Massachusetts	6 Mar 12	10	Nebraska	1 May 12	3
New Jersey	6 Mar 12	13	North Dakota	1 May 12	1
New York	6 Mar 12	29	Ohio	1 May 12	18
Pennsylvania	6 Mar 12	19	South Dakota	1 May 12	1
Rhode Island	6 Mar 12	2	Wisconsin	1 May 12	8
Vermont	6 Mar 12	1	Alaska	5 Jun 12	1
West Virginia	6 Mar 12	3	Arizona	5 Jun 12	8
Alabama	3 Apr 12	7	California	5 Jun 12	53
Arkansas	3 Apr 12	4	Colorado	5 Jun 12	7
Florida	3 Apr 12	25	Hawaii	5 Jun 12	2
Georgia	3 Apr 12	13	Idaho	5 Jun 12	2
Kentucky	3 Apr 12	6	Montana	5 Jun 12	1
Louisiana	3 Apr 12	7	Nevada	5 Jun 12	3
Mississippi	3 Apr 12	4	New Mexico	5 Jun 12	3
North Carolina	3 Apr 12	13	Oregon	5 Jun 12	5
Oklahoma	3 Apr 12	5	Utah	5 Jun 12	3
South Carolina	3 Apr 12	6	Washington	5 Jun 12	9
Tennessee	3 Apr 12	9	Wyoming	5 Jun 12	1
Texas	3 Apr 12	32			
Virginia	3 Apr 12	11			

Finally, the Brock Commission report noted:

> NASS points out that the rotating regional system builds upon a general movement towards regional primaries. Some regional states have coalesced to hold their primaries on the same day. In 1988, several southern states joined together to form Super Tuesday on the second Tuesday of March. Eleven states that would be in the southern region under the rotating regional plan participated in Super Tuesday in 1988, and six of those southern states held their primary on the second Tuesday in March of 2000. Seven of the states, which would be in the East region, had primaries on the same day in 2000, the first Tuesday in March. Also in 2000, there was an attempt by a few of the western states to create a Rocky Mountain primary on March 10. Three of those states, all of which would be in the West region under the NASS proposal, held their primary or caucus on the same date in 2000.[17]

NASS's appeal to the historical trend toward regional primaries as a justification for its preferred plan is curious, for it is exactly this trend that has resulted in the front-loading of the process. Pointing out the advent of regional primaries ignores the overall and dominant trend, which is that nearly all of the primaries that matter now occur within a one-week period. In this context, the concept of regional primaries is essentially meaningless.

Even a rotating regional primary system divided into four segments spread out over several months would blow out candidates with small campaign chests in the first round, because such candidates could not possibly compete in so many states simultaneously. They simply could not afford to get their messages out to one quarter of the entire nation. The Rotating Regional Plan pays lip service to retail politicking by preserving it in Iowa and New Hampshire while effectively outlawing it everywhere else. Obviously, such a system would result in fewer candidates even daring to throw their hats into the ring, thereby giving the people fewer choices.

Another criticism, raised by the Center for Governmental Studies at the University of Virginia, is that the Rotating Regional Plan does not address the practice of "homesteading," in which candidates campaign in Iowa and New Hampshire years in advance in order to build a local political network:

> This plan fails to break up the Iowa-New Hampshire monopoly. As a result, these two states will continue to set the tone for the entire race, and the candidates will continue to camp out in these states, preserving the permanent campaign. Homesteading may actually become more prevalent under such a plan. Because campaigns will know decades in advance which region will go first in any given election year, they may choose to spend even more time pandering to voters in an entire region. This predictability will likely dictate the timing of presidential bids by certain candidates, as they await a year in which the regional order benefits them. It may actually extend homesteading over several election cycles, rather than just years.[18]

Rotating regional primaries would give unfair advantage to a candidate from the region that holds its primary first. The Brock Commission noted the concern that "the rotating regional concept encourages a 'favorite son' candidate from the first region who could likely win the primaries and caucuses in that region, and as a result go into the next region with a significant advantage in the race for delegates."[19] The concern is a legitimate one. During the years when the South's Super Tuesday was a prominent feature of the early campaign season, six of the eight major party presidential nominees were from southern states (see Table 7.2).

Table 7.2: Home States of Major Party Nominees, 1988–2000

Year	Democratic Nominee	Home State	Republican Nominee	Home State
1988	Michael Dukakis	Massachusetts	George H. W. Bush	**Texas**
1992	Bill Clinton	**Arkansas**	George H. W. Bush	**Texas**
1996	Bill Clinton	**Arkansas**	Robert Dole	Kansas
2000	Al Gore	**Tennessee**	George W. Bush	**Texas**

Note: States in boldface are in the southern US.

The Rotating Regional Primary Plan gives an overwhelming advantage to one particular region in a given presidential year. On the other hand, the American Plan picks individual states at random rather than whole regions, thus tending to bring more geographic balance to the system. Also, in contrast to the Rotating Regional Plan, the American Plan allows a gradual ramp-up in the extent and expense of campaigning. Grassroots campaigns with shoestring budgets would be competitive through several election intervals, giving them time to gather momentum. This opens the process to the widest field of candidates, giving the American voter more choices and a longer time to deliberate. Rotating Regional Plan allows for no ramp-up, just Iowa and New Hampshire, then *boom!* It's all over. But that is the system we have already; the Rotating Regional Plan can only be viewed as an improvement if one imagines that it is still acceptable to have three-quarters of Americans ignored, as long as we rotate the insult and injury from one cycle to the next.

THE DELAWARE PLAN

The Delaware Plan was developed by Delaware Republican Committee member Richard A. Forsten and state chairman Basil Battaglia.[20,21] Under the final version of the plan adopted by the Brock Commission, the states would be grouped into four "pods" according to population, as determined by the decennial federal census. The smallest twelve states, plus federal territories, would go first, followed by the next smallest thirteen states, then the thirteen medium-sized states, and finally the twelve largest states. These four consolidated primaries would occur on the first Tuesday of each month, beginning in March and ending in June. In its original form, the Delaware Plan divided the states into five groups based on their populations. However, the Brock Commission had concerns about whether the first grouping of states adequately reflected the voice of minority voters, and whether the nomination would already be decided by the time the last group of states held their

Table 7.3: 2012 Delaware Plan Schedule

State or Territory	Date	Congressional Districts	State or Territory	Date	Congressional Districts
Alaska	6 Mar 12	1	Alabama	1 May 12	7
American Samoa	6 Mar 12		Arizona	1 May 12	8
Delaware	6 Mar 12	1	Colorado	1 May 12	7
District of Columbia	6 Mar 12		Indiana	1 May 12	9
Guam	6 Mar 12		Kentucky	1 May 12	6
Hawaii	6 Mar 12	2	Louisiana	1 May 12	7
Idaho	6 Mar 12	2	Maryland	1 May 12	8
Maine	6 Mar 12	2	Massachusetts	1 May 12	10
Montana	6 Mar 12	1	Minnesota	1 May 12	8
New Hampshire	6 Mar 12	2	Missouri	1 May 12	9
North Dakota	6 Mar 12	1	Tennessee	1 May 12	9
Puerto Rico	6 Mar 12		Washington	1 May 12	9
Rhode Island	6 Mar 12	2	Wisconsin	1 May 12	8
South Dakota	6 Mar 12	1	California	5 Jun 12	53
Vermont	6 Mar 12	1	Florida	5 Jun 12	25
Virgin Islands	6 Mar 12		Georgia	5 Jun 12	13
Wyoming	6 Mar 12	1	Illinois	5 Jun 12	19
Arkansas	3 Apr 12	4	Michigan	5 Jun 12	15
Connecticut	3 Apr 12	5	New Jersey	5 Jun 12	13
Iowa	3 Apr 12	5	New York	5 Jun 12	29
Kansas	3 Apr 12	4	North Carolina	5 Jun 12	13
Mississippi	3 Apr 12	4	Ohio	5 Jun 12	18
Nebraska	3 Apr 12	3	Pennsylvania	5 Jun 12	19
Nevada	3 Apr 12	3	Texas	5 Jun 12	32
New Mexico	3 Apr 12	3	Virginia	5 Jun 12	11
Oklahoma	3 Apr 12	5			
Oregon	3 Apr 12	5			
South Carolina	3 Apr 12	6			
Utah	3 Apr 12	3			
West Virginia	3 Apr 12	3			

primaries. To alleviate these concerns, the Commission proposed that the states be divided into only four groups instead of five, and recommended that the U.S. territories (American Samoa, Guam, Puerto Rico, Virgin Islands) and the District of Columbia be specifically included in the first group of states, in order to strengthen the voice of minority voters early in the process. Table 7.3 shows a possible schedule for 2012.

The Brock Commission recommended the Delaware Plan in its May 2000 report to the Republican National Committee; however, there were voices of dissent. Commission member Governor Frank Keating of Oklahoma preferred the Rotating Regional Primary Plan, but recognized:

> ... [E]ither it or the Delaware model specified in the report would be far superior to the current nominating system. Whether we rotate regional primaries or arrange them by size, these two models would do much to open and invigorate the process and to assure the fullest possible debate and participation.[22]

However, fellow commission member, Secretary of State Bill Jones of California, was vehement in his opposition to the Delaware Plan in his dissenting statement at the end of the report, and the failure of the commission to present a united front was fatal. The plan was rejected by the Republican National Committee's (RNC) Rules Committee at the July 2000 Republican Convention in Philadelphia due to opposition from the Bush campaign and from large-population states.[23, 24]

The plan has the advantage of delaying costly, high stakes campaigns in large states until later in the season, with the intent of allowing a wide field of candidates to run inexpensive campaigns in small states in early contests. In recommending the plan, the report of the Brock Commission stated:

> The party would achieve its goal of reducing front-loading through this plan's limitation on the number of states eligible to hold an early primary or caucus. Compression could be diminished due to the finite number of states that could hold their event within certain time periods.
>
> The plan could also lengthen the period of time for the primary contest. Instead of the nomination being effectively wrapped up by early March, it could be extended through the spring and into early summer. Sustained voter participation and media interest would surely follow. Such an extended primary season would allow for increased discussion of the issues and vetting of the candidates.
>
> Early "retail politics" could be enhanced by the graduated nature of the plan, giving opportunity for lesser-known (and less funded) candidates to gain traction in the primary process.[25]

Nevertheless, the Delaware Plan has serious flaws. The first pod encompasses seventeen states and territories, and although the populations of these jurisdictions are small, the net effect is that of forcing candidates to wage seminational campaigns. As New Hampshire Senator Bob Smith put it in June 2000:

The idea that a single grass roots candidate can appeal to 14.9 million people who are spread over the entire continental United States from Maine to Alaska, plus five different island regions, is not realistic.[26]

The Center for Governmental Studies concluded that the Delaware Plan might create four mininational campaigns:

Each grouping of states is spread out across the country, making it very difficult to have a concentrated effort anywhere. This plan would likely increase the wear and tear on candidates or the media. Moreover, having more than one or two small states at the beginning of the schedule would force candidates to choose among the group for more viable markets and opt to disregard others. Thus, candidates would probably end up saturating the other states with television ads and direct mailings to compensate for the lack of personal appearances. It is already very expensive waging a media campaign in the two major media markets reaching New Hampshire–Manchester and Boston. Imagine doing so in all of the states in the first pod.[27]

Another criticism of the Delaware Plan is that states are locked into the same schedule in every quadrennial cycle. The larger the state, the later it is always scheduled. This is inherently unfair to voters in large states. At the Republican National Convention in July 2000, Bush advisor and former RNC chairman Haley Barbour, who also served on the Brock Commission, said that the Delaware Plan is a "sincere" but "impractical" effort to fix the system. Barbour objected to a system that would allow a candidate to lock up the nomination before being tested in a big state like New York, Pennsylvania, California, Texas, or Florida.[28] It was believed that such a schedule might "permanently disenfranchise half the nation's voters, who are concentrated in the largest dozen states, [because] nominations would still be settled in the early primaries."[29] Other criticisms hurled at the plan included:

[T]he states at the end of the calendar would never have a chance to influence the process.[30]

The 12 largest states should not allow their voters to have their voices stifled.[31]

We're not excited about a plan that discriminates against the people of California because they happen to live in a large state.[32]

While proponents of the Delaware Plan contend that it preserves "the 'retail' side of politics, keeping candidates down on the ground talking to people where they live and work, not just up on the airwaves through expensive television ads,"[33] the American Plan far better achieves this goal. The current algorithm typically selects two small states or one larger state (a total of eight congressional districts) for the first interval. In contrast, the Delaware Plan's first pod consists of twelve states with a total of seventeen congressional districts, plus American Samoa, the District of Columbia, Guam, Puerto Rico, and the Virgin Islands.

At the same time, the American Plan is much fairer to large states than the Delaware Plan. For example, in the Delaware Plan, Virginia, being the twelfth most populous state, would always vote on the first Tuesday in June (the last pod), when 40 percent of the country had already voted; however, in the American Plan, Virginia would be eligible to vote as early as the first Tuesday in March (the second of ten intervals), and only two percent of the country would have voted in the previous round. Under the Delaware Plan, the percentage of the total US population voting before a given state ranges from zero to forty. Under the American Plan, based on the average eligibility of states to vote in the ten intervals, the relative advantage of the smallest states over the largest states is 13 percent, only one-third of the spread in the Delaware Plan. It is remarkable that this level of equitability is achieved in a system that deliberately gives preferential treatment to small states. Can the American Plan withstand the criticisms that Jones leveled at the Delaware Plan? Let us take them in turn:

> First, as has been noted by a number of experienced national political consul-
> tants, it would be extremely difficult for a candidate to raise enough money to
> begin the process in February or March, go through months of crisscrossing
> the country to campaign in the majority of small to medium size states and
> remain financially viable to mount a credible campaign in the larger and more
> populous states months later.[34]

Whereas seventeen states and territories—from the Caribbean across the International Date Line to the Western Pacific, and from the Arctic Circle across the equator to the southern hemisphere—are in play in the Delaware Plan's opening round, in most cases there are only one or two states in Round 1 of the American Plan, and there are generally only two or three states in Round 2. Although there might be a total of five states in the two rounds, this is a far smaller number than the seventeen jurisdictions in the Delaware Plan's first pod. Most candidates would survive these early rounds and move on to Rounds 3 and 4.

> Second, the Delaware Plan, which leaves the larger states until the end—
> permanently—does not take into account that it runs entirely against the
> momentum of the current political process, as we have witnessed this year,

wherein candidates raise money, compete in primaries and endeavor to capture the party's nomination as early in the process as possible. Based on the last 20 years of presidential primaries as well as the 2000 primary season, the states at the end of the primary calendar will never have a chance to matter in the process regardless of the number of delegates they may hold or their state's population.[35]

Obviously, any state scheduled at the end of the process is disadvantaged compared to one that is scheduled at the beginning of the process. In the American Plan, all states are eligible to be selected in Round 4, prior to which only 11 percent of party members have had the opportunity to vote or caucus. It is difficult to see how a nomination could be locked up before Round 4, thus all states would have a chance for meaningful participation in the process.

Perhaps most importantly, the Delaware Plan makes the assumption that our nation's most populous states will cede their vote and their voice to the smaller, less diverse states in perpetuity—a process that is certainly not fair or equitable for many Americans. By contrast, the Rotating Regional Presidential Primary will ensure that each state and region of the nation has the opportunity to influence the selection of the presidential nominees at least once over a period of two or three presidential election cycles. In short, the process must be fair for all or all will want to be first in the process.[36]

The American Plan makes a far smaller assumption, that our nation's most populous states will allow a slight scheduling advantage to low-population states in acknowledgement that retail-politicking in small venues allows more candidates to survive until the later rounds, thereby mitigating the disadvantage of being a larger and on average a slightly later state. This is a process that is fair and equitable for all Americans.

THE BEST OF BOTH WORLDS

If the quest for the presidency can be compared to climbing a mountain, then the time charts comparing the proposed reforms to the presidential primary schedule clearly show that the American Plan results in an initial slope that is gentle enough for many candidates to ascend at first, but one that becomes steeper over the ensuing weeks, ensuring that only the fittest candidates succeed in scaling the final summit. The slope of the American Plan is smooth and graceful, not jerky and discontinuous.

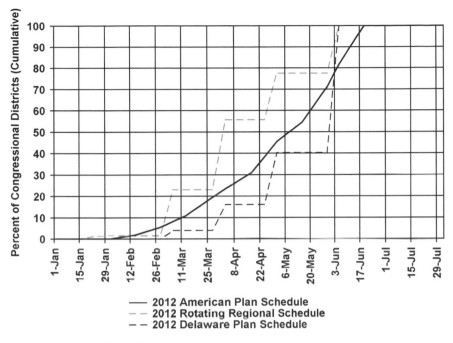

Figure 7.1: Comparison of reform plans.

No other proposed system of reform approaches its mathematical elegance (see Figure 7.1).

The Vanishing Voter Project at the Joan Shorenstein Center on the Press, Politics, and Public Policy (Harvard University) concluded that reform proposals, when it comes to the nominating process, should be judged on the basis of their ability to foster:

- A shorter campaign.
- A nominating process that remains competitive for a longer period of time in order to give the public a greater opportunity to engage the campaign and to become informed about the candidates.
- A briefer interval between the decisive contests and the conventions in order to help people sustain the levels of public engagement and information they had attained when the nominating campaign peaked.
- A system that increases the likelihood that voters in all states will have an effective voice in the selection of the nominees.[37]

The American Plan satisfies three of these criteria. As for a shorter campaign season, in 2008, we will see a twenty-two-day campaign from the Iowa caucuses on January 14 to the February 5 Mega Tuesday, after which campaigning will effectively cease. Indeed the Florida primary on January 29, only fifteen days after Iowa, may mark the end of the campaign. This situation is already a disaster, and making the campaign shorter still is an outstandingly bad idea.

Quite often during the Q&A period following my presentation of the American Plan, someone asks, "Doesn't a longer campaign season cost more money and hurt grassroots candidates?"

My answer is, "It's not about the total amount of money a candidate has to raise; what matters more is how much has to be raised when. How many people in the audience paid for their house in one lump sum? How many have a mortgage? But you end up paying more when you have a mortgage, don't you? Similarly, a longer campaign seasons would lower the barriers to entry, because many more candidates could afford to stretch their payments over a longer period of time."

Although the American Plan was developed in isolation from the other plans for reforming the presidential primary system, yet it includes the best features of some of these other systems. Like the Regional Lottery System and the Smith Plan it selects the order of states and territories in the schedule via a random process, thus all states are treated fairly. Also, as with the Smith Plan, and to a lesser extent the Regional Lottery System, the American Plan distributes the dates of individual primaries and caucuses so that they are not bunched together on the first Tuesday of each month. Like the Delaware Plan, the American Plan structures the overall primary schedule so that the number of delegates at stake starts out small and gradually increases, allowing a greater number of campaigns to begin at the grass roots level and build momentum.

Of all of the ideas for reforming the presidential nomination process, the top competitors to the American Plan are the Delaware Plan and the Rotating Regional Plan. Each has part of the correct solution. The Delaware Plan provides for a gradual escalation of the campaign, but keeps the states in a static order, with some permanently privileged, and some permanently penalized; it is inconceivable that the twelve states in the last pod, comprising 59 percent of the American population, will ever accept this. The Rotating Regional Plan allows for a dynamic ordering of the states, but does not allow for a gradual escalation of the campaign, thus Big Money will win over good ideas and good candidates.

Only the American Plan has both a graduated schedule to promote campaign competitiveness, and a dynamic, equitable ordering of the states. The Delaware Plan increases campaign competitiveness but is not fair to all states. The Rotating Regional Plan is fair to all states but does not increase campaign competitiveness. Only the American Plan increases campaign competitiveness and is fair to all states (see Table 7.4).

Table 7.4: American Plan, Delaware Plan, and Rotating Regional Plan

Criteria	American Plan	Delaware Plan	Rotating Regional Plan
Delays costly, high stakes campaigns in large states until later in the season, allowing a wide field of candidates to run inexpensive campaigns in small states in early contests.	*Yes.* The first three rounds involve a handful of states: Round 1: 1.8% of electorate. Round 2: 3.6% of electorate. Round 3: 5.5% of electorate.	*No.* All "pods" contain large numbers of states, making campaigning costly: Pod 1: Seventeen states and territories. Pod 2: Thirteen states. Pod 3: Thirteen states. Pod 4: Twelve states.	*No.* The first interval encompasses 25% of the American electorate, forcing candidates to wage quasi -national campaigns.
Enhances "retail politics" by the graduated nature of the plan, giving opportunity for lesser-known (and less funded) candidates to gain traction in the primary process.	*Yes.* Every candidate can compete in one or two small states in the first interval. The plan preserves retail politicking in small states early in the season. It gives an underfunded grassroots campaign a chance to catch fire and take off.	*No.* The first "pod" encompasses seventeen states and territories, forcing candidates to wage quasinational campaigns.	*No.* Retail politicking is impossible when candidates must campaign in 1/4 of the nation simultaneously. The nominee is determined in the first interval, thus all candidates spend all of their campaign money in this "do or die" round. Big Money wins the race.
Enables populous states early enough participation in the nomination process to have a strong influence on the outcome.	*Yes.* IL, PA, OH, and MI are eligible for Round 3, prior to which only 5.5% of the American electorate has voted. CA, TX, NY, and FL are eligible for Round 4, at which point only 11% of the American electorate has voted.	*No.* The twelve most populous states, from CA to VA, are always in the last "pod."	*Yes.* Each regional primary includes large and small states.

(Continued)

(Continued)

Criteria	American Plan	Delaware Plan	Rotating Regional Plan
"A nominating process that remains competitive for a longer period of time in order to give the public a greater opportunity to engage the campaign and to become informed about the candidates." —Vanishing Voter Project, Kennedy School of Government.	*Yes.* A graduated schedule allows campaign competitiveness to be sustained over a longer portion of the primary season. The plan gives candidates a chance to bounce back from early defeats.	*Marginal.* A graduated schedule promotes campaign competitiveness; however, even the first "pod" contains large numbers of states, making campaigning costly.	No. Competitive campaigning ends with the first regional primary. The remaining regional primaries are virtually uncontested.
"A briefer interval between the decisive contests and the conventions in order to help people sustain the levels of public engagement and information they had attained when the nominating campaign peaked." —Vanishing Voter Project, Kennedy School of Government.	*Yes.* The decisive contests do not occur until near the end of the primary season.	Yes. The decisive contests do not occur until near the end of the primary season.	No. The decisive contests occur at the beginning of the primary season.
"A system that increases the likelihood that voters in all states will have an effective voice in the selection of the nominees." —Vanishing Voter Project, Kennedy School of Government.	*Yes.* A graduated schedule allows campaign competitiveness to be sustained over a longer portion of the primary season, and increases the likelihood that voters in all states will have an effective voice in the selection of the nominees.	*Marginal.* A graduated schedule allows campaign competitiveness; however, with a large first "pod" campaigning is costly and candidates are likely to withdraw, or not even enter the race.	No. In effect, the first region to vote chooses the nominee. Most other candidates drop out of the race. The remaining 3/4 of the country are left with few choices, if any.

Changes made to the 2004 schedule were supposed to front-load delegates and essentially end the nomination battle early so energy could be focused on Bush. The commission seemed to think this idea failed. —DNC Commission on Presidential Nomination Timing and Scheduling.	*Yes*. The plan is specifically designed to end front-loading.	No. The plan institutionalizes front-loading by having 1/4 of the country vote on the same day. In comparison, after more than a month of voting, by March 1, 2004, the Democratic Party selected 23% of its delegates in the most front-loaded schedule in history.
There was some sense that a longer selection process helps: deflate the importance of early acting states, candidates get better known, issue positions get better developed and better understood by voters. —DNC Commission on Presidential Nomination Timing and Scheduling.	*Yes*. A graduated schedule reduces the importance of early acting states. A protracted, competitive campaign increases discussion of the issues and vetting of the candidates.	No. Competitive campaigning, and therefore the discussion of issues and vetting of candidates, ends with the first regional primary.

NOTES

1. University of Virginia, Center for Governmental Studies. 2001. *Report of the National Symposium on Presidential Selection*, 17. Charlottesville: University of Virginia. Available from http://www.centerforpolitics.org/reform/nssreport_entire.pdf; accessed January 4, 2003.

2. *Congressional Quarterly Weekly Report.* 1972. "Presidential Primaries: Proposals for a New System." July 8, 1650–1654.

3. Painter, Tom. 2000. "National Primary Day." Oped.com, June 1. Available from http://www.oped.com/archives/archive-G11.html; accessed January 4, 2003.

4. Marlantes, Liz. 2002. "Primary Races—Over in One Day?" *Christian Science Monitor*, January 18. Available from http://www.csmonitor.com/2002/0118/p01s02-uspo.html; accessed January 4, 2003.

5. *Congressional Quarterly* 1972, "Presidential Primaries: Proposals for a New System."

6. Parshall, Lisa K., and Franco Mattei. 2002. "Parties and the Presidential Nomination Process: Political and Constitutional Implications of 'Front-Loading,'" 37–38. Presented at the 2002 Conference of the Southern Political Science Association, Savannah, Georgia, November 7–9.

7. University of Virginia 2001. *Report of the National Symposium on Presidential Selection*, 17.

8. Republican National Committee, Advisory Commission on the Presidential Nominating Process. 2000. *Nominating Future Presidents*, 42. Washington, DC: Republican National Committee. Available from http://www.rnc.org/media/pdfs/brockreport.pdf; accessed February 13, 2003.

9. Lester, Will. 1999. "Regional Primary Plan Approved." *Washington Post*, February 13. Available from http://www.washingtonpost.com/wp-srv/politics/campaigns/wh2000/stories/primary021399.htm; accessed December 10, 2003.

10. Gorton, Slade, and Joseph Lieberman. 1999. "Regional Presidential Selection Act of 1999." Available from http://thomas.loc.gov/cgi-bin/query/z?c106:s.1789; accessed April 8, 2003.

11. Lieberman, Joseph. 1999. "Gorton, Lieberman Call for Presidential Selection Overhaul." News release, October 26. Available from http://www.senate.gov/member/ct/lieberman/general/r102699a.html; accessed January 4, 2003.

12. Gorton, Slade. 2000. "Testimony of Senator Slade Gorton (WA) Before the Committee on Rules and Administration," United States Senate, March 29, 2000. Available from http://rules.senate.gov/hearings/2000/032900gorton.htm; accessed January 25, 2003.

13. Republican National Committee 2000. *Nominating Future Presidents*, 30.

14. National Association of Secretaries of State. 2000. "Presidential Primary Plan." Available from http://www.nass.org/issues.html; accessed December 23, 2002.

15. Republican National Committee 2000. *Nominating Future Presidents*, 29.

16. Ibid., 29.

17. Ibid., 28.

18. University of Virginia 2001. Report of the National Symposium on Presidential Selection, 21.

19. Republican National Committee 2000. *Nominating Future Presidents*, 29.

20. University of Virginia 2001. *Report of the National Symposium on Presidential Selection*, 18.

21. Klett Rooney Lieber & Schorling. 2003. "Richard A. Forsten." Biography. Available from http://www.klettrooney.com/attorneys/alpha/f/forstenra.html; accessed February 13, 2003.

22. Republican National Committee 2000. *Nominating Future Presidents*, 45.

23. Walsh, Susan. 2000. "Primary Reform Clears GOP Hurdle." CBSNews.com, July 26. Available from http://www.cbsnews.com/stories/2000/07/27/politics/main219401.shtml; accessed February 13, 2003.

24. Lester, Will. 2000. "GOP Abandons Plan to Overhaul Primary Schedule." *Associated Press*, July 28. Available from http://archive.nandotimes.com/election2000/story/0,3977,500233467-500339806-501946106-0-nandotimes,00.html; accessed January 4, 2003.

25. Republican National Committee 2000. *Nominating Future Presidents*, 27–28.

26. Smith, Robert. 2000. "Senator Bob Smith's 'Fairness in Primaries' Plan." Memorandum to the Republican National Committee Members and Delegates. Available from http://www.gwu.edu/~action/smithplan.htm; accessed December 24, 2002.

27. University of Virginia 2001. Report of the National Symposium on Presidential Selection, 20.

28. Walsh 2000, "Primary Reform Clears GOP Hurdle."

29. Broder, David S. 2000. "GOP Begins Difficult Overhaul of Primaries." *Washington Post*, May 12.

30. Clymer, Adam. 2000. "G.O.P. Panel Sets Vote on Revising Primaries," *New York Times*, May 12.

31. Smith, Mike. 2000. "Republicans Debate Changes in Primary Schedule." CNN.com, May 12, 2000. Available from http://www.cnn.com/2000/ALLPOLITICS/05/12/primaries.gop.ap/; accessed January 2, 2003.

32. Schneider, Mary Beth. 2000. "Meeting Here, GOP Panel is Rethinking Primary System." *Indianapolis Star*, May 10.

33. Walsh 2000, "Primary Reform Clears GOP Hurdle."

34. Republican National Committee 2000. *Nominating Future Presidents*, 44.

35. Ibid., 44.

36. Ibid., 44.

37. Patterson, Thomas E. 2000. "Public Involvement and the 2000 Nominating Campaign: Implications for Electoral Reform," The Vanishing Voter Project, April 27. Available from http://www.vanishingvoter.org/releases/04-27-00prim-4.shtml; accessed February 13, 2003.

PART IV

THE JOURNEY

8

AN INTELLECTUAL EXERCISE

THE BACK OF THE ENVELOPE

Moving now from the political science behind the American Plan, the next few chapters recount my experiences in the on-the-ground politics that built support for the plan. It is structured as a narrative, with some occasional opinion-editorials, both published and unpublished. As such, these chapters veer away from the usual track of a political science book. However, the American Plan does not have its origins in a political science department in academe, although it developed with the aid of a professor. Neither does it have its origins in the political leadership of this country, although its rise to the national debate would have been impossible without the support of politicians. Rather, the American Plan is an insurgent idea in both venues, laying siege in each realm to the fortresses of the "not invented here" mentality. It is an idea thought up by one of the people, and then taken up one by one by other people.

I first noticed the front-loading of the presidential primaries in 1992, during the second presidential primary season to sport a Super Tuesday, and I said to myself, "This isn't good. It'll all be over before they get around to California. There has to be a better way." The last time the California primary had mattered was in 1976, when it put Ronald Reagan within striking distance of Gerald Ford. California ought to matter more often than that. Any state ought to matter more often than that, and no state should matter as much as Iowa and New Hampshire do.

It had been nearly twenty years since I had taken two lower-division political science courses at the College of San Mateo, one in American government, the other in state and local government. Ronald Reagan was still governor of

California, and Richard Nixon was president of the United States. After a short stint as an enlisted in the United States Air Force, I attended the University of Southern California on an Air Force scholarship and commissioning program, obtaining a bachelor's degree in aerospace engineering in 1978. Now, here I was, years later, out of the Air Force again after serving twelve years as an officer, watching Bill Clinton on the road to the White House, and thinking that road needs some straightening out. I suppose it offended my engineer's sense of design and system that the presidential nomination process had no design and had no system to it; rather, "it had jest growed that way." Given how meticulously the framers of the Constitution had crafted an elegant clockwork of interlocking governmental functions, the haphazard way we were nominating presidential candidates seemed to be an affront to their sensibilities and intellects. What we were doing was self-interested, shortsighted, and slipshod.

It was also spoiling my fun. During each presidential campaign in the 1970s I would try to anticipate which political party was going to have the tightest nomination race by the time the California primary rolled around in June, then I would register with that party. Front-loading put an end to that.

So, I took out my mental slide-rule and went to work. (Yes, I was one of the last engineers to graduate having learned on the slide-rule—handheld calculators were just coming in during the late 1970s.) I began it as simply an interesting mental exercise, however, not as a mission. After all, my bachelor's degree—now fourteen years old—was in aerospace engineering, not political science, and I simply wondered whether I could construct a mathematical solution to a political problem. It was the only fun I could look forward to in this 1992 primary season, since the California primary would come too late to matter.

Despite having so little academic background in political science, and no experience in politics except going to the polls regularly, I somehow understood that what had made the nomination process work as well as it did was that it was spread out over nearly four months, from the beginning of March to the end of June. No date on the primary calendar was decisive; rather, candidates had to go on, week after week like football players, and giving their best effort on every down. At its best, a campaign was a magnificent seesaw battle whose outcome was uncertain until the final gun. In 1976, the game had nearly gone into overtime, as both the Ford and Reagan teams prepared to slug it out at the Republican National Convention.

Another thing I was fairly sure of was that the campaign season should start out slow and small. That way, a lot of candidates could throw in their ante. Even if you had it, spending $50 million in New Hampshire wouldn't make any sense if you knew you were still going to need to win in Pennsylvania or Florida somewhere down the line. The strategy for all the candidates should be to spend just enough to win by just enough, and then move on to the next state.

Next, approaching the problem as an engineer, I needed to come up with a convenient way to mathematically model the system. The system had fifty states, which is a nice, round number, but it also had the District of Columbia, Puerto Rico, the U.S. Virgin Islands, Guam, and American Samoa. Although the last four didn't vote for president in the general election, they did send delegates to the party conventions. Now, each of the two major political parties had a drastically different total of delegates; the Democratic Party had about half again as many. Still more complicated was the fact that the number of delegates from each state was determined on the basis of party registration, not on the basis of its total population. However, the subtleties of this didn't matter so much to me, since my objective was to design a system for both parties, not one tailored to the idiosyncrasies of one or the other. In any case, party registration in a state could change over time; the Solid South had been solidly Democratic until the 1960s, and now it was solidly Republican. The system I designed had to be independent of such political shifts. So the mathematical model only needed to represent a reasonable approximation of the population, and the units of analysis should be a number that was stable over time.

Such a number was the total membership of the U.S. House of Representatives, 435. It had been static for eighty years and was probably going to remain so. And, the apportionment of the 435 members reflected the population distribution among the states. So far, so good. Each state could be modeled according to the number of its congressional districts. Yet, 435 wasn't the most convenient number with which to work; for a number of that size, it didn't have an outstanding number of nontrivial factors: 3, 5, 15, 29, 87, and 145. But, I had yet to account for the five territories. If I added them to the system, each counting as one congressional district, the result was 440, a much more elegant number. To begin with, it had lots of nontrivial factors: 2, 4, 5, 8, 10, 11, 20, 22, 40, 44, 55, 88, 110, and 220. After playing around with these numbers, I came to see the numbers 8 and 10 as the key:

$$\sum_{n=1}^{10} 8n$$

which is the short way of writing:

$$8 + 16 + 24 + 32 + 40 + 48 + 56 + 64 + 72 + 80$$

So, I could design a system in which there were ten rounds, incrementing by eight from one round to the next. The elements of the baseline design of Graduated Random Presidential Primary System were in place. I wrote an application in the BASIC programming language, and it worked. Intellectual exercise complete. Not having any idea how to implement it, or whether anyone would think it was a useful idea, I put the idea in a drawer for a few years. It seemed to me that the only way to implement the idea was via a constitutional amendment. When I considered that there had been only twenty-six amendments to the Constitution in its 200-year history, and of those, ten had been ratified in one shot early on and three others had been the aftermath of a civil war, that left only thirteen that had come into existence by what one might call normal processes. A nice idea . . . with a snowball's chance in hell.

LOST OPPORTUNITIES

I pulled my idea out of the drawer in 1997. I had just gotten interested in the Internet, and I figured that it might be a neat idea put on my website. Looking at what had happened with front-loading in the 1992 and 1996 presidential primary races, I was certain that 2000 would only be worse. Maybe someone else out in cyberspace felt the same way.

Someone else did. I forget who it was or where he was from, but someone phoned me in 1998. I think he may have been connected with some university, possibly the University of Virginia. He asked me if I had heard of some other plan (it might have been the Delaware Plan). I had not. Anyway, he indeed thought that it was a neat idea, and encouraged me to publicize it and to write to politicians. So, I did. But which politicians would see the idea as being in their bailiwick?

I guessed that as California's chief election official, Secretary of State Bill Jones might be interested. His e-mail response is in some long-dead PC clone with 640K of RAM somewhere in my attic, but my recollection is that in late 1998 he wrote back to the effect, "Thank you for sharing your ideas, but we have something we think is better: the Rotating Regional Plan." As I was to learn several years later, when I did some real research on the issue, Jones had then pretty much completed work on the Rotating Regional Plan with his coauthor, Massachusetts Secretary of the Commonwealth, William Galvin. Nor was Jones to be faulted for his opinion on my idea. It might have looked like a good idea to anyone but a Californian, for as my system was then designed, California would have been eligible for the random selection no earlier than the seventh of ten rounds.

On March 11, 1999, Assemblywoman Kerry Mazzoni wrote:

Thank you for your letter concerning your proposal for a random regional primary system. I find the concept intriguing and of the utmost importance.

Indeed, the amount of money involved in the primary process is extraordinary and of concern to many voters. The numbers provided in your correspondence are alarming and underscore the enormity of being a "player" in the process. I share your concerns over "big money" and will forward your proposal to my colleagues on Elections and Reapportionment Committees. Additionally, you may be interested in legislation by Senator Burton (SB 100) concerning Presidential Primaries.[1]

Mazzoni invited me to make an appointment to discuss my proposal in person. I had a foot in the door . . . and the shy, geeky engineer would not walk into the office. I was no one of importance, and certainly I couldn't claim to be an authority on the issue. Even scoring a success in a major metropolitan newspaper with the first opinion editorial I ever wrote didn't give me the confidence to follow up on Mazzoni's invitation.

Realign Presidential Primaries to Dilute Power of Region, Money

Philadelphia Inquirer
By Thomas Gangale
13 April 1999

We are less than a year away from a train wreck in presidential electoral politics.

California, New York and the New England states will hold their presidential primaries on March 7, 2000. A week later, the Rocky Mountain States will follow. Then, on March 21, the Southern states will hold their "Super Tuesday" primaries.

In the space of only two weeks, half of all the delegates to both the Democratic and Republican conventions will be chosen.

This is a front-loading frenzy, as each region scrambles to get an earlier say, and therefore more political clout, in the presidential primary process.

What does this mean for America? That the people will be forced into a rush to judgment, rather than being allowed to cast a carefully considered ballot. It means that the candidate who can afford to carpet-bomb the airwaves across several dozen states simultaneously will grab the most delegates and lock up the nomination. It means that Big Money will gain even greater control over our political system.

The traditional schedule of presidential primaries was simply that—a tradi-tion, one that evolved over decades, without rhyme or reason. New Hampshire always went first because, well . . . it was New Hampshire. The first significant break with tradition came in 1986–88, when a bloc of Southern states decided to hold their primaries on the same Tuesday in March. It came as no surprise that a governor from Arkansas won this Super Tuesday handily and walked away with the Democratic nomination. He was, after all, the South's favorite son.

But any region can play that game, and in 2000, a lot of them will. Last September, California decided to move its primary from June to the first week of March, leapfrogging Super Tuesday. A few months later, a bloc of Western states agreed to move their primaries to the week between California's new date and Super Tuesday.

Don't for a moment believe that it will stop there. New Hampshire already has had to move its primary to February to stay ahead of the pack. Clearly, March Madness will eventually give way to February Frenzy, and I invite you to come up with your own alliteration for January. In this brave new world of the 21st century, the word campaign will be obsolete in the political lexicon, to be replaced by blitzkrieg.

Now that the traditional schedule has collapsed, a formal national system needs to be established to return the process to a reasonable schedule so the nation can make an informed decision. The defect of the traditional presidential primary schedule was that the states voted in the same order year after year. A strong point, on the other hand, was that small states held the first few primaries, giving Big Money less of an early impact, since campaigning was almost literally door-to-door.

Early victories by less-moneyed candidates in small venues enable them to attract contributions that get them to later primaries. Such a process favors the candidate with the best message, rather than the loudest voice. A better presidential primary system, therefore, would meld the best feature of the traditional schedule—small early, bigger later—with the idea of moving the date of each state's primary from year to year.

Let's imagine a system featuring 10 two-week intervals, during which ran-domly selected states hold their primaries. (This 20-week schedule is the ap-proximate length of the current presidential primary season.)

In the first interval, a randomly determined combination of states with a combined total of eight congressional districts would hold their primaries, cau-cuses or conventions. For example, Kentucky and Nevada might vote in the first round, or Colorado and Hawaii. In the second period—two weeks later—the eligibility number would increase to 16. Every two weeks, the combined size of the contests would grow by eight congressional districts, until a combination of states totaling 80 congressional seats—nearly one-fifth of the total—would be up for grabs in the 10th and last interval toward the end of June. As the political stakes increased every two weeks, a steady weeding-out would occur, as less successful campaigns dropped out. Such a system would foster the widest possible political debate, which would resolve to one or two viable candidacies by the end.

The random determination of the schedule every four years would be administered by the Federal Election Commission. The system also would be reformulated every 10 years as districts were reapportioned based on the Census.

The schedule favors no one state or one region. And, as mentioned, the system enables the widest possible political debate early on. A successful candidate need not start out well-heeled but will cross the finish line fully vetted. He or she need not hail from any particular region of the country but must appeal to the whole nation. America deserves such a president, and America deserves a rational, systematic primary process for the 21st century.

The op-ed caused no real stir; at least, I received no feedback. My member of Congress, Lynn Woolsey, wrote on April 16, 1999:

> You have certainly presented an interesting method for nominating presidential candidates. Unfortunately, the Democratic National Committee (DNC), which plans the Democratic Party's presidential nominating procedure, has already finalized rules for the 2000 presidential cycle.[2]

Here was a clue, and I missed it completely: another route to changing the presidential primary system might be via changes to national party rules. It would certainly be easier than a constitutional amendment.

After this brief and ineffectual flurry of activity, I put the Graduated Random System in a drawer again. I could say that I had run out of ideas on how to sell the concept, but that wouldn't be entirely honest. The truth is that several responses from officeholders invited me to set up meetings to discuss the concept, and the truth is that I was scared to death at the thought of meeting with an elected official. The truth is that I gave up too easily on writing additional op-eds. The truth is that I failed to follow through.

Meanwhile, Bill Jones and William Galvin had pushed ahead with the Rotating Regional Plan. National Association of Secretaries of State (NASS) adopted the plan in February 1999. Given that the secretaries of state were state officers, the NASS worldview was that action should come from the individual state legislatures to implement the plan. This idea was a sure loser. A less impractical approach—a constitutional amendment—would merely require passage by two-third in the House and Senate, and ratification by three-fourth of the states. However, with the NASS approach, realistically, every single state, along with the federal territories that send delegates to the national conventions, would have to agree to the plan, since any jurisdiction not buying into the plan would be free to move its delegate-selection event ahead in the calendar, which would encourage other states to defect from the system. Furthermore, a constitutional amendment, once ratified, became the supreme law of the land, whereas the model state bill written by Jones and Galvin provided no enforcement mechanism, and any states initially buying into the plan would be free to defect from it without consequence at a later date.

Meanwhile, now that the Rotating Regional Plan had the visibility of NASS backing, Senators Slade Gorton (R-WA) and Joseph Lieberman (D-CT) introduced a federal bill to implement the Rotating Regional Plan. The bill was by no means the first attempt to clean up the untidiness of the presidential primary system via federal legislation. There had been dozens of bills introduced in past Congresses, and none of them had ever been reported out of committee. The Gorton-Lieberman bill (SB 1789) never saw the light of day either. The Rotating Regional Plan was in a drawer, too, just a more public drawer.

Like most Americans, I was unaware of the fact that during these same years that I had looked at the problem of presidential nomination calendar, the Republican Party had also struggled with the problem of front-loading. In 1996, Republican National Committee (RNC) Chairman Haley Barbour set up a task force headed by Jim Nicholson to look at the problem and to recommend solutions. The task force's solution was to award bonus delegates to states that voluntarily delayed their presidential primaries until later in the season. There were few takers. On the contrary, a number of states moved their primaries forward, including California. So in 1999, Jim Nicholson, now the RNC chair, established a commission under the leadership of former RNC chair Bill Brock, and including Haley Barbour and Bill Jones. The report of the Brock Commission remains a valuable document to anyone researching the problem of scheduling presidential primaries, in that, among many other things, it catalogues the large number of reform concepts on which the commission heard testimony. One of these was the Delaware Plan.

To Bill Jones' great dismay, the commission chose to back the Delaware Plan over the NASS-backed Rotating Regional Plan. He wrote a separate statement, essentially a dissenting opinion, which was included at the end of the Brock Commission report issued in May 2000. Given that the Delaware Plan permanently relegated California to last place on the presidential nomination schedule, Jones' stand against it was perfectly understandable. It also relegated Texas to last place, so it is equally understandable that the 2000 Republican presidential nominee, George W. Bush, opposed it as well. The Bush campaign blocked the Delaware Plan from coming to the convention floor for a vote. Such a vote would have been a foregone conclusion anyway, given that Bush had a huge majority of delegates willing to act on his cue. The Delaware Plan was the victim of "regime change." Before the 2000 primary season, Jim Nicholson had been the leader of a Republican Party that didn't occupy the White House; now, and for at least until the November 2000 election, Bush was the leader of the party. Another factor in the demise of the Delaware Plan was the fact that it was an attempt at top-down change. The front-loading problem was one that was much on the minds of the party elite, but the rank-and-file were largely oblivious to it. There was no constituency for changing the system, and so the Delaware Plan had no hope of surviving the regime change. It was put in a drawer.

The Democratic Party took a look at front-loading and liked what it saw, so neither the Rotating regional Plan nor the Delaware Plan was of the slightest interest.

NOTES

1. Mazzoni, Kerry. 1999. Letter, March 11.
2. Woolsey. Lynn V. 1999. Letter, April 16.

A REMARKABLE ACHIEVEMENT

AN INDEPENDENT STUDY

In the fall of 2002, I entered the undergraduate program in international relations at San Francisco State University (SFSU), with the objective of obtaining a second bachelor's degree. I was taking my first university courses in nearly a quarter-century. I still remember how strange it felt to be in a setting in which my peers were approximately half my age. It was an alien environment, and vaguely threatening. It was as though during those first few weeks of reacquainting myself with academia, there was a voice inside my head telling me, "You don't belong here. You're too late." To silence that voice, I had to prove that I wasn't too late, and that I did belong there, and I had to prove it with every exam I took and every paper I wrote. The voice faded over the course of a couple of months, but every exam and paper continued to be important. I forgot about the voice, but perhaps subconsciously, my way of keeping the voice from ever coming back was to swing for downtown every time I stepped up to the plate.

By October, I was comfortable enough in the academic setting to trot out my presidential primary reform idea. Marilyn Dudley-Rowley's first thought was to approach Peter Phillips, chair of the Sociology Department at Sonoma State University, where Marilyn was a lecturer. Phillips also ran Project Censored, which ostensibly looks for developing issues that are below the mainstream media's radar coverage, raises funds from the progressive community to support its efforts and the work of the alternative media, and produces a yearbook of the most underreported important news stories. Marilyn asked Phillips' advice on how she and I could raise a few hundred dollars to fund a mini mail campaign to state secretaries of state and other lawmakers regarding my presidential primary reform plan, and on how to engage the academic and progressive communities on an important political issue. "Sorry, can't help you," he wrote with disinterested brusqueness. So, the American Plan ought to rank fairly high among Project Censored's most underreported stories.

Next, I asked one of my international relations instructors, Dr. Glenn Fieldman, for advice, and she referred me to Professor Robert Smith in the Political Science Department. Smith suggested that I present a paper at the National Conference of Black Political Scientists (NCBPS) in Oakland in March 2003, so I submitted my abstract. Another SFSU student, Arafa Moma, received word of her paper's acceptance in early December. Two weeks later, I still hadn't heard anything about my paper, so I began casting around for other alternatives. Glenn suggested the American Political Science Association (APSA) conference, but the deadline for abstracts for the September 2003 conference had already passed. In a way that was good; it would give me nearly another year to do some more work on the Graduated Random System. I still hadn't done any research in the subject area. Glenn also advised:

> Before the APSA proposal deadline rolls around, you might want to cultivate a couple of the PLSI [political science] profs who specialize in elections. You could talk to Robert Smith, but I think Rich DeLeon might also be helpful. He's partly retired, but will teach next semester. He's a great guy. You could make an appointment to see him or maybe e-mail him what you e-mailed me (or send it to me again when the semester starts and I'll forward it to him). The reason is (surprise!) that these conferences are political . . . he might know someone who's putting together a panel that would be appropriate—assuming that he likes your proposal.[1]

During the winter break, I did some preliminary research, and on January 12, I proposed a special study project to Professors Smith and DeLeon:

> Not having heard back from the National Conference of Black Political Scientists regarding my submission last October, I am planning a new strategy for my Graduated Random Presidential Primary System. I have updated my paper (see attached) with a view toward submitting it for publication in the American Political Science Association's "*PS*" journal. Is this the appropriate journal for such a paper, or is there a more suitable option? The submission deadline for the June 2003 issue is February 25. I would be very appreciative of any comments and advice you may have.
>
> While "*PS*" limits articles to 15 double-spaced pages, I plan to do more work on this subject than can be included in a paper of this length. I would like to do a more in-depth analysis of other proposed reforms to the presidential

primary system and compare them to my Graduated Random Presidential Primary System.

I would also like to collect data on the primary/caucus schedules for 1988 and earlier to study how the phenomenon of frontloading has developed over time and the impact it has had on the nomination processes to the major political parties.

At the conclusion of this study, a report might be sent to the National Association of Secretaries of State, the Center for Governmental Studies, the national committees of the Democratic and Republican parties, as well as other entities.

Would such a project be suitable for credit as a PLSI 899 Special Study?[2]

Smith wrote back that *PS: Political Science and Politics* seemed an appropriate place for the paper, and he also advised me to follow up with the Section Chair on the NCBPS paper.[3] Rich DeLeon's reaction was that it sounded like an interesting project, and he invited me to drop by his office sometime once the spring semester began.[4] On January 21 I received notice that my presentation had been accepted for the NCBPS conference.[5] Then, on February 3 I was notified that it was disaccepted![6] Fortunately, I had already come up with a Plan B and was putting it into motion. I was anything but a scholar; I was a dilettante with a vague ambition of becoming a scholar.

By January, the Fall 2002 grades were reported, and I had received "A's" in both international relations courses. I was becoming more confident. I had enrolled in two more IR undergraduate courses for the Spring 2003 semester, but I was beginning to set my sights on a higher goal. There were a whole lot of general education course requirements for a bachelor's degree at SFSU that I had not had to fulfill for my bachelor's in aerospace engineering at the University of Southern California (USC) in 1978. I didn't see this as anything but a waste of time. On the other hand, I looked at the curriculum for a master's degree in international relations, and calculated that in the time it would take me to get a second bachelor's, I could get a master's instead. Well, why not? At that point, my only concern was Inspector Javert. I had scraped by at USC with a grade point average of 2.4, not exactly a great selling point when applying to a graduate program. It was the loaf of bread I had stolen more than twenty years before, and it was still on my record. Was there a statute of limitations, or was I going to be punished for my old crime? There was only one way to find out, and that was to apply.

I knew that to succeed in getting a paper published on my presidential primary reform concept, I would need to do some research. Dr. Marilyn Dudley-Rowley, a sociologist whom I had met at a Mars conference in 1999, had taught me the importance of a "history of ideas" section in a scholarly paper. Beyond this, I wanted to collect historical data on the progression of front-loading over the years. So, writing this paper was going to be a research project, and I might as well get academic credit for the work. To get a foretaste of what life would be like as a graduate student, I decided to propose a graduate-level special study to the Political Science Department.

I met with Rich DeLeon on February 5 and outlined my objectives for the special study. He was intrigued with my proposal. He had come to San Francisco from the Midwest during the 1967 Summer of Love, had decided to stay, and he had made himself the expert on the electoral politics of San Francisco. However, he had never studied the presidential nomination process, so he was curious as to what I might come up with. He was initially puzzled by the fact that I was in the international relations undergraduate program, yet wanted to do a graduate-level special study out of the Political Science Department. I explained to Rich that the presidential nomination process had long been an interest of mine, and that I wanted to take that interest to a scholarly level. He revealed to me that the two departments had a decades-long history of infighting. Well, yes, that was interesting to hear, but it was also above my pay grade. I was a student, and how the faculty got along was another matter. Indeed, as I would later learn, the International Relations Department didn't get along with itself! Rich then explained that special studies were a kind of "a la carte;" the number of semester-hours depended on the amount of work I intended to do, anywhere from one to four hours, and he expected a final paper of ten pages per hour. I was confident that I could deliver forty pages, so I told him I would enroll for four hours.

A final point of discussion was my proposal to also write a paper for publication in *PS: Political Science and Politics*. Rich expressed some skepticism. "That is not an easy publication to get into. It is very competitive, and they reject papers from PhDs. If you were to get published in *PS*, it would be a remarkable achievement."

So, I was setting up quite a challenge for myself. In addition to four hours of special study in political science, I was enrolled in two international relations courses, for a total of twelve hours. Whereas five months earlier I had had some trepidation about becoming a part-time student, I was now a full-time student. I was also working full-time, and I had never before done both simultaneously. But, I was genuinely fascinated in the subject material, especially in the special study, and I threw myself into it.

By mid-February, the APSA Web site announced that they had slipped the deadline for submitting papers for the June 2003 issue of *PS: Political Science and Politics* to March 25, which gave me an additional month to get the manuscript in shape. In early March, Rich wrote detailed comments on the work I had done so far. "[T]his field isn't my specialization, as you know, but I hope some of this is useful to you."[7] It sure was! He posed questions that took my thinking in new directions. A good chunk of this book is the product of the special study, considerably more than Rich had expected.

Since I was simultaneously studying international political economy under Glenn Fieldman, I was inclined to draw an economic analogy:

> The political parties compete in the marketplace of ideas. As self-interested entities, they naturally seek to maximize the outcome of each transaction. However, specifically who gains the maximum advantage from each outcome is not the concern of the market system. The broader issue is whether the marketplace is maximally open to participation and competition. The political parties should not operate in an environment in which they play it safe within narrow limits by erecting, as they have, barriers to political competition; rather they should operate in an environment in which they are equally empowered to take risks, and to more openly and efficiently appeal to constituencies that have historically been marginalized. The "invisible hand" is prevented from evolving such a market because the major parties constitute an oligopoly.[8]

As Glenn said of Rich, "You couldn't have a better ally."[9] He forwarded my message containing the above paragraph to Rob Richie and Steven Hill of the Center for Voting and Democracy (also known as FairVote), inside the DC Beltway. In a few years, these would prove to be very useful connections. Also in early March, Rich encouraged me to apply for the John Randolph and Dora Haynes Fellowship. "I would definitely nominate you."[10] As honored as I was, there was a wrinkle in this; the fellowship was to be awarded "to an outstanding graduate student in political science interested in and committed to improving governance and the polity of California."[11] Neither my work in political science nor in international relations was focused on the "governance and the polity of California." What was going to be my angle? For the first time, I looked squarely at the fact that the baseline design of the Graduated Random Presidential Primary System (GRPPS) severely disadvantaged California in relation to other states. About the same time, I was looking at the patterns of anomalous ethnic population distributions in early round states in the computer simulations I had run on the GRPPS. A week later, on March 17, 2003, I replied to Rich:

> I have been considering the Haynes Fellowship for the past week. My concern has been to define an appropriate intersection of my work on the national issue

of presidential primary reform and the fellowship's emphasis on "improving governance and the polity of California."

Meanwhile, this week I continued to pursue a line of inquiry you raised in your detailed comments. I graphed 12 simulations to study anomalous ethnic distributions in the early voting samples. While the additional simulations confirmed my preliminary results—that the cumulative anomalies tend to converge on the national average to within five percent by the fourth round of primaries, I noticed that the initial overrepresentation advantages tended to alternate between whites and African-Americans, while Asians and Hispanics were consistently underrepresented. No matter how may simulations I studied, I could not find a case in which either of these latter two groups enjoyed a significant initial advantage. I then decided to graph the ethnic distributions of the total eligibility pools for each interval, and I found that whites and African-Americans were overrepresented, while Asians and Hispanics were underrepresented, in the eligibility pools until the seventh round. These discrepancies only amounted to two percent or less, but the biases were nevertheless there. At that point, the reason became obvious. The only state that is left out of the eligibility pools until the seventh round is California, the 600-pound gorilla. Accounting for one-eighth of the population of the U.S., California has double the percentage of Hispanics and triple the percentage of Asians compared to the national average, and so the effect is significant. There is no way to balance the ethnic books in the early voting rounds without advancing California's eligibility.

I considered several options, including splitting the state into northern and southern congressional districts in order to make each section eligible in the fourth interval, but that idea is unattractive for a number reasons. I then looked at reshuffling the order of the intervals, inserting the seventh round between the third and fourth round, and seeing how this affected the shape of the overall schedule curve. The effect, in my view, is insignificant. I then went even further and inserted the eighth interval between the fourth and fifth, and the ninth between the fifth and sixth intervals, and while the departure from the smooth, graceful theoretical curve is greater, I still consider it acceptable. In any case, it's possible to make a minor adjustment in the time-phasing of some of the re-ordered intervals so that the deviation from the baseline curve is negligible.

By identifying and solving one political problem—the underrepresentation of Asians and Hispanics in early rounds—I also ended up solving a second political problem: that the GRPPS significantly disadvantaged California in comparison with the other states. As much as I tried to sugarcoat this in my original proposal, it would still have been a bitter pill for California, possibly even a poison one that would block support for the proposal's implementation. The modified system brings the treatment of California in line with that of the other large states: Florida, New York, and Texas. Attached is a new section of my paper. It doesn't specifically address the ethnic demographic issues. I'll work that up next. As always, I invite your comments.

> Having arrived at this point yesterday evening, I discussed what I had written with Dr. Marilyn Dudley-Rowley, a Sociology lecturer at Sonoma State, who pointed out that I might well have stumbled upon that suitable confluence of my work and the Haynes Fellowship's focus on California. Accordingly, I hereby announce my candidacy for the Haynes Fellowship.[12]

Through asking a question on my work, then suggesting the Haynes Fellowship, Rich had led me to put the "California" in the California Plan, as I began to call the GRPPS. Also on March 17, I mailed my manuscript to *PS: Political Science and Politics.* Now, in addition to completing my research paper for the PLSI 899 special study, I had to write a research proposal for Haynes Fellowship. Marilyn Dudley-Rowley, who in addition to teaching at Sonoma State University also ran the OPS-Alaska research cooperative, was of great help as I put together the proposal.

Unfortunately, the fellowship required the applicant to be a "graduate student in political science." I was an international relations student, and by mid-April 2003 it became clear that this was a firm requirement. In order to be eligible for the fellowship, I would need to apply for the SFSU graduate program in political science. Rich and I didn't see a problem in my applying simultaneously to the international relations grad program and the political science grad program; however, the SFSU Graduate Admissions Office did. Its system wasn't designed to handle a student applying to two programs, and it insisted that I choose one or the other. Now I also appeared to be caught in the rivalry between the two departments. In a telephone conversation in late April with Dr. David Tabb, then the graduate coordinator for the Political Science Department, he made a vaguely hostile comment that he would not look kindly on my using his graduate program as a backdoor into the international grad program, whose entrance requirements were higher.

So, I could abandon the International Relations Department for the Political Science Department, where I had a better shot at getting into the graduate program and a good shot at the Haynes Fellowship, and where I could be a "scientist," or I could stay the course. I informed Dr. Tabb of my decision on May 2, 2003:

> I originally came to SFSU last autumn with the intention of earning a degree in International Relations. I have already applied to that department's graduate program through the Graduate Admissions Office, which has subsequently forwarded my application to the International Relations department. Having initiated this process, I feel honor-bound to see it through to its conclusion.[13]

Although a disappointing turn of events, the Haynes Fellowship exercise had lead to solving the "California problem" in the Graduated Random System. Making it even easier to put this episode behind me was the response from *PS: Political Science and Politics*:

> In the midst of this dismal mess, there is a ray of sunshine. I came home from the Asilomar conference last night to find a letter from the editor of "*PS: Politics and Political Science.*" He is interested in publishing my essay, contingent on incorporating some recommendations from the reviewer. No big deal. I need to revise it anyway to reflect the Mod 2A version of the concept, which I hadn't yet thought of when I sent the manuscript to *PS* back in February.
>
> I also had a chance to mention the California Plan to Senator Joseph Biden at Asilomar on Friday night. In reference to the Delaware Plan, I said, "With all due respect to your constituent, Basil Battaglia. . . . "
>
> The Senator smiled and said, "I know what you're going to say. It was a bad plan. I agreed with that decision," referring to the Delaware Plan's being shot down at the 2000 Republican National Convention.
>
> I briefly explained that the California Plan preserved the best feature of the Delaware Plan, that of beginning the primary season with small venues and gradually working up to larger ones, but did so in a way that should be palatable to large states. He asked for the details, so I arranged to have a copy of my report sent to him.[14]

Which was the more remarkable achievement: that I had written a manuscript that *PS* was interested in publishing, or that I had spoken to a U.S. senator where four years earlier I had quavered at the thought of meeting with a member of the California Assembly?

Toward the end of April 2003, Marilyn Dudley-Rowley and I had paid a visit to my eighty-eight-year-old father and took him out to lunch. "You've wasted your life," he told me. "You could have been a scientist."

"You're wrong!" Marilyn insisted politely but firmly. "He is a scholar. You just don't know it yet."

Rich and I had our end-of-semester meeting on May 15, 2003. I turned in a research paper comprising 120 pages of text, eighty pages of figures, tables, and references, and eighty pages of appended material. In terms of ensuring a grade of "A" it was overkill. In terms of learning enough to have some confidence that I had a solution to the problem of front-loading the presidential nomination calendar, it was sufficient. In terms of killing the inner ghosts of my unscholarly past, it wasn't nearly enough. I would do battle with them for several more years.

Later in the month I revised the *PS* manuscript according to the reviewers' comments and sent it to Rich for his final comments. On May 28, 2003, I received a telephone call from my father's first cousin. My father was dead. Three days later I received a letter from San Francisco State University welcoming me to the International Relations Department's Master of Arts program as a fully classified graduate student. The letter was dated May 22, but the envelope wasn't postmarked until May 29.[15] Had it been mailed promptly, I would have received the letter in time to tell my dad before he died.

THE RETREAT FROM DEMOCRACY

On June 26, 2003, I sent executive summaries of my research paper to the Republican National Committee and the Democratic National Committee, urging changes to the parties' rules, as well as to Lynn Woolsey (D-CA), my member of Congress, and to Senators Diane Feinstein (D-CA) and Barbara Boxer (D-CA), proposing legislation.[16] I also imagined that it might be an item of interest to a dozen or so candidates for the 2004 presidential nomination. Woolsey's July 28, 2003 response:

> It is important that we ensure the Presidential primary is about the candidates and their issues, not the amount of money they raise. I commend you for being proactive on this issue and presenting me with your bill idea. We must improve the integrity of our election system. You can be sure that I will keep your bill idea in mind as Congress works to improve our election system in the 108th Congress.[17]

Ed Gillespie, the new RNC chair, replied with bland and noncommittal prose during the first days in his position.[18] DNC Chairman Terry McAuliffe never responded at all, nor did my U.S. senators, nor did any of the presidential candidates. On August 5, 2003 I wrote to the following institutions:

- Center for Politics at the University of Virginia
- Governance Studies Program at the Brookings Institution
- Alliance for Better Campaigns
- Center for Responsive Politics
- Center for Voting and Democracy
- Common Cause
- Demos.[19]

Not one responded.

On August 18, 2003, *PS: Political Science and Politics* editor Stephen Yoder informed me that my manuscript, "The California Plan: A 21st Century Method for Nominating Presidential Candidates," was slated for publication in the January 2004 issue.

Clearly, writing journal articles and letters wasn't going to change the world. However, I had to do what I had shrunk from doing four years earlier. I phoned Rep. Woolsey's district office to inquire how I might pursue the matter. With not much back and forth, we arranged for me to meet with Rep. Woolsey during her "district office hours" in San Rafael on September 6, 2003. In our meeting, she informed me that a bill on presidential nomination reform was out of the question given the toxic environment on Capitol Hill. I pointed to the bills sponsored in recent years by Senators Gorton and Lieberman, and by Rep. Sander Levin. "And what happened to them?" she asked. I conceded that they had died in committee. "I don't write many bills, but I write the ones I think I can get passed. I like to work efficiently." She was being straight with me. I took a different tack, explaining why I thought the most promising approach was via changing the party rules. I asked her if she would write to Terry McAuliffe, and she said yes. After some exchanges with a member of Rep. Woolsey's campaign staff, her letter went out on October 30, 2003, with a final draft of the *PS* article attached.[20]

McAuliffe, the patron saint of front-loading, responded on December 10, 2003:

> I truly appreciate the in-depth research and thought-provoking concept of this proposal. I have forwarded the "California Plan" to our Political Division, Elections Strategist, and the Rules and Bylaws Committee for review.[21]

Later in December I wrote once again to all of the presidential candidates, Chairman McAuliffe, Rep. Woolsey, Senators Feinstein and Boxer, California Republican Party chair Duf Sundheim, California Democratic Party chair Art Torres, California Governor Arnold Schwarzenegger, and all of the secretaries of state.[22] This time, I attached the final draft of the *PS* article. Meanwhile, for 2004, McAuliffe had engineered the most front-loaded nomination season in American history, furthering the trend of making all but the earliest caucuses and primaries meaningless. As a direct result, a number of states were coming to the conclusion that the declining voter turnout in pointless presidential primaries weren't worth the expense.

Canceled Primaries Diminish Democracy

San Francisco Chronicle
By Thomas Gangale
6 January 2004

While Americans are working to bring democracy to Iraq, we will have a bit less of it here at home during the coming presidential election: A number of states—including Colorado, Kansas, Maine, Michigan, Utah and Washington—have canceled their presidential primaries.

This marks a sharp reversal of a 40-year trend in presidential politics. In 1960, there were only 18 presidential primary states; in 2000, primaries were held in 45 jurisdictions, including the District of Columbia and Puerto Rico. This trend away from party caucuses and conventions in favor of more primary elections has opened the political system to more Americans. In earlier times, it was customary for a few of the party faithful to gather in an auditorium to determine the composition of state delegations. The process has evolved to reach out to the electorate as a whole, and to include millions of voters.

But this year finds American democracy in retreat. States claim they cannot afford the millions of dollars it costs to hold presidential primaries. How ironic that at the same time, the federal government is spending billions of dollars to build democracy in Iraq. The idea that Americans cannot afford democracy is profoundly disturbing. What are our values if we consent to be less free just so we can save a few bucks?

In an attempt to justify the decisions to cancel the presidential primaries in these six states, it is pointed out that fewer voters participate in them. This is true; however, the proper response to this problem is more democracy, not less. The reason that fewer people bother to vote in the primaries is that fewer people believe that their vote makes a difference. Unfortunately, they are right. By early December, political pundits were already declaring Howard Dean the de facto nominee of the Democratic Party.

On what basis did they make such a pronouncement? Did they count the votes? Of course not. The Iowa caucuses were still weeks in the future, and the New Hampshire primary after that. No, they made this prediction by counting the money. Dean has a commanding lead in fund raising; ergo he is the presumptive nominee. According to a 2000 report from the Republican National Committee, in every presidential campaign since 1980 and in both parties, the nominee was the candidate who had raised the most money by Dec. 31 of the year before the general election. The primaries and caucuses merely rubber-stamp the decision already determined by money. Money matters; people's votes do not. This is not democracy.

Yet, while money continues to determine the outcome of the primaries, states are now claiming that there is not enough money to hold the primaries in the first place. Clearly, millions of dollars are available to the electoral process; it is simply a matter of priorities, and of re-engineering the system so that it works better for everyone.

The biggest problem with the system is the front-loaded schedule. By March 15, more than 70 percent of the delegates to the national party conventions will be selected. In order to successfully compete in all of these individual state contests simultaneously, candidates must raise vast sums of money up front, well before these elections and caucuses are held.

The campaign schedule was far more gradual in the 1960s and throughout most of the 1980s. This allowed poorly funded campaigns to get their messages out in small venues via door-to-door politicking. Those who scored early victories in a few states were then able to attract the contributions that allowed them to compete in later primaries. This process fostered more competitive campaigns. It was politics on the installment plan, and it gave more candidates meaningful access to the political system.

In contrast, running for president today is like paying cash to buy a house. Most Americans would be homeless in such a system, so it should come as no surprise that most presidential candidates are left out in the cold, with no chance of winning.

Relaxing the primary schedule will loosen the grip of money on the electoral system and return political power to the voters. Canceling primaries only takes power from the voters. Reforming the presidential nomination process will require the voters who are disenfranchised by the system to speak up by writing to the national committees of their respective parties. It also falls to the presidential candidates who are forced to campaign for dollars rather than for votes; this year's candidates must urge the national party chairmen to reform the rules of the nomination process. It is in the interests of Democrats, Republicans and independents to make this happen. If we do not solve the problem in this presidential election year, we will be stuck with the same mess—and possibly worse—in 2008.

I sent this article to all of the people I had written to in December, plus RNC Chairman Ed Gillespie.[23] His January 22, 2004, response was the same old same old, but at least he responded:

Please be assured that I have forwarded your letter and attachments to the Republican National Committee Rules Committee.[24]

From the Gubernator's office came James Minor's response of February 18, 2004:

The issue you have written about is Federal in nature and not under State jurisdiction.[25]

Really? Then why did the National Association of Secretaries of *State* have a reform plan? Minor went on to suggest that I contact Senator Feinstein:

In addition, you may wish to contact your Representative in Congress. To find out who your local Representative is, please visit the "Write Your Representative" webpage at www.house.gov/writerep.

Apparently, Mr. Minor was under the misapprehension that someone who was informed enough on American government to write in a scholarly journal was not informed enough to know who his member of Congress was, or even how to find out!

On May 3, 2004, Sen. John McCain, the Great Reformer, responded *in full*:

Thank you for contacting me. I am pleased that you took the time to share your views with me.

It is very important to convey your concerns, opinions and views to me and my staff. Your contribution on this matter and any interest of various issues in the future are of much value to me.

Again, thank you for your recent correspondence.[26]

Translation: American government is deaf to ordinary citizens. It doesn't care what we think, because we couldn't possibly know what we're talking about. The professional politicians have all the answers they need. I have stacks of similar responses. If you strip off the letterhead and the signature, and shuffle them, it is impossible to determine who is responding to what. In recent years we have come to expect the plague of robo-calls during campaigns; what the few who persevere in writing to politicians soon come to learn is that nearly all responses are robo-letters.

"I am a machine!"

—Arnold Schwarzenegger, *Terminator 3*

Uh-huh, and so are all the others. So, since we don't have a government of the people and don't have a government by the people, how can we be sure that it is really a government for the people? And, for which people?

Although the Center for Voting and Democracy had not responded to my August 5, 2003 letter, its thinking in regard to the presidential nomination process was very much in tune with mine.

Primary Solutions

Baltimore Sun
By Rob Richie and Steven Hill
2 March 2004

Maryland Democrats heading to the polls today can take some satisfaction that they still have a choice among candidates in the race for the presidential nomination.

But backers of candidates who have dropped out will have to settle for a smaller, less diverse field because of choices made in earlier primaries and caucuses.

Sen. John Kerry of Massachusetts has a clear edge, having so far won 18 of the 20 contests electing delegates. But Sen. John Edwards of North Carolina is pushing him hard. Dennis Kucinich and The Rev. Al Sharpton are still pursuing their long-shot candidacies.

The Iowa caucuses and the primaries that followed knocked out the five other major contenders. The candidate most focused on Maryland last year, former Vermont Gov. Howard Dean, has stopped campaigning, as have retired Gen. Wesley K. Clark, Rep. Dick Gephardt of Missouri, former Sen. Carol Moseley Braun of Illinois and Sen. Joseph Lieberman of Connecticut.

The rushed primary schedule has cost Marylanders their power of a full choice, as it did for everyone in the 32 states voting after Mr. Kerry's critical win in Wisconsin Feb. 17. Front-loading the primaries effectively has disenfranchised most Democrats and allowed front-runners to avoid the intense scrutiny they would have faced in a more competitive race—and that the Democratic nominee certainly will get from President George W. Bush's re-election campaign.

Perhaps most importantly for both the November election and beyond, if today's 10 primaries virtually lock up the nomination, Democrats won't have any incentive in the remaining primaries to mobilize new voters and encourage more attention to their case for the White House.

In retrospect, Mr. Kerry apparently gained a huge advantage by his surprise win in Iowa, which led to his convincing follow-up victory in his home territory of New Hampshire. The rushed primary schedule gave him nearly unstoppable momentum.

Some Democratic Party leaders would be pleased with a quick win that allows them to focus on fund raising for November, but they are making a serious mistake—both for winning in November and building their party and a strong democracy over time.

The nominating process should be fairer and more inclusive and effective. Reform is hardly far-fetched: Republicans nearly overhauled their primary schedule in 2000 and Democrats plan a major review by 2006.

Reform should enhance what already works. In contrast to most general elections, contested presidential primaries offer a meaningful range of views with real diversity of opinion. The intense focus on Iowa and New Hampshire encourages candidates to have sustained contact with ordinary voters rather than wage campaigns solely from TV studios. Potential nominees must withstand challenges that test their mettle.

But parties could strengthen themselves—and democracy—with new approaches:

Rotate opening states. A lottery among small and mid-size states should determine the first to hold primaries. Iowa and New Hampshire should not be the sole focus of candidates' grass-roots campaigning. Different states have different concerns, particularly those with bigger cities and more racial diversity.

Create an inclusive, sensible schedule. To avoid a nine-month general election campaign of sniping and personal attacks—and yes, it's already started—primaries should return to running from March to June. After the opening primaries, small states would vote in a "mini-Super Tuesday," followed by a break that would allow voters to give front-runners a second look. Bigger states would then vote, followed by more breaks, until the biggest states would vote in a decisive final round.

Require full representation. In Democratic primaries and caucuses, candidates win a fair share of convention delegates through full representation, in which 25 percent of the vote earns a proportional 25 percent of delegates.

Republicans, however, mostly use a winner-take-all system in which the first-place finisher receives all delegates. This distorts results and can allow an unrepresentative candidate to win big when the opposition vote is split among several candidates. Both parties should consider lowering the 15 percent threshold required by Democrats to win delegates.

Adopt Iowa's "second choice" system. Voting in a public meeting, Iowa's caucus participants can vote for stronger candidates if it's clear that their first choice can't win delegates. Primary voters would gain this enhanced power if they could indicate their second and third choice candidates rather than just vote for one. More voters would help elect delegates (in this year's early primaries, more than a quarter of voters supported candidates who didn't win delegates), and candidates would be more likely to reach out to supporters of other candidates and run positive campaigns.

Remember young voters. They are most likely to be unregistered and are disproportionately registered as independents and would benefit from being able to register on the day of the primary and vote even if registered as an independent. New Hampshire's primary rules allow these provisions, but Maryland's do not. And, while youth turnout remained low this year, young voters participated in bigger numbers than in 2000—400 percent more in Iowa and 50 percent more in New Hampshire.

Fix the financing. When leading candidates like Mr. Kerry, Dr. Dean and Mr. Bush opt out of public financing, the system is broken. A 4-to-1 public match for small donations should be provided and participating candidates given additional funds when opponents opt out.

We deserve elections in which more of us make a difference, choices are meaningful and our votes count. Parties can adopt most of these changes without congressional legislation. Let's reform so that in 2008, Marylanders—and the rest of the nation—have a better choice.

Rob Richie is executive director of the Center for Voting & Democracy in Takoma Park. Steven Hill is the center's senior analyst, based in San Francisco.

Meanwhile, between my January 6, 2004, op-ed in the *San Francisco Chronicle* and the article in the January 2004 issue of *PS: Political Science and Politics,* I began to get on some people's radar screens. On March 12, 2004, I received a message from Liss Palamkunnel, a senior research assistant for Judge Richard A. Posner at the University of Chicago Law School. Judge Posner was working on a project in which he was interested in the effects that caucuses and primaries have on election results. Having read the *San Francisco Chronicle*, she thought that I might have data on which states had caucuses and which had primaries for the years 1960 through 2004.[27] Indeed I did, and I was happy to share it. About the same time, Garry Young, a political science professor at The George Washington University in Washington, DC, wrote a commentary on the *PS: Political Science and Politics* article on his blog site.[28] On May 13, I received e-mail from Mike McNamee, deputy Washington bureau chief of *Business Week*, who was working on a story about reform of the Presidential nomination process. He found my Web site to be "a one-stop shopping center for information on primary reform." He wanted to talk to me about the California Plan and my sources of data for how the various plans would work.[29] We talked for quite some time about the California Plan, Delaware Plan, and Rotating Regional Plan; however, when McNamee's article appeared in the June 14, 2004 issue of *Business Week*, a lot of what we talked about was in it, but there was no mention of the California Plan.[30] I guess I got the business that week.

NOTES

1. Fieldman, Glenn. 2002. E-mail, December 19.
2. Gangale, Thomas. 2003. E-mail, January 12.
3. Smith, Robert. 2003. E-mail, January 15.
4. DeLeon, Richard. 2003. E-mail, January 20.
5. Fair, Terry. 2003. E-mail, January 21.
6. Nobles, Melissa. 2003. E-mail, February 3.
7. DeLeon, Richard. 2003. E-mail, March 3.
8. Gangale, Thomas. 2003. E-mail, March 7.
9. Fieldman, Glenn. 2003. E-mail, March 14.
10. DeLeon, Richard. 2003. E-mail, March 10.
11. DeLeon, Richard, Michael Graham, and David Tabb. 2003. E-mail, February 21.
12. Gangale, Thomas. 2003. E-mail, March 17.
13. Gangale, Thomas. 2003. E-mail, May 2.
14. Gangale, Thomas. 2003. E-mail, May 6.
15. Tsygankov, Andrei. 2003. Letter, May 22.
16. Gangale, Thomas. 2003. Letter, June 26.
17. Woolsey, Lynn V. 2003. Letter, July 28.
18. Gillespie, Ed. 2003. Letter, August 4.
19. Gangale, Thomas. 2003. Letter, August 5.
20. Woolsey, Lynn V. 2003. Letter, October 30.
21. McAuliffe, Terrence R. 2003. Letter, December 10.
22. Gangale, Thomas. 2003. Letter, December 22.
23. Gangale, Thomas. 2004a. Letter, January 10.
24. Gillespie, Ed. 2004. Letter, January 22.
25. Minor, James. 2004 Letter, February 18.
26. McCain, John. 2004. Letter, May 3.

27. Palamkunnel, Liss. 2004. E-mail, March 12.

28. Young, Garry. 2004. "Reforming the Nomination Process." Available from http://nopanaceas.blogspot.com/#107894018283459882; accessed March 13, 2004.

29. McNamee, Mike. 2004. E-mail, May 13.

30. McNamee, Mike. 2004. "No Way to Pick a Nominee." *Business Week*, June 14. Available from http://www.businessweek.com/magazine/content/04_24/b3887076.htm; accessed May 30, 2007.

A CALL FOR REFORM

THE FRONT-LOADED FIASCO

You scream, I scream, we all scream with Howard Dean!

Iowa and New Hampshire went to John Kerry, and he never looked back. By early February the Dean campaign had come off the rails, and he suspended his campaign on the nineteenth of the month. Although John Edwards would stay in the race for a few more weeks, he was far behind Kerry in the delegate count. Terry McAuliffe had his wish fulfilled; the Democratic Party had determined its nominee early. As the old saying goes, be careful what you wish for . . . you may get it! In the five months between the suspension of the Dean campaign and the July 2004 Democratic National Convention in Boston, whatever the President of the United States said or did was newsworthy. Meanwhile, most Americans forgot about . . . uh, that other guy. As the national television audience waited for the other guy to come to the podium and deliver his nomination acceptance speech, a talking head intoned that this was John Kerry's chance to tell the American people who he was. Funny, once upon a time, the campaign for the nomination had served that purpose!

Fortunately, I was not the only one working on the problem; I merely had the dubious distinction of being the least heeded. At the Democratic National Convention, forces led by Senator Carl Levin (D-MI) brought a resolution to the floor, calling for a commission to study the timing and scheduling of the presidential nomination process. It stated in part:

> Whereas, the timing of the delegate selection process and the scheduling of presidential primaries and caucuses is a critical component in the nomination of a candidate for president by the Democratic Party; and

Whereas, over the last 2 decades individual states have moved their respective contests earlier and earlier in the calendar year; and

Whereas, for years, objections have been raised to a calendar that some believe gives a disproportionate influence to a few early states; and

Whereas, based on the abovementioned issues, some Party leaders have called for an examination of the scheduling of future Democratic presidential primaries and caucuses.

Therefore Be It Resolved, that the 2004 Democratic National Convention shall create the Commission on Presidential Nomination Timing and Scheduling; and

Be It Further Resolved, that the Commission shall be charged with the responsibility of studying the timing of presidential primaries and caucuses and developing appropriate recommendations to the Democratic National Committee for the nominating process beginning in 2008; and

Be It Further Resolved, the Commission shall examine all substantive, systematic, and incremental reform proposals while evaluating how specific proposals would be implemented; outlining measures to ensure compliance; and bearing in mind the Party's commitment to a presidential nominating process that is open and fair to all Democratic candidates and voters and that produces the strongest possible nominee; and

Be It Further Resolved, that the Commission members . . . be appointed by the Chairman of the Democratic National Committee within 30 days following the 2004 general election, and

Be It Further Resolved, that the Commission shall hold a series of regional hearings/meetings throughout the country and shall hold its first meeting within 90 days following the 2004 general election; and

Be It Further Resolved, the Commission shall issue its report and recommendations to the Democratic National Committee by December 31, 2005 for consideration and action by the Democratic National Committee.[1]

So, here was a statement that during the year from December 2004 to December 2005, the Democratic Party would empanel a commission "charged with the responsibility of studying the timing of presidential primaries and caucuses and developing appropriate recommendations to the Democratic National Committee for the nominating process *beginning* in 2008," would "examine all substantive, systematic, and incremental reform proposals," and would "hold a series of regional hearings/meetings throughout the country." As 2005 unfolded, the reality was quite different. The commission made one tentative "regional" foray to Chicago, and then scurried back to the safety of the Beltway. For the most part, the commission, like Hamlet on the ramparts of the castle Elsinore, contemplating the rocks below, wrung its hands endlessly over what it to was to be or not to be, finally settling on the much more circumscribed purpose of wrangling over what timid changes it might recommend for 2008, while giving only cursory thought to a broader vision for systematic reform that might be implemented beyond 2008.

The bright spot was that one of the commission's members was the chairman of the California Democratic Party (CDP), former state senator Art Torres. That this was a bright spot would take many months to become apparent. Immediately upon hearing of Terry McAuliffe's empanelling of the commission in December 2004, I carpet-bombed all the members with a mail campaign of information packages on the California Plan.[2] I didn't hear back from any of them.

GRANITE AND GOLD

I also carpet-bombed all of the secretaries of state with letters[3] and received two responses.

It was one of those rare and brief moments when I wasn't online. The phone rang, joyfully doing something it hardly ever had the chance to do in the days when I had a dialup modem connection to the Internet, and I was startled, being unaccustomed to the sound. It was the Honorable William Gardner, Secretary of State of New Hampshire. We talked for an hour and a half about the California Plan, New Hampshire's historical position as the "first in the nation" presidential primary, and the Granite State's unique political culture.

As one would expect, he presented an impassioned defense of New Hampshire's position. "We don't have a baseball team, we don't have a football team. This is our World Series, this is our Superbowl. Please don't take it away from us." I assured him that while I had argued against Iowa and New Hampshire retaining their preferential treatment, I was open to counterarguments. More importantly, Secretary Gardner and I recognized our common ground in wanting to preserve the door-to-door nature of campaigning in small, early states, with a gradual ramping up of the campaign that allows this "retail politicking" to continue as long as possible before minor candidates get overwhelmed by big-budget campaigns carpet-bombing the air waves in huge media markets. While Secretary Gardner wanted New Hampshire to begin the campaign, he didn't want it to end the campaign as well, as we saw happen in 2004.

Several times, Secretary Gardner invited me to come to New Hampshire and see for myself how their presidential primary process works and its uniquely intimate venues. The way he described it, it sounded more like interviewing for a job than running for a public office. That must be something to see! I promised him that I'd try to come to New Hampshire in two or three years . . . on the campaign trail.

The Gardner phone call was an extraordinary event. What could explain the fact that a longtime secretary of state had spent an hour and a half with an ordinary citizen on the other side of the country? Marilyn Dudley-Rowley's view was that it was evidence that a conversation about the California Plan was taking place between Gardner and other secretaries of state. Possibly, but Gardner might have acted alone, without discussing the California Plan with any of his colleagues. It was consistent with the political culture he had described to me, in which the barriers that normally exist between presidential candidates and the electorate did not exist. It might be that they also did not exist for officeholders either, and that it was not unusual for Bill Gardner to talk extensively to an ordinary citizen. As for my being on the other side of the country, again, the political culture of New Hampshire was that people from all over the country came there to campaign. In a sense, I was running a political campaign, not for a presidential candidate, but for a process for nominating future presidential candidates. New Hampshire has a very strong interest in the current process, and Bill Gardner's job was to protect that interest.

I also received a phone call from National Association of Secretaries of State (NASS) Executive Director Leslie Reynolds. She acknowledged receipt of my letter, but indicated that the presidential nomination process was not on the agenda for the upcoming NASS meeting.

Another development from my mail campaign to NASS members was that Pedro Cortes, the Secretary of the Commonwealth of Pennsylvania, forwarded the material I had sent him to the Pennsylvania Election Reform Task Force, a panel of citizens he had formed. The California Plan turned up in the task force's February 17 meeting minutes, which were posted online.[4] If many of the people I was writing to weren't writing back, at least in some cases I was able to track their resultant actions via the Internet.

ALLIES AND FRIENDS

In December 2004, I reached out to Richard Forsten, the principal author of the Delaware Plan, in the hope of rekindling interest in reform in the Republican Party.[5] He responded on February 4, apologizing for the delay and pleading having been swamped with work.[6] I tried to engage him several more times throughout 2005, but a relationship never developed.

On January 6, 2005, a year to the day after my op-ed in the *San Francisco Chronicle*, Marilyn Dudley-Rowley and I stepped into an elevator with former Senator George McGovern (D-SD) on our way to a meeting of the World Affairs Council of Northern California in San Francisco, where the senator was about to speak. Here was the man I had come to respect as the father of the modern presidential primary system. I gave him my elevator speech on the California Plan, and followed up with a letter the following day.[7] I never heard from Senator McGovern.

My carpet-bombing letter campaign to various civic organizations on February 10[8] elicited two replies. On February 23, Chellie Pingree, president of Common Cause, send me a handwritten card thanking me for my interesting proposal, and informing me that she had passed it along to Ed Davis, Common Cause's vice-president of policy.[9] The other public policy organization to respond was the Center for Voting and Democracy (a.k.a FairVote), based inside the DC Beltway in Takoma Park, MD. On February 27, executive director Rob Richie wrote:

> I think you make a very strong argument, and I think we'd be open to working with you in drawing attention to the proposal. I've copied Rich DeLeon given your acknowledgement of him—he's a remarkable resource for all of us.[10]

FairVote's interest in the California Plan grew. It always competed for resources with FairVote's other projects (initially instant runoff voting, and later an interstate compact on the national popular vote for president as well), but at last the California Plan had gained what would prove to be a reliable ally. On March 2, 2005, Rob wrote, "The Democratic commission on presidential nomination meets next week, I believe. Are you working with anyone on that commission?"[11]

I wished! I told Rob of my repeated efforts. He wrote back, "I know one person on the commission pretty well and will talk to him about it."[12] Rob asked me for information he could pass along to his contact, and I sent him the January 2004 *PS* article. On March 15, Rob reported:

> Was at Common Cause today, and we talked some about the California plan. Ed Davis there is looking at it, and seems interested.
>
> Dems had their first meeting on Saturday. They don't seem to be up for major changes, perhaps, but the ball is rolling.[13]

On March 4, 2005, I wrote to Art Torres, California Democratic Party (CDP) chair and member of the Democratic National Convention's (DNC)

Commission on Presidential Nomination Timing and Scheduling (a.k.a. the Herman-Price Commission after its cochairs, former Secretary of Labor Alexis Herman and Representative David Price), asking to be invited to present the California Plan to the commission.[14] I also wrote to California Secretary of State Kevin Shelley.[15] Shelley, however, was being dragged down by a political scandal and he resigned a few days later. Governor Schwarzenegger appointed Bruce McPherson as his replacement, and I wrote to McPherson on March 31, the day that the California Senate confirmed him.[16] I also wrote to Pedro Cortes on March 29.[17] I received no reply from Torres, McPherson, or Cortes. In time, however, I would meet with all of them.

Since the silence from Art Torres was deafening, on March 26, 2005, I decided to ask Representative Lynn Woolsey to write a letter to Senator Torres in support of the California Plan.[18] On the same day, I pitched to Rob Richie the idea of a joint FairVote/OPS-Alaska news release announcing FairVote's support of the California Plan.[19] Ideally, Common Cause would be on board as well; however, Rob reported, "Common Cause is juggling a lot of priorities/decisions to make—I suspect this just hasn't reached the tipping point for it feeling it needs to decide."[20]

In December 2004 and early 2005 I began to get acquainted with the local Democratic Party in Marin County, California. I met Greg Brockbank, who had declared his candidacy for the Sixth Assembly seat being vacated by termed-out Joe Nation, and also Dotty LeMieux, who had run for the county Board of Supervisors in the 1990s. Marilyn Dudley-Rowley and I joined the Sixth Assembly District Committee in January. At the next Sixth AD Committee meeting on March 21, at the Mill Valley Community Center, I spoke for the first time about the California Plan to rank-and-file Democrats. The response was encouraging. Although I didn't have time to explain the plan in detail, there was general agreement that the presidential primary system had to change. It had been three decades since any Californian had cast a meaningful vote for the presidential nomination in either major political party. I asked Dotty LeMieux's advice on getting Art Torres' attention at the upcoming California Democratic Convention. She had run the local arm of the 2004 Dennis Kucinich presidential campaign, and on March 28, 2005, she wrote of putting together a campaign for the California Plan. As for getting to Art Torres, he was "a slippery one," and she suggested that we talk about whom else to approach.[21] She also felt that the name "California Plan" wouldn't be popular in other parts of the country.[22] My reaction was, how unpopular had been the name "Delaware Plan?" It wasn't the name that had defeated it.

Around the middle of April 2005, Representative Woolsey agreed to write a letter to Senator Torres. After a couple of weeks of working with campaign staffer Holly Butler on the text, the letter went out on May 2.[23]

On April 27, David Phelps, Vice Chair of the Democratic Party of the San Fernando Valley and a delegate to the Los Angeles County Democratic Central Committee, e-mailed me:

> I have been studying your California Plan and am a big supporter. I am active in the Democratic Party and would like to see this considered before the DNC's Commission on Presidential Primary Scheduling this year.
>   Are there any high profile Democrats that are supporters of your plan?[24]

I could not have imagined how significant this contact would be. I had no idea of how the California Democratic Party (CDP) was structured or how to use that structure to advance a political initiative. I had no idea of how pushing the California Plan through the CDP would translate into support at the level of the DNC. Having joined the Sixth AD Committee at the beginning of the year and having attended a few meetings, I had a dim idea of using that venue to advance the California Plan, but I wasn't at all sure of how to go about it. Thanks to David and his associate, Damian Carroll, these things would become much clearer in the course of the next six months. Over the previous three years at San Francisco State University I had learned how to do research, but over the next few months I would learn from David and Damian how to take a reform idea out of the classrooms and into the committee rooms.

Although it was doubtless a positive development, I didn't give the e-mail exchange with David a great deal of thought at the time. I was scrambling to recover from my having changed my international relations thesis topic well into the semester, and to turn in the required work for the Thesis Selection and Methods seminar as the end of the semester approached. Then early in May, my twenty-four-year-old son Darius phoned me out of the blue from Dayton, OH. He was very distraught. He felt that he was stuck in an unproductive routine and that his life was going nowhere. I asked him if he wanted to move out of Dayton, and he said yes. I had no room for him; however, my mother, who lived in Sausalito, agreed to take him in. Marilyn Dudley-Rowley and I had already committed to traveling across the country in June to present several papers at the New Trends in Astrodynamics II conference at Princeton University, so we adjusted our plans to pick up Darius along the way. So, in April through June, I was focused on my international relations coursework, the astrodynamics conference, and family matters, and not so much on southern California interest in the California Plan.

Also in May, I tried everything I could think of to get on the agenda of the Herman-Price Commission's May 14 meeting. They continued to ignore me. They did, however, hear a presentation by Leslie Reynolds, NASS Executive Director, on the Rotating Regional Plan. It was beginning to look as though the California Plan would be completely shut out of the commission's proceedings and deliberations.

Meanwhile, another venue presented itself. On May 3, 2005, Rob Richie alerted me to a link he had with the Commission on Federal Election Reform, cochaired by former President Jimmy Carter and former Secretary of State James Baker.

> Do you have a good, tight two-pager on your proposal or would it be easy to convert it into one? I'm on the academic advisory committee of the Carter-Baker electoral reform commission, and they would be interested in one.
>
> Attached is an example of one that I did on instant runoff voting. The thing you'd have to look at is what *federal* laws should be changed.[25]

I had long since come to the conclusion that federal legislation was not the way to go. Roughly a hundred bills had been introduced on Capitol Hill in the past three decades, and not one had seen the light of day.

> Regarding federal law . . . it requires no change in federal law if it is implemented via the rules of the major national parties. There are several U.S. Supreme Court rulings that have given the parties broad discretion to organize themselves as they see fit, including the process of choosing presidential nominees. Since the Republican Party nearly approved the Delaware Plan in 2000, and we have a Democratic commission studying presidential primary reform this year, the party rules route is clearly the way to go. In the past, several bills to reform the presidential primary system have been introduced in Congress, but they all have died in committee. That is not the way to go.[26]

Rob replied:

> If you're thinking federal law is not the way to go, not sure if Carter-Baker would act on it, but it might possibly advocate action on the general principle.[27]

Still, I sent him the two-pager, we massaged it a bit, and Rob passed it along to two members of the Carter-Baker Commission, Daniel Calingaert and Robert Pastor, who were based at American University in Washington, DC:

> This seems to us a particularly [achievable] reform that would have a major impact on Americans' faith in their electoral process. The fact that both Democrats and Republicans seem open to reform (with Republicans nearly adopting the Delaware Plan in 2000) seems particularly promising.
>
> Attached is the draft of a two-pager we're working on with Tom Gangale, who developed this excellent proposal. Tom has much more additional information on what he calls the California Plan. We don't think calling it the California Plan captures its inclusive qualities, so call it the American Plan.[28]

Perhaps Dotty LeMieux had been right about the need for a name change. I responded to Rob:

> The AMERICAN Plan? AMERICAN University? You really are a political guy . . . talk about your shameless pandering! Just kidding, of course. Way to go![29]

From this point, the name "American Plan" began to take hold and the "California Plan" gradually fell into disuse. On May 9, Daniel Calingaert signaled that the Carter-Baker Commission was interested in the issue of the presidential nomination schedule.[30]

In late May, Marilyn Dudley-Rowley and I started on our journey eastward to pick up Darius in Dayton, then headed to the June 3–5, 2005, astrodynamics conference at Princeton University. Mindful of the fact that we were near Grover's Mill, New Jersey, where legend has it that a Martian invasion force landed on the night of October 30, 1938, conference organizer Edward Belbruno arranged for a showing of George Pal's 1953 film, *The War of the Worlds*, for an evening of relaxation at the end of a day's heavy-duty presentations. Incredibly, the world's leading astrodynamicists clustered around the videocassette player for about half an hour and were unable to get it to operate properly. No one would have believed that in the first years of the twenty-first century, intellects vast and cool and accustomed to contemplating the complexities of navigating sidereal space would have been defeated by something as ordinary as an item of consumer electronics. In lieu of the movie, J. Richard Gott read passages from the first chapter of H. G. Wells' text.

After the Princeton conference on, Marilyn, Darius, and I traveled to the DC area. On June 8, I met with Rob Richie, Chris Pearson, and Adam Johnson at the FairVote offices in Takoma Park, and I got to see this set of allies face to face for the first time. A FairVote intern, whose name unfortunately has not survived in my records, asked an intriguing question that I hadn't considered: would the random selection of the order of the states from one cycle to the next be with or without replacement? In other words, if a given state had a certain position in one cycle, would the same position be open or closed to the state in the next cycle? As I thought about it after the meeting, I could see that if a state were selected for Round 10 in two successive cycles, its electorate would probably be rather disgruntled. To address this concern, I created the One Time No Replacement Option.

The following day, while Marilyn, Darius, and I were in the Columbia, SC, area to visit Marilyn's cousins and friends, David Phelps called me on my cell phone. I must have sounded terribly distracted as Marilyn directed me left and right with hand signals through unfamiliar territory. David and Damian Carroll had presented a resolution of support for the California Plan to the Democratic Party of the San Fernando Valley (DP/SFV) Executive Committee on June 6 and it had passed.

DP/SFV Resolution to Support California's Impact on Democratic Presidential Nomination Process

WHEREAS California's impact in determining the presidential nominee of the Democratic Party for the last several elections has decreased, and

WHEREAS the current front-loaded primary system often results in fewer than 200,000 Iowans and 300,000 New Hampshire voters in the first weeks of January in effect choosing the Party's nominee before being tested in larger states like California, and

WHEREAS California, as the highest populated state in the nation, deserves greater influence in determining the party's nominee than simply serving as the fundraising capital for national candidates and their campaigns,

THEREFORE BE IT RESOLVED that the Democratic Party of the San Fernando Valley (DP/SFV) encourages presidential primary reform efforts that will:

- Allow a greater number of campaigns to begin at the grassroots level and build momentum;
- Provide a nominating process that remains competitive for a longer period of time in order to give the public a greater opportunity to engage the campaign and become informed about the candidates;
- And create a system that increases the likelihood that Democrats in all states will have an effective voice in the selection of nominees, and

RESOLVED that the DP/SFV calls on the Democratic National Committee's (DNC) Commission on Presidential Nomination Timing and Scheduling to seriously consider the California (or Graduated Random System) Plan which features a schedule consisting of 10 two-week intervals, during which randomly selected states will hold their primaries. This 20-week schedule is the approximate length of the traditional presidential primary schedule, and

RESOLVED that DP/SFV distribute copies of this resolution to the Los Angeles County Democratic Central Committee, California Democratic Party and the DNC for consideration and support.

Drafted by David Phelps, 2nd Vice-Chair

Approved unanimously by the Political Action Committee 8–0 on April 26, 2005 and unanimously by the Board of Directors on June 6, 2005.

Their next steps were to present the resolution to the Los Angeles County Democratic Party (LACDP) and to the California Young Democrats (CYD). By the time we returned to the Bay Area in late June, I was developing a strategy for garnering support for the American Plan in the Democratic Party organizations in the North Bay using the resolution process. What David and Damian were doing, Marilyn and I should copy. I began working with Evelyn Woo of Marin County to present a similar resolution to the Sixth AD Committee, and with Dotty LeMieux to present the resolution to the Democratic Central Committee of Marin. The Sixth AD Committee didn't have any meetings scheduled in the near future, but Evelyn thought it would be possible to pass the resolution in an e-mail vote.

On June 23, 2005, a bolt came out of the blue. McGraw-Hill Higher Education publishing group faxed me a contract regarding the use of my Web site material about the California (American) Plan, to be published in the tenth edition of *Points of View: Readings in American Government and Politics,* edited by West Virginia University political science professors Robert E. DiClerico and Allan S. Hammock.[31] This was amazingly good fortune. It meant that within a year or so, political science students around the country would be reading about the American Plan. I signed the contract and faxed it back to McGraw-Hill.

Two days later, Damian Carroll reported, "[T]his afternoon California Young Democrats passed the DP/SFV Resolution advocating the California Plan. The vote was unanimous."[32] The resolution would now go to the Young Democrats of America for consideration at its convention in San Francisco in August.

THE NAME GAME

Perhaps in response to Damian Carroll's use of the old name "California Plan" in announcing its adoption by the California Young Democrats, Rob Richie wrote on June 26:

> Should we take a moment to see what we want to call the plan? I know why Tom called it California Plan at first, but I don't think that's a particularly good selling point in other states. . . . That's why we came up with American Plan (in contrast to the Delaware plan), trying to spin it that we have the plan that ensures all Americans have a reasonable chance to vote in a meaningful primary.[33]

I responded, "I have no problem with the name change. This is something Dotty LeMieux suggested several months ago."[34] And, since it was originally her suggestion, I cc'd Dotty. She piped up:

> I [think] a name change is good, but in any "branding" situation, you need something that captures the [essence] of the product. So let's think of something catchy, memorable and informative, that is having to do with fair voting.
> I'll give it some thought myself.[35]

I took a stab at it:

> Well, Rob has already warned me that math is scary to most people, but I can't help thinking like a rocket scientist. In my view, the heart of the plan, the engine that makes it go, the thing distinguishes it from all others, is its mathematical progression:

$$\sum_{n=1}^{10} 8n$$

> Is calling it the Sigma Primary Plan too scary? Half the houses on Frat Row have a Sigma in their name. Is it catchy? Is it memorable? Is it informative?[36]

Rob Richie stuck by his suggestion of "American Plan." Miles Kurland, the local Democracy for America organizer in Santa Rosa and an early supporter of the California Plan in the blogosphere, suggested that it be called the "Gangale Plan."[37] That was a nice head rush, but it was also way too much personalization for my taste. I had no wish to be the center of a personality cult, not least because I didn't think I had the personality for it!

Concurrent with the name game was a discussion to delete the California Plan's mathematical formula from the handout materials.

> Please hide that mathematical formula and never reveal it again. We don't want this to become known as the Nerd Plan!
> (Just kidding.)
> In all seriousness, the way to pitch this plan should be its tendency to require candidates to compete in many different states over an extended period, so that they become battle tested. Perhaps a sporting metaphor is in order (to help us pick up the jocks!) Maybe the Marathon Plan? Or the Decathalon Plan (we have ten rounds, after all)?[38]

FairVote's Adam Johnson chimed in, "How about the equal opportunity plan, or the equality plan?"[39] David Phelps asserted the need to keep calling it the California Plan while working for its support around the state, and suggested that the transition to the American Plan label could begin after that.[40] My eyes were beginning to roll around in my head . . . where was all of this getting us? Then Dotty, as promised, gave us her thoughts:

> Here's my suggestion of a possible direction for the new name:
> Gangale Uniform Presidential Primary Initiative (GUPPI)
> It gets the point across, gives you credit and has an easy to remember acronym.[41]

Her suggestion drowned the debate, and there was silence. With a name like GUPPI, the plan would end up "sleeping with the fishes."

FairVote's Chris Pearson had been cc'd on this debate but had not participated. Instead, he was doing useful work, writing a FairVote news release featuring the American Plan. I received an anxious call from him. "Is there something wrong with the name?"

"*I* don't think there's a problem," I assured him. "Let's go with Rob's suggestion: American Plan."

Marilyn Dudley-Rowley, who had run the public relations for Representative Don Young's 1980 reelection campaign, helped to close the debate:

> . . . [L]et's not get too wrapped up in this name business. Part of OPS-Alaska's evolution comes from my public relations, marketing, political and labor campaign management, etc. businesses since the late 70s and into the 1980s.

My gut tells me not to get too wrapped up with this. I think Adam said something, too, along these lines—perusing all your e-messages.

Just talk the Plan itself up.[42]

That was the end of the name game. We had bigger fish to fry.

NOTES

1. Democratic National Committee, Commission on Presidential Nomination Timing and Scheduling. 2005. *Report of the Commission on Presidential Nomination Timing and Scheduling,* December 10; 11. Available from http://a9.g.akamai.net/7/9/8082/v001/democratic1.download.akamai.com/8082/pdfs/20051215_commissionfinal.pdf; accessed December 27, 2005.

2. Gangale, Thomas. 2004. Letter, December 31.

3. Gangale, Thomas. 2004. Letter, December 31.

4. Pennsylvania Election Reform Task Force. 2005. "Meeting Minutes," February 17. Available from http://www.dos.state.pa.us/election_reform/lib/election_reform/Proposed_Minutes_(PERTF_2-17-05)_(Final).doc; accessed March 3, 2005.

5. Gangale, Thomas. 2004. E-mail, December 20.

6. Forsten, Richard A. 2005. E-mail, February 4.

7. Gangale, Thomas. 2005. Letter, January 7.

8. Gangale, Thomas. 2005. Letter, February 10.

9. Pingree, Chellie. 2005. Letter, February 23.

10. Richie, Rob. 2005. E-mail, February 27.

11. Richie, Rob. 2005. E-mail, March 2.

12. Richie, Rob. 2005. E-mail, March 3.

13. Richie, Rob. 2005. E-mail, March 15.

14. Gangale, Thomas. 2005. Letter, March 4.

15. Gangale, Thomas. 2005. Letter, March 4.

16. Gangale, Thomas. 2005. Letter, March 31.

17. Gangale, Thomas. 2005. Letter, March 29.

18. Gangale, Thomas. 2005. Letter, March 26.

19. Gangale, Thomas. 2005. E-mail, March 26.

20. Richie, Rob. 2005. E-mail, March 26.

21. LeMieux, Dotty. 2005. E-mail, March 28.

22. LeMieux, Dotty. 2005. E-mail, March 28.

23. Woolsey, Lynn V. 2005. Letter, May 2.

24. Phelps, David. 2005. E-mail, April 27.

25. Richie, Rob. 2005. E-mail, May 3.

26. Gangale, Thomas. 2005. E-mail, May 3.

27. Richie, Rob. 2005. E-mail, May 3.

28. Richie, Rob. 2005. E-mail, May 6.

29. Gangale, Thomas. 2005. E-mail, May 7.

30. Calingaert, Daniel 2005. E-mail, May 9.

31. Gangale, Thomas. 2006. "The Graduated Random Presidential Primary System." In *Points of View: Readings in American Government and Politics.* 10th edition. Ed. Robert E. DiClerico and Allan S. Hammock. New York: McGraw-Hill.

32. Carroll, Damian. 2005. E-mail, June 25.

33. Richie, Rob. 2005. E-mail, June 26.

34. Gangale, Thomas. 2005. E-mail, June 27.

35. LeMieux, Dotty. 2005. E-mail, June 27.

36. Gangale, Thomas. 2005. E-mail, June 27.

37. Kurland, Miles. 2005 E-mail, June 27.

38. Carroll, Damian. 2005. E-mail, June 27.

39. Johnson, Adam. 2005. E-mail, June 27.

40. Phelps, David. 2005. E-mail, June 27.

41. LeMieux, Dotty. 2005. E-mail, June 28.

42. Dudley-Rowley, Marilyn, 2005. E-mail, June 20.

ROAD WARRIORS

THE MARCH ON ROME

Years ago, a friend remarked to me, "In California, San Francisco is Athens, and Los Angeles is Rome. San Francisco is the seat of culture, and Los Angeles is the seat of power." An oversimplification, to be sure, yet the aphorism had its insights. As Rome had been, so Los Angeles is known for its roads and aqueducts, and indeed, Los Angeles has its own imperialist past, during which it had laid claim to distant resources . . . principally to water.

David Phelps was working to get the American Plan resolution on the agenda for the July 12, 2005, meeting of the Los Angeles County Democratic Party (LACDP).[1] He also sent the resolution to the Orange County Democratic Central Committee.[2] Additionally, the Young Democrats of America convention in San Francisco was coming up in August, and the LA Boys were angling for a meeting there to educate delegates on the American Plan.

Meanwhile, I hoped to get the American Plan resolution considered by the Sixth AD Committee, thereby getting action going in the Democratic Party in northern California. Evelyn Woo shepherded the resolution through a virtual meeting of the Sixth AD Executive Committee that was conducted by e-mail. After a request for more information on the plan, she wrote, that the committee was in the process of voting.[3] An incorrect e-mail address delayed my making contact with the chair of the Democratic Central Committee of Marin (DCCM), John Alden, until July 6, and by then it was too late to get on the agenda for the committee's July 7 meeting. However, Dotty LeMieux was helpful in getting the contact closed, and getting on the DCCM's August 5 agenda looked like a good possibility.

The next Herman-Price Commission meeting, scheduled for July 16, was fast approaching. Again, I had not been invited to present the American Plan. What impact Lynn Woolsey's May 2 letter may have had on Art Torres was unknown. David Phelps had a contact at the Democratic National Committee (DNC) who was supporting the Herman-Price Commission. David passed along from him:

> As for the "California Plan," Commission members have received information regarding the plan, as well as many others. The agenda for the July 16 meeting is full as of now, but I am more than happy to pass along any additional information you may have to Commission members. I, of course will forward the documents that you had sent on Friday to the Commission as well.
>
> The October 1 meeting will be the venue for final decisions to begin to be discussed. It is impossible at this time to know what form that will take, but I am more than happy to keep you updated. Suffice to be said that Commission members are looking at a variety of proposals, and it is difficult to pin down the "chances" of any one plan.[4]

Our hopes for pulling off an event that would make the commission's radar screen in advance of its upcoming meeting rested on getting the Los Angeles County Democratic Party's endorsement on July 12. Perhaps then I would be invited to present the American Plan. Why would the vote of one county central committee matter? Because Los Angeles County wasn't just any county, it was one-fourth of the population of California; as a separate state, it would rank between Ohio and Michigan.

Chris Pearson made contact with the DNC:

> I spoke with Phil [McNamara] who is apparently the staffer for the Presidential Nomination Timing and Scheduling commission at the DNC. I asked if he knew of the plan and what the commission was all about. He mentioned passing along information to the leadership a few months ago. Seems they are interested in reforms that they could "actually get done." Typical.
>
> Anyway, he invited me to observe the meeting on the 16th which I plan to do.[5]

So much for the commission's mandate to "examine all substantive, systematic . . . reform proposals." It sounded as though it were really just interested in incremental reforms.

While the news out of the Herman-Price got steadily more discouraging, we continued to make progress locally. Miles Kurland introduced Marilyn and me to the chairman of the Sonoma County Democratic Central Committee,

Jim Grau, at a Democracy for America event at Sonoma State University on July 7. I talked about the American Plan, naturally, and Jim shared with us his vision of developing a network among Democrats in neighboring counties. On July 11, Evelyn Woo announced that the sixth AD Committee had passed the American Plan resolution. Since the Sixth AD included all of Marin County and most of Sonoma County, this vote should strengthen our position in the DCC of Marin, and also give us entree to the Sonoma County DCC.

That same afternoon, David Phelps reported regarding the next evening's Los Angeles County Democratic Party meeting:

> They finally got back to me today about this, and they are saying they have 5 minutes for you to talk. I'm not sure that would be worth it for you.
>
> I will see about getting you the main presentation time for the August meeting which may be more worth your time and a better buy in from the [committee] members on the Plan.[6]

Five minutes was barely enough time to pique their interest; it certainly wasn't enough time to get them the in-depth information for putting the resolution to a vote. However, Marilyn and I agreed that it was important to be there in person, to show the flag, and for the author to seize any opportunity to speak for his work. In any case, I had already accepted David's invitation to present the American Plan that same day at a lunchtime meeting of the Valley Industry and Commerce Association, where David Phelps was then employed. So, Marilyn, Darius, and I left Petaluma at 3 A.M. and drove the eight hours to Los Angeles, arriving just in time for the lunch gig. Afterward, we drove down to Wilshire Boulevard and spent a leisurely afternoon in the lounge of a hotel near where the Los Angeles County Democratic Party would be holding its meeting that evening. It happened to be near where the Ambassador Hotel had once stood, where, on a June night long ago, a presidential campaign had ended in a moment of horror.

That evening, we met Damian Carroll for the first time. Together, David and I presented the American Plan. He had managed to squeeze another five minutes into the schedule, for a total of ten, which still wasn't enough time to fully explain the plan, although it was unarguably better than five. There were many questions from the floor. A debate on the DP/SFV's American Plan resolution followed. It was clear that we had managed to ignite a great deal of enthusiasm in just a few minutes, but it was also clear that a number of people wanted to hear more details and take some time to digest them. Someone motioned to table the resolution for later consideration, and a rather impassioned debate ensued on that motion between those who wanted more time and those who wanted an immediate vote on the resolution. When the question was called and the motion to table passed by a narrow margin, there was an audible sigh of disappointment throughout the room and a few muttered obscenities.

It was a long drive back to the Bay Area that night. This being the first vote on the American Plan at which any of us had been present, our initial reaction was that it was a setback. It really wasn't. Actually, that night set the pattern for all the victories to come. We had clearly built support during the meeting—in only a few minutes—and the chances of the resolution being called for a vote at the next meeting in August seemed very good. We would be back. Meanwhile, David and Damian set about inserting an article about the American Plan in the LACDP newsletter to bring the committee members up to speed for the August meeting. We arrived in Petaluma at 3 A.M. the next morning, completing the round trip to Los Angeles in twenty-four hours. My after action report on the LA sortie later that morning read:

> It was really terrific meeting both of you yesterday. It was a very effective sortie down to LA. I didn't expect the California Plan to be put to a vote last night. The fact that we nearly defeated a "motion to table" in the largest Democratic county central committee in the nation after just a few minutes' presentation on what is arguably a complex concept, the fact that there were anguished sighs and a few mutterings of "Aw, shit!" when the close result of the vote was announced, speaks volumes as to the power of this idea and the enthusiasm it has attracted. I think it's clear that people are ready to support a well-considered redesign of the system over any band-aid half-measures. Marilyn and I will be back next month, we'll make a full presentation, and I have little doubt that the resolution will pass.
>
> Equally important were the contacts we made yesterday, both within the LA business community and within the LA Democratic Party. It is my hope that the business contacts will lead to dialog with Republicans in the state. It must be remembered that Republicans were very active on the issue of reforming the presidential nomination process in 1996 and 2000, when the DNC was saying, "We love front-loading, and we want more of it!" Also, the contacts we made within the Los Angeles County Democratic Central Committee have the potential to open doors to the Executive Board of the California Democratic Party. If you could send me the appropriate e-mail addresses, Marilyn and I would like to send "thank notes" for allowing us to present at these venues yesterday.
>
> It was also a fun trip. This nerdy introvert never realized how exhilarating it could be to get involved in the "rough and tumble" of politics "on the ground." Although I have some academic understanding of politics, I'm a novice to

politics in the real world. Marilyn is an old hand at this sort of thing, but I'm learning a great deal from all of you who are receiving this message.

I'm very happy with the way things went yesterday. We're picking up momentum and allies; however, we're in a race against the schedule of the DNC Commission on Presidential Nomination Timing and Scheduling, and so the question is, are our voices going to be loud enough to get the attention of the commission before it makes irrevocable decisions?[7]

OUT OF COMMISSION

Progress was slow in Marin County. At last, the Resolutions Committee, which Dotty LeMieux chaired, was looking at the American Plan resolution and the background materials that the American Plan team had developed over the past few months. According to Dotty, the committee wanted to know if there was an easy way to understand the plan. She suggested that I come to talk to the Central Committee in August.[8] I wasn't sure there was an "easy" way to understand it. The problem of the presidential nomination process was a complex one; it took us decades to screw it up, and understanding both the problem and the solution necessarily took time and effort. Still, we had to find ways of refining our message, distilling it down to the essentials, to the point where a wider audience could grasp it more quickly and with less effort. It had to look less like rocket science. Over the next couple of days, Chris Pearson and I worked over the two-page summary again. I sent it to Dotty's committee, and Chris got it into the hands of Carl Levin's staffer at the July 16 Herman-Price Commission meeting. Chris reported his observations on the meeting a couple of days later:

The Herman-Price Commission, 16 July 2005 Meeting

Memorandum
Chris Pearson
18 July 2005

At one point a commission member noted they didn't have a clear idea of what question there were supposed to be answering.

I got the sense they want to think of a system that will help them strategically to win the office. Changes made to the '04 schedule were supposed to front load delegates and essentially end the nomination battle early so energy could be focused on Bush. The commission seemed to think this idea failed.

All of the interests groups wanted the chance to go first recognizing that first is very different from acting early. [AFL-CIO President John] Sweeney offered that any state that is allowed to act ahead of the window must be matched by a state that is heavy with labor and minority voters since they are the Democratic base.

There was some talk of fairness. There was some discussion about the failure of the public financing system needing changes to stay relevant.

There was a general consensus that retail politicking was valuable.

There was some sense that a longer selection process helps: deflate the importance of early acting states, candidates get better known, issue positions get better developed and better understood by voters.

Steps for us:

- We have to frame this as a strategic answer to help the Democratic Party choose a winning candidate. They are not interested in doing something because it's right or fair but because it will help them win power.
- We have to figure out realistically how this would get implemented. Are we talking federal legislation, concurrent state legislation or what?
- We have to have a solid answer to what it costs because states are understandably shy of holding two primaries—one presidential and one for state offices.

We need concerted outreach to commission members. I put the AP two-pager into the hands of Sen. Levin and will follow up with his office. My dream would be for someone like him to get behind the idea and then help us create a strategy to influence other members. Rob will reach out to Rock the Vote who has a member on the commission and we are also close to a few other members who might be willing to help.

The next meeting is in October. We should do everything in our power to present at that meeting. It is a hard issue to organize on because the reality of constituent pressure is unlikely. But, perhaps an opportunity with Levin or another member can open some doors.

Hours before I received Chris' report, I had commented, "By every indication, this is a commission that is listening to the people with its fingers firmly planted in its ears."[9]

In mid-July, FairVote sent letters to former members of the Brock Commission to see if they remained interested in reforming the presidential nomination process. The first to respond was former California Secretary of State Bill Jones. Chris followed up with a phone call:

I talked with Bill Jones today who followed up on our letter from last week. I'll make a round of calls to the other recipients starting tomorrow.

In a nutshell, Bill wants to see the system shaken up. He did not support the Delaware Plan in 2000 because it strongly favored small states and left CA out to dry. He helped coauthor NASS' rotating regional primary plan, and supports it in part because I think he believes it could actually get implemented. For example, he mentioned that regions are already lumping themselves together to some extent.

But, he wishes us luck as anything that shakes up the process would be good for the system and therefore good for the country. I told him I'd be back in touch if anything really heats up.

He mentioned I should speak to George Munro at NASS to get an update on what was happening with the regional plan. George reported that the DNC commission heard a description from NASS at their April meeting.

He admitted it seems hard to gage where the DNC commission is at.

I sent him our two pager. I think it's worth noting that at least the DNC commission took testimony on the regional plan. Seems the excuse of "only looking at realistic tweaks to the current system" was not valid for NASS.

Yesterday I sent a follow up e-mail to Sen. Levin's staffer. I think a top priority has to be finding a way to get in front of the commission![10]

My response:

Absolutely, getting in front of the commission is the top priority. If we can get enough presentation time, we can sell this thing.

If Bill Jones will give me a half-hour in his office, I'll bet I can even sell it to him, despite his coauthorship of the Rotating Regional Plan. I think he's fair-minded enough to give us a fair shake. You also have to like his spirit: shake up the system! Does that sound like a Republican to you? In 1998, the Democrats swept all of the statewide offices in California except for secretary of state; Bill Jones was the last Republican standing.

Yes, it is difficult to read exactly what is going on with the DNC commission. They appear to have finally acknowledged that Terry McAuliffe's front-loading strategy failed, but they seem to be at a loss as to where to go from here. The fact that they heard testimony on the Rotating Regional Plan, but apparently not on any other comprehensive solution (certainly not ours), is an indication of how half-assed they are (so are they semi-donkeys?). In marked contrast, the Brock Commission considered about a dozen proposals before settling on the Delaware Plan.

The DNC commission may not have the depth of knowledge on this issue that Republicans acquired through dogged experience, so they might well repeat the error that the Republican commission made in 1996 and recommend band-aid measures, rather than go for a systemic solution as the Brock Commission did in 2000. If so, then another blitzkrieg campaign looms in 2008, and a small portion of the American electorate will be buried in the rubble of sound-bite rhetoric, while the majority will be left disenfranchised. After another disaster, the Democrats will empanel yet another commission, and we'll do this whole thing over again four years from now.[11]

Chris doubted that pursuing Bill Jones would yield results:

My sense is that there is little point in following up personally with Bill Jones. If we pick up any steam then it will make sense. The chief reason I say this is that he didn't even have a clue where things stood with the rotating regional plan that he loves so much. It was clear he is unplugged to a certain degree.[12]

Who could blame him? I didn't imagine he had relished the idea of running against Barbara Boxer for her Senate seat in 2004; my guess was that the Republicans had asked him to do a dirty job and he had dutifully done it. He ended up raising very little money, and she clobbered him. It was a hell of a way to end a career of public service. Even if Jones was burned out on politics and had no desire get back into any fray, I felt that in talking to him I might gain some valuable insights. He had been some of the places I was hoping to go, and more. He had been an advocate of reforming the presidential nomination process, an issue with no obvious constituency, out of conviction rather than calculation.

The Unfair Power of the Primaries

Newark Star-Ledger
By Rob Richie and Ryan O'Donnell
27 July 2005

Political junkies had a field day at the opening of the annual meeting of the National Governors' Association in Des Moines, Iowa. Everywhere you looked was a would-be presidential candidate.

Govs. Mitt Romney, George Pataki, Jeb Bush and Bill Richardson are among those now gracing the pages of countless political horse-race columns and Internet blogs. Even Arnold Schwarzenegger may be pining for the White House (if only he could find a way to change the Constitution's inconvenient provision banning immigrants from running for president). These governors had to be thrilled to be in Iowa, a state that makes or breaks candidates by virtue of its first-in-the-nation time slot in nominating presidential candidates.

Iowa Gov. Tom Vilsack, himself a dark-horse presidential hopeful, would no doubt benefit from his roots in his home state. After all, the "Iowa effect" can be formidable. John Kerry's presidential bid seemed dead in the water until he surged forward in Iowa's caucuses. After his surprise win, Kerry coasted to victory, as a party eager to defeat George Bush ratified Iowa's decision in the rapid-fire series of primaries that offered no time for second thoughts.

In effect, one small state, boasting low turnout and an overwhelmingly white population, picked the party's nominee.

The problem is not Iowa; it's the parties' every-state-for-itself system. New Mexico Gov. Richardson has made news with a modest plan to reschedule primaries for eight states and create an early Western primary in 2008 that would include Arizona, Colorado, Idaho, Montana, Nevada, New Mexico, Utah and Wyoming. Fluent in Spanish, Richardson would presumably run well in several of those states with rising Latino populations.

Richardson is no fool. History shows that candidates do well to concentrate time and money on the states with the earliest primaries. Not surprisingly, other states now left sitting on the sidelines have reacted to this imbalance by moving their primary dates earlier. In June, acting Gov. Richard Codey signed a bill shifting New Jersey's primary to late February.

Continually going earlier might work if we wanted to wind up with 2012 presidential election starting in 2009. Though New Jersey will no longer vote last in the nation, other states are bound to follow suit, triggering a primary avalanche across the country. These moves make sense to each state individually, of course. Iowa and New Hampshire certainly like their position, and states like New Jersey will benefit from rescheduling. Unfortunately, the rest of the country loses out.

As the gaggle of would-be presidential candidates pressed flesh and courted the press at barbecues during the meeting in Des Moines, another important meeting quietly took place. The Democratic Party's Commission on Presidential Nomination Timing and Scheduling met to debate changes to the presidential nomination calendar. Making such changes is not beyond reach.

In 2000, the Republican Party nearly adopted a dramatic overhaul of the primary schedule called the Delaware plan, which would have set up four groups of states that would vote in order of population, with a month off between primary days. After support from a party commission, the proposal made it to the convention floor before George Bush's backers decided against it at the last minute, fearing the plan might boost potential competitors in 2004.

Republicans will have another chance at their 2008 convention, but Democrats can act now. A good option on the table is the "American plan," Thomas Gangale's proposal recently endorsed by the California Young Democrats. Like the Delaware plan, the American plan would create gaps between primaries and would move from states with small populations to states with bigger populations. Unlike the Delaware plan, however, it would create chances for all states to be part of earlier primaries, thus better balancing the interests of large states like New Jersey and California and small states like Iowa and New Hampshire.

Not long ago, party conventions dominated the selection process. Primaries were created to transfer the power to pick candidates from party bosses to the people. As we ponder future contenders for the presidency, we should realize that the transfer of power is far from complete. It's time to ensure that all Americans, not just those living in a handful of states, can play a meaningful role in selecting the president.

CENTER FIELD

Dotty LeMieux arranged for me to address the Democratic Central Committee of Marin at its August 4, 2005, meeting. Both she and Evelyn Woo asked whether Marilyn Dudley-Rowley and I planned to attend the California Democratic Party (CDP) Executive Board meeting in Sacramento at the end of July. We figured, why not? We had never been to an E-Board meeting, had no idea what it was about, and here was an opportunity to learn more about the inner workings of the CDP.

We had no idea what a smart move that was.

Within a few hours, we happened to stumble into a gold mine in the form of Barbara Pyle, a member of the Fresno County Democratic Central Committee. She had been active in the party for years, and being a consummate net worker, she apparently knew just about everyone in the state party. Through her, we met Mary Longmore, chair of the Nevada County DCC, as well as Mark Knaup and Michelle Borzoni from Lake County. We ended up having dinner with many of these new friends that evening. After dinner, Barbara, who had taken the train from Fresno and was staying at the Longmores' house in Grass Valley, found that she had a logistics problem: the Longmores needed to return home, but Barbara needed to find the person in whose hotel room she had temporarily stored her luggage. Marilyn and I told her, no problem, we'd drive her to Grass Valley later in the evening. It would be an opportunity for us to get better acquainted.

Among the Fresno County people to whom Barbara introduced us was Joel Murillo, an attorney from Fowler, CA, whom she said had the ear of retired state Senator Art Torres, chair of the California Democratic Party and member of the Herman-Price Commission. Joel later turned out to be golden in a more material sense; when the American Plan effort badly needed "keep alive" funding, Joel was far and away its most generous benefactor. Joel took an immediate interest in the American Plan as I explained it to him over breakfast on the second day of the meeting. He fired one question after another, as though he were deposing a witness. I also imagined that I was getting a taste of what it was like to orally defend a thesis or dissertation. Over the next few months we became good friends. I never knew whether he spoke to Art Torres about the American Plan. This was the first of many examples of planting seeds here and there, reaping a crop several months later, but never knowing exactly which seeds had sprouted. Later, one could infer that some actions had occurred behind the scenes, even though direct intelligence of such actions was lacking.

Almost incidental to all of this networking was the fate of the American Plan resolution that had been passed by the Sixth AD Committee. I was entirely unfamiliar with the party apparatus and its process for considering resolutions. The best I can do is surmise in retrospect that the Steering Committee bounced it to the Resolutions Committee, which then couldn't consider it until the next E-Board meeting in Manhattan Beach in October. My recollection is that the Sixth AD committee also had been unfamiliar with the resolutions process at the state party level, and the American Plan resolution had been sent to the wrong committee. Not a problem. We were just getting started, and we weren't anywhere near being ready for a vote at the state level. By October, we would be much stronger.

ATHENS AND ROME

The Young Democrats of America held its convention in San Francisco from August 3 to 7, 2005. Damian Carroll took the point for the American Plan on this mission, and although Marilyn Dudley-Rowley and I were there to get a visual of what went on, most of the action took place in the form of whispered conversations during the Platform Committee's meeting on August 5, out of our earshot, between Damian and Leighton Woodhorn, who represented the California delegation in the committee, and the other delegations. The committee had a long agenda, it took longer than scheduled for them to slog through it, and early afternoon wore into late evening.

Damian and Leighton put the time to good use. We had expected that there would be trouble from the New Hampshire delegation . . . except that they hadn't come out to the West Coast for the Young Democrats of America (YDA) convention. However, the New York delegation undertook to represent New Hampshire's interests, and they raised objections to the American Plan resolution. Another wrinkle was that the Michigan delegation also had a resolution on reforming the presidential nomination process. The latter problem was easily solved; the two delegations agreed to support each other's resolutions. New York was a tougher sell, but as Damian built support behind the scenes, the Empire State delegation agreed to abstain. Both Michigan's resolution and the American Plan resolution passed in the Platform Committee, and the committee's report was sent to the convention floor the following day. The floor vote, when it came, was anticlimactic, without any debate, lost among the hubbub of the crowd, the speeches, and the music.

That's it?

That was it. We now had the Young Democrats of America.

My hat is off to both of these guys. The fact that there was no real fight over the resolution is a testament to the lobbying they did behind the scenes (that and IA and NH didn't show up). Damian and David are teaching me how to do politics "on the ground." If I were to put on my air force cap and extend the metaphor, I'd say that my campaign of letter-writing to politicians and op-eds to newspapers over the years has been high-altitude bombing, and only marginally effective. The classic airpower theorists notwithstanding, wars are still won on the ground. If the metaphor seems a violent one, recall that Carl von Clausewitz declared that "war is the extension of politics by other means." I suppose the reverse is also true.[13]

Adam Johnson reported on a phone conversation he had had recently with Tom Sansonetti, a member of the Brock Commission and former chair of the RNC Rules Committee:

He seemed to like the plan, though he still favored [the] Delaware [Plan] (thought ours was 2nd best). FYI his major hesitations with the plan were:

- It could force states to hold multiple primaries, which is an expensive pain in the ass, and in some cases could force state Republican parties to finance their own primaries.
- In large states this would be impractical.

- He was afraid that the plan would discriminate against medium sized states (i.e., the Arizona sized states would still be likely to be shunted into the later rounds, and overshadowed by CA, TX, NY, etc.).

He seemed to favor set dates for primaries, rather than have them be randomized.[14]

Actually, Arizona would be eligible for the first round in the American Plan. And, how did California, Texas, New York, etc., feel about set dates that always set them dead last? These and other comments from Sansonetti underscored the need to engage people in conversation long enough to make sure they were clear on the implications of the plan's features, and its advantages over the facets of other plans. We needed to get into a debate.

States would NOT be forced to hold multiple primaries! States would be free to choose whether to hold consolidated primaries or separate the presidential primary from state and local races. I envision that eventually, when both parties have implemented the American Plan, if enough states wanted to separate their primaries and they had a compelling case, the two parties might agree to federal funding to relieve the states.

What Sansonetti calls a "medium sized state," the American Plan treats like a small state and Delaware Plan treats like a large state. Arizona is eligible for the first round in the American Plan, but is relegated to the third pod in the Delaware Plan. . . . A slightly larger mid-sized state, Virginia is eligible for the second round in the American Plan, but is dead last in the Delaware Plan. Put in these terms, we can see that not only is the Delaware Plan a raw deal for the large states, it ain't that great of a deal for the mid-sized states either.

The inescapable consequence of [the set schedule] idea is that someone is always in the front of the bus and someone is always in the back of the bus.[15]

As we looked forward to the August meeting of the Los Angeles County Democratic Party, the American Plan continued to make progress in the North Bay. Sonoma County chair Jim Grau suggested that I contact Issues and Legislation Committee chair Ray Gallian and arrange to present the plan to the committee. Eva Long, a member of Marin County's Resolutions Committee, asked me for a copy of the American Plan resolution; I thought this was odd . . . hadn't Dotty LeMieux distributed it to her own committee?

To prepare the ground for the LA vote, David Phelps and Damian Carroll had arranged for the LACDP's August newsletter, which had been mailed to the membership before the meeting, to carry a one-page description of the plan. It might have been the newsletter article that drew the attention of Bob Mulholland, campaign advisor for the California Democratic Party, who reported directly to Art Torres. He asked if the American Plan was the one that would have some congressional districts in California voting on one day in the presidential primary and other districts on other days.[16] David Phelps undertook to correct Mulholland's misconception, and to pitch for Art Torres' intercession:

> In answer to your question, this plan DOES NOT split up any states. States become eligible in each of the ten rounds based on how many CDs are available in that round. For example, Round 1 starts with 8 CDs, with each succeeding Round adding 8 more. In the first round, a state having 9 or more CDs is not eligible. In the second round, a state having 16 or more CDs is not eligible, and so on. Every state would be eligible in every Round beginning in the 4th Round.
>
> With endorsements from DP/SFV, CYD, and now YDA, this proposal is now receiving significant and worthwhile support from dedicated grassroots and party organizations throughout California and the nation. The L.A. County Democratic Central Committee (next Tuesday), along with central committees from throughout the state will be considering resolutions on this Plan at their August and September meetings.
>
> We would appreciate further consideration from Chairman Torres and the CDP before the next DNC Commission meeting October 1. Let me know if there's anything I can do (Phelps, 12 August 2005).

Mulholland's response was that it is far too confusing, and wanted to know how the American Plan would get the Democratic more votes in November.[17] A few days later I asked David if he had gotten Mulholland straightened out.[18] He replied:

> [N]ot really. [H]e just quieted down. I [am] going to go through the Resolutions Committee route. He can't ignore them. I'm just waiting for the LACDP to endorse before I really move forward. I [am] working on letters of support from our current supporting organizations.[19]

Then it was back to Los Angeles. This time, rather than sortie from Petaluma and return the same day, as we had a month earlier, Marilyn Dudley-Rowley and I decided to remain overnight at the Bonaventure Hotel, a few blocks from the LACDP meeting at the Department of Water and Power headquarters. (Actually, water *is* power, for all aqueducts lead to Los Angeles. An earlier Mulholland had made sure of that.) We came better prepared with lots of handouts to explain the American Plan. However, there was a new wrinkle this time; it was candidate endorsement night, and everyone who hoped to be elected in November had a speech to make. It was the endorsement process that had priority on the agenda, so it wasn't guaranteed that the American Plan would come up for a vote that night.

The Los Angeles County Democratic Party must be like no other in America. It's so huge they have to meet in an auditorium. As the evening unfolded, we were treated to a couple of unscheduled spectacles. One was a series of disruptions by a young cadre of Lyndon LaRouche acolytes, annoying but harmless. More troubling, as I stepped out of the auditorium into the hall to retrieve an additional box of American Plan handouts, was to find the LACDP chair, Eric Bauman, locked in an exchange with a very heated and irrational man who insisted on being allowed to vote in the meeting despite the fact that he was not a member of the Central Committee. I moved in closer as the argument continued, with some vague idea of backing up Eric in case the situation got out of hand. Even though he had a meeting of several hundred people to run, Eric was patient with the guy, but also firm: he could sit in the meeting, but he couldn't vote because he wasn't a Central Committee member. "I've been a member of the Democratic Party for thirty years, and now you're telling me I can't vote!" Still, Eric appeared to be containing the situation with his calm demeanor, and it didn't look like he needed a total stranger butting in, so I returned to my seat in the auditorium next to Marilyn. A few minutes later, Eric and his assailant were at it again, this time at the front of the auditorium, below and to stage left. This nut was taking up too much of Eric's time, so I decided duck out of the auditorium again and alert building security to the situation in case Eric found it convenient to have the guy escorted from the building. However, when I returned to the auditorium, I found him wandering up and down the aisles with something resembling a voting card in his hand, except that his was pink and everyone else's was yellow. In the end, Eric had found a way to defuse the situation, appearing to give the guy what he wanted, but in fact giving him a card that was probably never counted anytime he held it up during a vote.

Eventually, the candidate endorsements were completed, and it was time for other business. Marilyn, David, Damian, and I began passing the American Plan handouts through the audience. I was still intent on this task, taking a bit of time to say a few words to each Central Committee member, when David came up to me told me, "That's it. It passed." It had happened so quietly, Marilyn and I completely missed the vote we had driven eight hours to see. There hadn't even been a debate this time. The newsletter article had done its work. Also, by that hour, people were probably ready to rush out of the auditorium and go home.

That's it?

That was it. We had Los Angeles County, the largest local party organization in the country, representing about a quarter of all the Democrats in California. By comparison, the vote of the Sixth AD committee in July had represented one-eightieth of state Democrats. What we had just accomplished in LA was equivalent to carrying Michigan or Ohio; however, it set us up to vault an even taller hurdle: the California Democratic Party. The next Executive Board meeting would be from October 1 to 2, on Manhattan Beach. We needed to get at least 50 percent of the party behind the American Plan . . . in the next two months.

NOTES

1. Phelps, David. 2005. E-mail, July 1.
2. Phelps, David. 2005. E-mail, July 5.
3. Woo, Evelyn. 2005. E-mail, July 5.
4. Phelps, David. 2005. E-mail, July 6.
5. Pearson, Chris. 2005. E-mail, July 8.
6. Phelps, David. 2005. E-mail, July 11.
7. Gangale, Thomas. 2005. E-mail, July 13.
8. LeMieux, Dotty. 2005. E-mail, July 14.
9. Gangale, Thomas. 2005. E-mail, July 18.
10. Pearson, Chris. 2005. E-mail, July 20.
11. Gangale, Thomas. 2005. E-mail, July 21.
12. Pearson, Chris. 2005. E-mail, July 22.
13. Gangale, Thomas. 2005. E-mail, August 7.
14. Johnson, Adam. 2005. E-mail, August 8.
15. Gangale, Thomas. 2005. E-mail, August 8.
16. Mulholland, Bob. 2005. E-mail, August 11.
17. Mulholland, Bob. 2005. E-mail, August 12.
18. Gangale, Thomas. 2005. E-mail, August 15.
19. Phelps, David. 2005. E-mail, August 15.

TACKLING TORRES

TARGETS OF OPPORTUNITY

Meanwhile, things appeared to be progressing toward consideration of the American Plan resolution by the Democratic Central Committee (DCC) of Marin at its September meeting, and Democracy for America-Marin was also showing interest. Sonoma County was dead still; Jim Grau had taken an extended holiday from the Central Committee, and I had yet to hear from Ray Gallian. And, there was no headway with the Herman-Price Commission. Chris Pearson observed:

> [Price] and the DNC in general (Dean or staffers) need to feel the pressure. All we can do is get them to listen to us. At some level that will be a step in the right direction, even if we understand they are not at all likely to adopt the plan, or even seriously entertain it. To me, speaking realistically, it would be a win if the commission did whatever lame tiny tweaks they were going to but put a little clause about liking the American Plan and something about comprehensive reform. . . .
>
> In other words, since they're never going to push that hard this year, maybe we can get a few steps ahead for the battle years down the road.[1]

David Phelps and Damian Carroll followed up aggressively on the LA victory:

> [Damian and I have been divvying up follow-up responsibilities among the L.A. area groups. DP/SFV distributed letters this week to Art Torres and all the California members of the DNC Commission. We are asking the same of the other groups.[2]]

Just then, Fresno County DCC member Barbara Pyle phoned Marilyn Dudley-Rowley and me with a valuable piece of intelligence: Art Torres would be speaking at a fundraising picnic being put on by the Nevada County Democratic Central Committee in Grass Valley in a couple of days. "If I were you, I'd go up there and get Mary [Longmore, the DCC chair] to introduce you to Art." So we did just that. As I was to learn over the next couple of years, one of the artful things about Art is his ability to dodge a public function as soon as he has done his bit. He did his best this time—he and state insurance commissioner John Garamendi had a black sedan waiting to whisk them away—but Marilyn (sometimes known as Dudley-Flores) and I had him in double coverage. In the act of rising from his seat and turning to dart off, His Artfulness nearly drove his nose into Marilyn's cleavage. Without skipping a beat, Marilyn handed him her business card. "Torres, I'm Flores. This man works for me. You need to listen to him."

Conversation with Art Torres

Memorandum
By Thomas Gangale
20 August 2005

GANGALE: I want to talk to you about presidential primary reform.

TORRES: Yeah, I'm on the Commission.

GANGALE: The word I've heard is that the commission is talking about doing incremental tweaking here and there. We can't afford to do that. If we do that, we'll hand the Republicans a huge opportunity.

TORRES: Yeah.

GANGALE: We need to implement a systemic reform. Are you familiar with the history of the Republicans on this issue?

TORRES: Yeah, I'm familiar from the material that the Commission has been studying.

GANGALE: The Nicholson Task Force in 1996, the Brock Commission in 1999–2000.

TORRES: Yeah, I know about that.

GANGALE: They'll come back to this issue if we don't solve it first. We have the ball now. But if all we do is run three plays and punt, the Republicans are going to score on their next possession.

TORRES: Absolutely. We ought to look at regional primaries.

GANGALE: Are you familiar with the American Plan?

TORRES: Yeah.

GANGALE: Last Tuesday, the Los Angeles County Democratic Party endorsed it.

TORRES: Yeah, you know how I heard about that? Eric Bauman told me.

GANGALE: And two weeks ago the Young Democrats of America endorsed it.

TORRES: Yeah, at their national convention in San Francisco. I'm on top of this.

GANGALE: I'd like to present the American Plan to the commission in October. All I have to do is explain how it works, and the plan will sell itself.

TORRES: Have you sent it to the Commission?

GANGALE: Already did that, no response.

TORRES: The separate members?

GANGALE: Done that, no response.

TORRES: We'll be in touch.

GANGALE: I need to be at that meeting in October.

TORRES: I'll see what I can do.

GANGALE: Thank you, sir. It's been an honor talking with you.

THE MAN WHO KNEW TOO EARLY

Two days after my chat with Art Torres, I left a voicemail message with Bill Jones, who was now CEO of Pacific Ethanol, based in Fresno. Chris Pearson hadn't thought that his phone call with Jones had been very productive. His impression of Jones was that he has completely retired from politics, both mentally and emotionally, and was out of touch with what was happening with the presidential primary reform issue. I wasn't terribly surprised. He had coauthored the Rotating Regional Plan with Massachusetts Secretary of the Commonwealth William Galvin in 1998, and although the plan had received the NASS endorsement the following year, it had then hit a brick wall. In 2000, the Brock Commission passed it over for the Delaware Plan. Ultimately the Bush campaign had quashed the Delaware Plan before it could come the floor of the Republican National Convention (RNC), but in the intervening years the Rotating Regional Plan (RRP) had made no measurable progress. The final straw for Jones was his thrashing at the hands on Barbara Boxer in his campaign for her senate seat. My guess was that the California Republican Party had sent him out on a political suicide mission, and now he was in the political afterlife, running an ethanol company in his hometown of Fresno. But I had some idea of the time and effort he had devoted to presidential primary reform during his tenure as secretary of state and as a member of the Brock Commission. I had admired him for it even though he had turned aside my plan when I had sent it to him in 1998, and he was the only Republican I voted for in the 1998 elections when he had run for reelection (the Democrats swept the state offices except for his). Surely, I thought, he must still have some interest in presidential primary reform, and would be willing to offer some advice. I felt it was worth making a follow-up phone call to him. He returned my call the following morning. I introduced myself as the author of the American Plan, and I reminded him of his conversation with Chris Pearson of FairVote a few weeks earlier.

Conversation with Bill Jones

Memorandum
By Thomas Gangale
23 August 2005

GANGALE: I know you worked vigorously on presidential primary reform during your tenure as secretary of state. Few people realize how important this issue is. It doesn't grab any headlines. Quite frankly, sir, you are one of my heroes.

JONES: Thank you for saying that. But let's not forget Bill Galvin [Secretary of the Commonwealth of Massachusetts, his coauthor on the Rotating Regional Plan] and other members of the NASS.

GANGALE: I think that a systemic reform of the presidential primary system would be the most significant change in the American electoral system since the 1965 Voting Rights Act. Millions of Americans are disenfranchised during the primary season by the current system, and that needs to change.

JONES: Absolutely!

GANGALE: Naturally, I believe I have a very good plan. I believe it combines the best features of the Rotating Regional Plan and the Delaware Plan. If I could come to Fresno and have an hour of your time, I think I could sell you on it, even though you coauthored the Rotating Regional Plan.

JONES: I don't know that it would be worth your time to come down here. I'm retired now.

GANGALE: I understand.

JONES: You need to get some support in the NASS. Of course, the small states wield an enormous amount of political power. Have you sent your plan to the NASS?

GANGALE: Yes, sir. I've gotten responses from several individual members. [Secretary of the State of New Hampshire] Bill Gardner called me up and we talked for an hour and a half.

JONES: He's a great guy. Very friendly.

GANGALE: He sure is! He invited me to come to New Hampshire and he's show me around. He wants me to see how the political process works during primary season.

JONES: Now, on the Republican side, you have the problem of a specific window. They have to wait until the national convention to implement anything.

GANGALE: But they can form a commission prior to that.

JONES: That's right, and we did that [with the Brock Commission in 1999]. On the other hand, the Democrats can implement a change at any time.

GANGALE: Would it be possible for you to arrange a meeting with [Secretary of the State of California] Bruce McPherson?

JONES: I could do that. But first, let me put you in contact with Beth Miller of Wilson & Miller. She's the staffer who worked with me on this issue when I was Secretary of State. If your plan sounds good to her, she can get you a meeting with Bruce McPherson. I don't think he's knowledgeable on this issue, so what she has to say will carry great weight, both with him and with me.

GANGALE: I'd greatly appreciate that. All I need is to get in the game, and I will perform. How is your relationship with Art Torres?

JONES: It's pretty good.

GANGALE: He's on the DNC commission that's studying the presidential nomination process, with a view to changing things for 2008. I spoke with him at a fundraiser in Grass Valley on Saturday. I think that the more people who talk to him about this issue, the more apt he is to promote a systematic reform plan.

JONES: Well, I haven't talked to Art in several years. Let's see what Beth says first. I wouldn't want to talk to anyone about this before it's been vetted.

GANGALE: Oh, certainly! I understand.

JONES: What's your background?

GANGALE: I have an aerospace engineering degree from the University of Southern California, and I'm finishing up a master's in international relations at San Francisco State University. I'm also a former Air Force officer.

JONES: How did you get involved in this issue?

GANGALE: Actually, I originally came up with my plan in 1992, when I saw the effect that front-loading was having on the nomination process. I wrote to you about my plan in late 1998, and you had some criticisms of the plan that I think were fair. So, I went back to the drawing board a couple of years ago and came up with a revised plan that's fairer to California. My plan allows some of the small states to go first so that we preserve retail politicking, but at the same time gives large states such as California the opportunity to go early enough in the schedule to have a real impact on the outcome.

JONES: Well, that sounds good. I'll get in touch with Beth and tell her to expect your call. Then we'll see how things go from there.

GANGALE: Fair enough. Thank you for your time, Mr. Secretary.

JONES: Keep up the effort in this.

GANGALE: Oh yes sir! "Once more unto the breach!" We have to keep at it unto we get the job done.

JONES: That's right! Have a good day.

GANGALE: You too, sir.

COUNTY INROADS

Things were now slowing down in Marin County. The DCC chair, John Alden, wrote that it looked as though they weren't going to be able to move on the American Plan resolution until October.[3] Still, the frustrations with Marin County were offset by progress elsewhere. Barbara Pyle and Kurt Gripenshaw in Fresno County, and Susan Rowe in Madera County, had signaled that their DCCs would consider the American Plan resolution at the next opportunity, and San Joaquin County DCC chair David Burr had invited Marilyn and me to the September 3 meeting in Lodi. David and Damian were working on Orange County.

Primary (Reform Under False) Colors

Berkeley Daily Planet
By Thomas Gangale
26 August 2005

The greatest political issue of 2005 is flying under the public's radar: how shall we decide who gets to be on the November 2008 ballot? Ah! To nominate or not to nominate, that is the question!

In 2004, Iowa and New Hampshire nominated John Kerry, then it was all over but the shouting. The voters in later states didn't really matter. By the time Howard Dean threw in the towel in mid-February, only a fifth of the American electorate had spoken.

In 2008, California will have no voice. The state legislature has moved the primary to June. That'll be about four months after the shouting, unless there is a complete redesign of the nomination process.

The Democratic National Committee has a commission studying possible reforms. How are they doing? An eye-witness to the DNC commission's July 16 reported, "At one point a commission member noted they didn't have a clear idea of what question they were supposed to be answering." After seven months of work, the commission is still looking for a mission statement.

Taking a look at the commission's website, most of the links on it result in a "Page Not Found" error. There is no way for the ordinary citizen to know what the commission has done, is doing, or will do. Also, this commission was supposed to hold meetings around the country and get lots of input, but all of its meetings have been meeting in Washington. The new DNC chairman Howard Dean has promised a more open and activist Democratic Party, but this commission is the blackest of the black holes, the smokiest of the smoke-filled rooms. The analysis and decision-making that go into determining how the 2008 primary schedule will be laid out ought to be conducted in the full light of day, which as much participation as possible by the party rank and file. This is an issue that all Democrats own, yet it might just as well be locked away at Guantanamo Bay.

This year's Democratic commission may not have the depth of knowledge on this issue that Republicans acquired through dogged experience, so they might well repeat the error that a Republican commission made in 1996 and recommend half-hearted measures, rather than go for a systemic solution as another Republican commission did in 2000 (which George Bush helped to shoot down). If so, then another blitzkrieg campaign looms in 2008, and a small portion of the American electorate will be buried in the rubble of sound-bite rhetoric, while the majority—including all Californians—will be left politically orphaned.

2008 is the grand opportunity. For the first time since 1928, no incumbent president is running for re-election, and no sitting vice-president is running for the top job. The planets are all lined up, and the Democrats are acting like they're not ready to launch.

A systemic solution is possible, but it must be fair to populous states even as it preserves "retail politicking" in the intimate venues of low-population states in the early part of the campaign season. It would be far better for the two parties to take this leap of faith, if not simultaneously, at least with some confidence that one will follow the other. We, the people, deserve this. The report of the bipartisan Miller commission stated:

"No political process in the United States is more important than our method of nominating presidential candidates, yet none has given rise to so much dissatisfaction. From both ends of the political spectrum come demands for change. A growing resolve on the part of concerned Americans to find a solution to this problem unites Democrats and Republicans, liberals and conservatives.... This new movement knows no partisan cast, nor does it seek to benefit any one candidate or faction. It is motivated solely by the belief that the public interest is ill-served by the current nominating system. Its conviction is as simple as it is significant: there must be reform."

That was in 1982. My watch says, "Half past 2005." How about yours?

A FAILURE TO COMMUNICATE

At the end of August, Marilyn and I drove to Long Beach to present some papers at Space 2005, an annual symposium of the American Institute of Aeronautics and Astronautics. In the evenings we sat aghast in the hotel bar as New Orleans drowned on huge television screens.

Christ Pearson reported on a conversation he had on August 26, 2005, with David Lyles, Carl Levin's chief of staff:

Conversation with David Lyles

Memorandum
Chris Pearson
30 August 2005

He was familiar with the plan as I had sent it to their office in July after handing the 2 pager directly to the Senator at the DNC meeting. I didn't get the chance to figure out where David stood on the question because he immediately explained we were too late. The time for outside testimony in front of the commission had passed. We're months too late, he explained.

I countered that I and others had been talking to commission staffers for many months and that it didn't seem right the only comprehensive plan they heard was NASS's rotating regional plan. He didn't have anything to say.

> I explained about the recent grass roots success and our partisan push about having to follow the GOP down the road but it was falling on deaf ears.
>
> Lately I've been toying with the idea that maybe the commission could just reference our plan. In other words, make the small tweaks it is targeted to make and then ad something about future commissions that should examine the American Plan and the Rotating Regional Plan.
>
> Something that would give us a leg up in the future. I asked if he had any suggestions about helping this idea along and he said flatly, NO.
>
> My hope at this point is we can convince one commission member to suggest something along these lines. If that happens, and we've been pressuring others perhaps they would chime in to support the idea (even if they refused to take the lead). What do others think? At this point I feel it's the best we can hope for from the commission.

We were months too late? What a joke! I had sent the American plan to every single member of the commission the previous December! The Herman-Price had ignored us for eight solid months and had nearly run out the clock. We had just time for a Hail Mary pass. David Phelps agreed on what our last play should be:

> We need to make a personal and real connection with just one of these Commissioners. Then get them to at least raise the Plan as a viable systemic reform to be considered by the next Commission.[4]

Chris had made the pitch to Carl Levin in a letter, citing both his conversation with him on July 16, and his conversation with Lyles:

> If it is indeed too late for a full hearing in front of the Commission I wonder if it might be possible to make sure the plan is at least mentioned in the final report and also to have action on this considered in Congress? Such support would be consistent with the party's new "'50 State Vision." Could you include something that urges future Commissions to consider comprehensive reform like NASS's rotating regional plan or the American Plan? At this point it seems this is the best we can hope for and I wonder if you might consider supporting the plan with a request along these lines.[5]

On a parallel track, on September 4 I sent a letter to Senator Levin's brother, Representative Sander Levin, who on two occasions had introduced in Congress his own plan to reform the presidential nomination process.[6]

While still in Long Beach, I wrote to Fresno County DCC member Barbara Pyle for help:

> I have written (by mail) to Chairman Torres four times, and Rep. Lynn Woolsey has written to him once on behalf of the American Plan. I also spoke to the commission's lead staffer once, e-mailed him several times, and sent him hard copies. On all of these occasions I asked to present the American Plan to the commission in person. I never received a response from anyone. Now the commission is saying, "The time for outside testimony in front of the commission has passed. You're months too late."
>
> This is not my idea of how the Democratic Party should run, how about you?
>
> If Joel Murillo and anyone else has Art Torres' ear, now is time to speak up. I appreciate all that you have done for the American Plan so far, and I hate to ask more, but the next couple of weeks is do or die.[7]

Barbara forwarded my message to Nevada County DCC chair Mary Longmore, asking her if she had any ideas. Mary responded, "This does not surprise me a bit." But I was new to politics:

> I get the same reaction from the more experienced political hands: "This does not surprise me a bit." But it surprises me, and I think it would dismay thousands of people across the country who were energized and brought into the party by the candidacy of Dean in particular and to some extent that of Kerry as well. Dean gave a lot of people hope that the party would open up to more rank-and-file participation. On the issue of presidential primary reform, this has certainly not been the case! When I read the report of the 2000 RNC Brock Commission, they had a much more open process, and they cast a wide net, considering a broad range of reform ideas. When the Republicans are more open than we Democrats, we have a problem.[8]

What we had here was a failure to communicate. However, not all of the communications failures were on the other side. Having lived all of my life in California, except for my time in the Air Force, I had never been to Lodi. On September 3, Marilyn Dudley-Rowley and I arrived at Dee Dee's restaurant at 8 P.M. . . . And found ourselves stuck in Lodi without dinner. The restaurant was closed. I called David Burr on my cell phone. Yes, we were at the right place, but at the wrong time; the San Joaquin County DCC meeting had been at 8 A.M. Another snafu occurred on September 13, when Marilyn borrowed my car to teach a class at Solano Community

College that night, leaving the keys to her car in some unfathomable place, and I was supposed to present the American Plan to the Sonoma County DCC that same night. Whatever was going around was highly contagious; Chris Pearson confessed that he had neglected to actually mail his letter to David Lyles.[9]

TWO-MINUTE DRILL

The game clock running down at the Commission on Presidential Nomination Timing and Scheduling (CPNTS) had implications for the American Plan resolution now being considered by a dozen Democratic central committees:

> At some point in time, the language in the resolutions that have been passed so far and are presently under consideration will be outdated, in that there will clearly be no point in calling on "the CPNTS to seriously consider the American Plan." We should come to an agreement on what that point in time is, and what the new language should be. Regarding time, I'm thinking in terms of any resolution that cannot come to a vote prior to 1 October, or possibly even 15 September. Regarding language, here are two options:
>
> 1. Cite the clauses in last year's resolution at the national convention that called this commission into existence, which the commission has failed to live up to, and call upon Howard Dean to empanel a new commission that will live up to these clauses.
> 2. Call upon the DNC to adopt and implement the American Plan.
>
> The first option seems useless to me, although resolutions with this language would undoubtedly be easier to pass. The danger is that Dean will shrug and say that the work of the present commission is good enough, so we don't need a new one. My feeling is that he is inclined to do this, given his remarks a couple of weeks ago that only "minor surgery" is needed. The second option is unequivocal, and if passed by enough committees, would force Dean to empanel a new commission that would "seriously consider the American Plan." The problem is, that being so clear and unequivocal, a resolution with this language might be a tougher sell.[10]

Damian Carroll suggested a great third option: "Can we split the difference, and call on Dean to empanel a new commission that would seriously consider the American Plan?"[11] I tweaked the resolution accordingly and sent the revision to all DCCs that were considering it. Most of them wouldn't bring it to a vote until after the October CDP Executive Board meeting (which was on the same weekend as the Herman-Price Commission meeting), so if the revision resulted in a month's delay, the tradeoff for a stronger resolution was a good one. Meanwhile, Barbara Pyle informed me that the Fresno County DCC passed the old version on September 7.

> OUTSTANDING! Thank you for your effort on this. Also, as I have said before, your network of contacts around the state has been a godsend. Marilyn and I look forward to celebrating many future victories with you on the American Plan, the 58 County Plan, and other issues of vital interest to the Democratic Party.[12]

Also, as Madera County DCC chair Susan Rowe informed me a few days later, her committee adopted the resolution on September 8. Damian and David advised me that conflicts between the old and new resolution language could be resolved (no pun intended) once they reached the CDP Resolutions Committee. The Placer County DCC adopted the American Plan resolution on September 12. In Lake County, Becky Curry, whom Marilyn and I had met at the July CDP Executive Board meeting in Sacramento, was having a problem with a balky committee.[13] In any case, David Phelps reported that the American Plan was on the Resolutions Committee agenda for the CDP Executive Board meeting in Manhattan Beach.[14]

Despite the list of organizations that had endorsed the American Plan resolution so far, David was not as sanguine as his note sounded. To better ensure our success, he was trying to arrange for a face-to-face meeting with Art Torres before the next E-Board meeting. He pointed out that if Torres wanted to tank the resolution, the Resolutions Committee would do just that. David and Damian saw an opportunity on September 18, "to make a personal and real connection with just one of these Commissioners."

Conversation with Art Torres

Memorandum
Damian Carroll
19 September 2005

I am pleased to report that David and I finagled a meeting yesterday with none other than Chairman Art Torres!

We were at an event in Woodland Hills called the Minority Outreach Symposium. Art Torres appeared as a guest speaker, and David and I talked him into meeting with us for a few minutes in a back office room. We were helped in this endeavor by John Heaner, our local area rep to the CDP, who sat in with us at the meeting.

I cannot promise Thomas's tape-recorder memory, but this is basically how it went down . . .

DAVID: (Thanked Chairman Torres for meeting with us. Told Torres we have a resolution we are introducing to the CDP in October regarding the American Plan. Briefly outlined the rapidly growing grassroots coalition supporting the plan. Gave Art a packet of information regarding the plan. Said frankly that we knew this resolution would not go forward in the CDP without his support, and asked for his backing.)

TORRES: (Confirmed that this was about the American plan. Said he was familiar with the plan, and had run into the plan's author at a meeting a couple months ago. Said he was good friends with Bill Richardson, that they had come up the ranks together as politicians, and that Richardson was advocating for a regional primary (that is, a mega-primary of Southwestern states, *not* the rotating plan—DC) but that so far Richardson was not including California in such a primary. Also said that he had spoken with Howard Dean and Sen. Levin on the subject, to discuss workable solutions to the primary calendar. Said that he was going to the next meeting in DC. (Art has attended one meeting of the commission, the first—DC.)

DAVID: Are you familiar with the plan? Do you have any questions we could answer?

TORRES: I am familiar with the plan. My initial reaction is positive. Let me do some additional research and get back to you.

DAMIAN: It's fitting that we discuss the plan here at the Minority Outreach Symposium, because the intention of this plan is to restore fairness to the system and increase participation by voters in more states and among more populations. Please keep in mind while you are doing your research that there are two ways for primaries to be viewed as "important"—they need to vote early in the schedule or they need to be big, like Super Tuesday. This plan distributes those attributes throughout the calendar—primaries are either small and early or later and big.

TORRES: As you know California is now at the back of the calendar again.

DAVID: Yes, we believe this plan is California's best chance at moving earlier. Under the present system, whenever California schedules their primary earlier, many other states follow suit.

TORRES: I know, if we continue like that the first primaries will be in October.

DAMIAN: It will continue that way until all the states can agree on a broad framework that they think is fair. As you know we are not requesting any special treatment for California, we only want to have the same treatment as other states, including Iowa and New Hampshire.

TORRES: I have to sit next to the Iowa delegate at the Commission meetings, but I speak my mind anyway.

DAVID: What can we do to assist you?

TORRES: I will give you (David) a call on this next week. We can talk about next steps then.

(Thank-yous all around, Torres went back to the forum. Dave and Damian high fived.)

Obviously the next step is the phone call next week between David and Torres. We need to plan ahead because we don't know exactly when Art will call. What further message should we relay? Keep in mind that David may have a short amount of time to speak.

Finally, it looked like we might have an inroad with the Herman-Price Commission. I was guardedly optimistic. Thinking of Torres' power to "tank the resolution," I wrote:

> One thing I would impress upon Art is that we would have had a lot more resolutions by now if it weren't for everyone having to focus on the special election [the party was mobilizing to defeat six ballot initiatives backed by Governor Schwarzenegger]. There are a lot more resolutions coming down the pike. We have 20 counties in play, and the avalanche is going to come in November and December. Art needs to understand that this is a bandwagon that he needs to get on.[15]

COPYING SOMEONE ELSE'S HOMEWORK

Here's a case where that concept failed miserably. That same day, Rob Richie alerted me that the Carter-Baker Commission report was out:

> You saw that Carter-Baker recommends the NASS regional plan? The description of why speaks of course to the American Plan—good op-ed opportunity.[16]

Presidential Primary Schedule

Report of the Commission on Federal Election Reform
19 September 2005

The presidential primary system is organized in a way that encourages candidates to start their campaigns too early, spend too much money, and allow as few as eight percent of the voters to choose the nominees. The Commission believes that the scheduling of the presidential primary needs to be changed to allow a wider and more deliberate national debate.

In 2000, the presidential primaries were effectively over by March 9, when John McCain ended his bid for the Republican nomination and Bill Bradley left the race for the Democratic nomination. This was less than seven weeks after the Iowa caucus. In 2004, the presidential primary process was equally compressed. Less than 8 percent of the eligible electorate in 2004 cast ballots before the presidential nomination process was effectively over.

The presidential primary schedule has become increasingly front-loaded. While 8 states held presidential primaries by the end of March in 1984, 28 states held their primaries by March in 2004. The schedule continues to tighten, as six states have moved up the date of their presidential primary to February or early March while eight states have decided to cancel their presidential primary.

Because the races for the presidential nominations in recent elections have generally concluded by March, most Americans have no say in the selection of presidential nominees, and intense media and public scrutiny of candidates is limited to about 10 weeks. Moreover, candidates must launch their presidential bids many months before the official campaign begins, so that they can raise the $25 to $50 million needed to compete.

The presidential primary schedule therefore is in need of a comprehensive overhaul. A new system should aim to expand participation in the process of choosing the party nominees for president and to give voters the chance to closely evaluate the presidential candidates over a three- to four-month period. Improvements in the process of selecting presidential nominees might also aim to provide opportunities for late entrants to the presidential race and to shift some emphasis from Iowa and New Hampshire to states that more fully reflect the diversity of America.

Most members of the Commission accept that the first two states should remain Iowa and New Hampshire because they test the candidates by genuine "retail," door-to-door campaigning. A few other members of the Commission would replace those states with others that are more representative of America's diversity; and would especially recommend a change from Iowa because it chooses the candidate by a public caucus rather than a secret ballot, the prerequisite of a democratic election.

While the presidential primary schedule is best left to the political parties to decide, efforts in recent years by political parties have failed to overhaul the presidential primary schedule. If political parties do not make these changes by 2008, Congress should legislate the change.

Recommendation on Presidential Primary Schedule

We recommend that the Chairs and National Committees of the political parties and Congress make the presidential primary schedule more orderly and rational and allow more people to participate. We endorse the proposal of the National Association of Secretaries of State to create four regional primaries, after the Iowa caucus and the New Hampshire primary, held at one-month intervals from March to June. The regions would rotate their position on the calendar every four years.

Out of a hundred-page report, the commission devoted little more than a page to the presidential nomination process. The commission's description of the problem was accurate; however, it provided no rationale as to how the NASS Rotating Regional Plan addressed the problem. It was a "just so" story, one that was easy to shoot down. What had the commission members been thinking? On this issue, it hadn't thought very hard. George Washington University professor Spencer Overton, who was both a member of both the Carter-Baker and Herman-Price commissions, said that presidential primary reform was one of over fifty issues the Carter-Baker Commission tackled, and they only spent fifteen to twenty minutes considering that presidential nomination reform.

Bad Plan for Elections Just Won't Go Away

San Francisco Examiner
By Thomas Gangale
21 September 2005

The recently released report of the Carter-Baker Commission on Federal Election Reform devoted 550 words to the problem of the presidential primary schedule, about the length of this opinion article.

The report from the commission headed by former President Jimmy Carter and former Secretary of State James Baker wastes most of that verbiage expounding on the obvious—that things need to change. The commission's recommendation actually contains only 75 words, so perhaps they just didn't give this part of the report much thought: They endorsed a system of four regional primaries, the order of which rotates from one cycle to the next.

Why this particular recommendation? This remains unexplained. You're supposed to just accept this on faith. Will a rotating regional presidential primary system "allow a wider and more deliberate national debate," as the report suggests? Wider than what?

When Bill Bradley and John McCain threw in their towels in early March 2000, just under half of the delegates to the Democratic and Republican national conventions had been selected. When the Howard Dean campaign collapsed in late February 2004, less than a quarter of the delegates had been chosen. The other way of looking at it is that more than three-quarters of the nation's Democrats had absolutely no say in the nomination of John Kerry. That's democratic?

The rotating regional plan would permanently disenfranchise three-quarters of the electorate in both parties. Because the winner of the first regional primary would look like "The Winner" and the others would come off looking like also-rans, every candidate would spend all of his or her time, energy and money in those first states in a do-or-die effort. The rest of the country would be completely ignored.

Since no resources would remain for any real campaigning after this electoral Armageddon, the states in the remaining three regional primaries would get on the bandwagon with The Winner of the first primary. Win one, get three free. Any politician can do that math.

The lucky first 25 percent would rotate from one four-year cycle to the next. Your particular region would get to cast a meaningful vote once every four cycles, or once every 16 years. You would be privileged to choose your party's nominee three or four times during your life. That's enough voting privileges for one lifetime, right?

The rotating regional presidential primary idea dates back to the early 1970s, when Oregon Republican Bob Packwood introduced a bill for such a plan in the U.S. Senate. The bill had only two co-sponsors and it died in committee. Thirty-two similar bills have been floated in Congress over the past 30 years, and they have met the same fate. Quite simply, this is a plan that can't survive outside the committee room.

It's an idea that goes nowhere, again and again. Think about it. This plan was designed around the same time as the space shuttle. Its saving grace has been that—unlike the shuttle—thank God, it has never been launched. Now they're seriously talking about reanimating this creaky old idea and launching it.

According to H.L. Mencken, "For every complex problem, there is a solution that is simple, neat and wrong." This is one of them. There are much better alternatives out there, but politicians are ignoring them so they can continue riding their tired old hobbyhorses. That's much easier than studying new solutions based on solid political science.

THE MAN WHO DID HIS HOMEWORK

In the course of the next few weeks, Rob Richie and Chris Pearson at FairVote arranged for telephone conferences with several former members of the Brock Commission, including Tom Sansonetti and Jim Nicholson. Marilyn Dudley-Rowley and I were in on the conversation with Bill Brock, and immediately afterward we captured the conversation to relay to David and Damian.

Conversation with Bill Brock

Memorandum
Thomas Gangale
22 September 2005

The sense I got, along with Chris Pearson's impression of Jim Nicholson on Tuesday, is that they're both still pretty cheesed off that the Bush campaign wouldn't let the Brock Commission's recommendation go to the floor at the 2000 Republican convention, and a year of effort went down the drain. According to Chris, Nicholson described Brock as still being passionate on the issue.

Brock did not disappoint. He started out by saying we might talk for 15 to 20 minutes, and he gave us about 50 minutes.

When Rob asked him why his commission decided not to go with the Rotating Regional Plan, he replied bluntly (and this sounded so lovely in his Tennessee drawl), "We just didn't think it made any sense. It won't increase voter turnout, or increase grassroots participation, or help lesser-known candidates, or reduce the influence of money."

Brock came out very strongly for the American Plan, stopping short of an outright endorsement only because he still likes the Delaware Plan as well. He acknowledged that the American Plan would be more palatable to populous states. "But no plan can be perfect. All of them have warts. Yours has one of the same warts as the Rotating Regional Plan, that of shuffling the dates of the primaries around. The secretaries of state are going to resist that."

Except, of course, that since the National Association of Secretaries of State backs the Rotating Regional Plan, they can hardly raise this point in opposition to the American Plan.

Brock was surprisingly dismissive of the Rotating Regional Plan, to the point that I wondered if I were hearing my own echo. "Let them try it once and they'll see how bad it really is. It won't do any of the things they think it will. But then, any reform we try will deteriorate in a few years." I took this as a needed note of realism. It was the McGovern-Fraser reforms of 1972 that eventually produced the mess we're in now. Every good intention has unintended consequences. It may unnerve some to ask this, but as a scientist and engineer, I must ask it: what have we not thought of in the American Plan? Asking such questions is how we make it better: find what's broken, fix what's broken.

Brock suggested that Ohio Republican Secretary of State Ken Blackwell might be a fracture point in the NASS's backing of the Rotating Regional Plan. He was also encouraged to hear that my contact with Bill Jones might result in access to California Republican Secretary of State Bruce McPherson.

Brock sees the need for a bipartisan strategy. He was pleased to learn of our success among California Democrats, and is interested in getting a similar effort going in the Republican Party, both at the local level, through the Young Republicans, and by talking to party leaders. We talked about getting access to party activists who could serve as ignition points for grassroots efforts.

Brock expressed concern over what might happen if our California Democratic effort was stymied at the state level, that we'd be dead in the water nationally. I took this as an indirect way of saying that he hopes that we succeed. He said that we really need to get a party in one or two populous states to endorse. That was one of the things that went wrong with the Delaware Plan. He mentioned Illinois' opposition to the Delaware Plan, and there's evidence that Texas and California Republicans also opposed it. Another cause of the failure was not communicating the issue adequately outside of the commission. That's what makes our effort in California unique: it's bottom-up rather than top-down. I think he's surprised that we've been so effective in getting grassroots buy-in on such a complex issue.

Brock also discussed the relative merits of the Republican and Democratic Party rules. "The Democrats are more flexible because they can implement a change in mid-term, whereas the Republicans have to get approval at their national convention." He expressed despondence over the dearth of creative thinking in his party, but I assured him that there was little evidence of it in the Democratic Party. I'm not sure that was any comfort. He'd like to think there are a few neurons firing somewhere.

Rob mentioned that Dean had already stated publicly that any changes out of this year's DNC commission would be small, and that New Hampshire would remain first. In reference to bowing before New Hampshire, Brock grated derisively, "Everyone has to go through that charade."

Brock said that while his commission was doing its work, they stayed in contact with the DNC. When Rob asked him whether this year's DNC commission had contacted him, he said, "No." Rob said this fact, or for that matter the fact that the commission didn't bring me into its proceedings, spoke volumes about the quality of this commission's work.

Brock sees little hope for an openly bipartisan effort because of the lack of civility "in this town," meaning Washington specifically, but I think also as a metaphor for American politics in general. "The best you can hope for is that while one party is effecting a systemic change, it keeps the other informed and tries to address any concerns the other party might have. Let's face it: once one party does it, the other is going to find it very difficult not to follow, because the present system is so bad. It's really very damaging, and it can't go on much longer. The nominees in both parties are being chosen by a few ideologues, a few nut cases."

Everyone agreed that the Carter-Baker Commission's recent endorsement of the Rotating Regional Plan is an opportunity to raise this issue's visibility, but no one thinks they gave it much thought. "It's been a very closed process, a few people sitting in a room." Brock expressed some frustration over the fact that the press doesn't cover this issue very well because it's technical and substantive. "And where is the Brookings Institution on this? Or CSIS [Center for Strategic and International Studies]? Or some of the other big research institutions?"

Rob suggested putting together a C-SPAN event, and Brock was all for it. He suggested a few "formers" who might be interested: Lee Hamilton, Jim Nicholson, George Mitchell, Elliott Roosevelt. And he would like to be in on the action, too. "I'm not running for anything, so I'll take no prisoners."

I wasn't running for anything either. None of us were. But we couldn't afford a "no quarter" policy. When we took a prisoner, we had to try turning him into an ally. The delicate balance was in beating on their armor enough to get their attention, without upsetting them too much. Who really knew where that balance was? Rob Richie and Steven Hill played "good cop" to the Carter-Baker Commission, where I had played "bad cop."

What Baker-Carter Got Right

TomPaine.com
By Rob Richie and Steven Hill
27 September 2005

Last week's release of the report of the election reform commission headed by Jimmy Carter and James Baker has drawn fierce fire from civil rights and electoral reform organizations for recommending that voters be required to present photo identification at the polls. Because the ID recommendations in isolation would shrink the electorate, many reformers have pronounced the Baker-Carter recommendations DOA.

We believe it a mistake to condemn the entire report because of the understandable voter ID objections. Dominated by aging politicians of the creaky two-party duopoly, the Commission on Federal Election Reform certainly was less than bold in many important areas. But building on his vast experience observing elections around the world and experiencing elections in the South, Carter earned bipartisan support for several forward-looking recommendations.

The commission's boldest call is for universal voter registration, a practice used by many democracies around the world in which all eligible voters are automatically registered to vote. Universal registration would add more than 50 million unregistered Americans—nearly three in 10 eligible voters—to the voter rolls. These potential voters are disproportionately under 25, low-income and people of color. Their absence from the voter rolls helps to explain the shocking disparities in our voter turnout based on traditional measures of class status: income, education and race.

Of course, the devil is in the details, and the commission fails to outline a clear plan for how the government would ensure that all eligible voters are registered. But if implemented fully, this would be one of the single most important government civil rights actions since the Voting Rights Act of 1965.

Remarkably, James Baker, architect of the Bush campaign's post-election strategy in Florida in 2000, joined Carter in a New York Times op-ed on September 23rd calling for universal registration. They wrote that the government should "assume the responsibility to seek out citizens to both register voters and provide them with free ID's that meet federal standards. States should open new offices, use social service agencies and deploy mobile offices to register voters." Once registered, people would stay registered; the report's goal is that "people would need to register only once in their lifetime."

Other commission recommendations respond directly to problems in our recent elections. They include:

Nonpartisan election officials. In the wake of presidential races in which Florida's former secretary of state Katherine Harris and Ohio's Ken Blackwell made clearly partisan decisions affecting a tightly fought national race, the commission calls for nonpartisan election officials. This would help rid our elections of the appearance of fraud—and might dissuade actual fraud.

Paper trails. Heeding a rising tide of grassroots activism founded on a mistrust of the privately owned voting equipment companies that run our elections, the commission calls for a paper audit trail that has been verified by each individual voter.

National elections assistance. Challenging the majority view of the old guard National Association of Secretaries of State that in February voted to restore what essentially amounted to the pre-2000 decentralized regime for administering elections, commissioners instead call for ongoing federal funding of elections. They also would strengthen the Election Assistance Commission, established in 2002 to administer some national guidelines.

A revamped presidential primary schedule. The commission supports a dramatic overhaul of the presidential primary schedule. The current system is absolutely bankrupt, with states chaotically advancing their primaries in the hope of gaining candidate attention—but collectively making it even more likely that Iowa and New Hampshire will be the only states that matter. The commission's recommendation will help boost an alternative dubbed the American Plan, recently supported by the Young Democrats of America.

Although they would bring the United States up to international norms, none of these proposals are the transformative changes that might truly shake up partisan calculations. There's no call for direct election of the president despite the Electoral College's malfunction in 2000 and the ever-declining number of contested states. Commissioners neglect the potential of instant runoff voting despite recent high-profile elections with non-majority winners and "spoilers."

The report is equally silent on establishing a constitutional right to vote, despite the obvious adverse impact on elections of having more than 13,000 jurisdictions able to make independent decisions about running federal elections. It overlooks how nonpartisan redistricting, campaign finance reform, fusion and proportional voting are necessary means to take on the shocking lack of voter choice and distortions in representation in our legislative elections. It doesn't even propose ideas like citizens assemblies to at least put such fundamental reform proposals on the table.

In addition, liberals on the commission had to accept a trade-off to secure conservative support for policies designed to increase the voter rolls so dramatically. That tradeoff was a series of measures designed to address concerns about voter fraud, such as presenting photo IDs at the polls, regulating voter registration processes and preventing people from registering to vote in more than one state.

Some of these anti-fraud proposals are problematic, particularly if adopted in isolation by states ignoring other recommendations in the report. Absentee voters—who are disproportionately well off—need only sign their ballot to prove validity, while voters who show up at the polls would have to present a photo ID. And although the commission recommends IDs be free, some states may still charge fees and establish other practical barriers that would be tantamount to a modern-day poll tax.

The reality is that the number of votes affected by fraudulent activities is dwarfed by voting barriers like lack of universal voter registration. But if a candidate you prefer loses because of fraudulent votes, as some argue happened in last year's razor-close gubernatorial race in Washington, fraud is a very big deal. Voters certainly demand that politicians "play by the rules," and in exchange for universal registration, democracy advocates should agree on what steps to prevent fraud would be acceptable.

The commission's greatest flaw is calling on states to lead what should be a national system. There is no doubt that some states will abuse these recommendations, jumping to require photo IDs while not acting to register all eligible voters. The current leadership in Congress and many states certainly has put pro-democracy advocates on the defensive, struggling simply to maintain access to the polls for racial minorities and the poor.

But Republican and Democratic leaders are both now unpopular among most Americans, and ignore reasonable steps toward free and fair elections at their political peril. Advocates should make fixing our elections a litmus test of support. As part of a proactive democracy strategy, we should not be afraid to support what's good in the commission's report and oppose what's bad.

Certainly it is high time to call for clean and complete rolls with 100 percent registration as enjoyed by many other democracies. Who would have thought that James Baker would help lead that call?

A FOOT IN THE DOOR

Darius had declined to come on the road trip to Manhattan Beach with Marilyn Dudley-Rowley and me. He loved to discuss political issues, but he wasn't comfortable in crowds. Like me, he was a loner at heart. That was unfortunate, as from across the room at the July LACDP meeting, Marilyn and I did not fail to notice that several young women attempted to strike up conversations with him. He could be quite engaging when he wanted to.

When Marilyn Dudley-Rowley and I arrived in Manhattan Beach that evening, I was feeling rather frustrated that once again I hadn't been invited to present the American Plan to the Herman-Price commission, and my attitude regarding politicians in general was...well, surly. I was tired of being ignored and of being blown off with *pro forma* letters that said nothing.

The Idiot Politician

Unpublished Op-Ed
By Thomas Gangale
30 September 2005

Mark Twain once said, "Suppose you were an idiot, and suppose you were a member of Congress; but I repeat myself."

Are politicians really idiots? In order to prove that proposition, one would have to subject a statistically significant sample of them to IQ tests, and of course, they would have to be idiots to comply with such a testing program. It is better to be thought a fool than to actually be proven one.

But they really do appear to be idiots. Write a letter to one sometime and see if you get a response. Chances are you won't, but if it's your lucky day, you'll receive a bland acknowledgement that in no way addresses the issue you raised in your letter. In fact, you'll wonder whether they actually wrote to you or they misaddressed their unresponsive response that was intended for some other hapless constituent.

A former senator, cabinet secretary, and national party chair asked me last week, "Do you really think people read their mail?" Stupid me! No, I think their staffers read only enough to figure out what the issue is according to some vague metric, then they weigh all the letters they receive on that issue on a postal scale. Below a certain weight threshold, it's not an important enough issue, so they do nothing.

Now, repeat the experiment. Write another letter, but this time include a $2000 check. Of course, the change in response isn't proof of intelligence...even a plant turns toward the sun.

The tragedy is that most politicians start out as moderately intelligent, well-intentioned people. Then they get into power, and over the years they have less and less contact with their constituents and more and more contact with big donors, lobbyists, fellow politicians, and staffers. They forget that they were once constituents themselves. The arrogance of entrenched power seduces them into a belief in their own omniscience and that of the others in the "in" crowd. But in this closed-loop information system, the same old stale ideas get passed around and around, and through this process of increasing insularity, the best and brightest degenerate into idiocy. There is no better evidence of the unintelligent design of the universe than the devolution of politicians.

But we can reverse devolution. We can turn unintelligent design into intelligent design. We can be the evolutionary force that transforms politicians.

Write your politicians. If they don't write you back, write them off, and write yourself in at election time. This will accomplish several things.

First of all, you can be confident about your choice. When you vote for yourself, you know you're not voting for an idiot.

Second, although you won't win office, you'll take market share from the professional politicians. They'll really hate that. No politician wants to be forced into a run-off election. And, suppose neither runoff candidate wins a majority. You can make this happen simply by voting for yourself again and again. Your victory is to deny them victory. Your power is in disempowering the powerful.

Third, the more who people write themselves in, the more it will stuff up the electoral system. Election officials have to count each write-in ballot by hand. Each election could take weeks to sort out. If you don't like the two-party machine, throw sand in the gears until it grinds to a halt.

Finally, the cumulative effect of all of this will be to transmit a loud and clear message of voter disgust over politics as usual.

Let's retire these 20th-century dinosaurs. Either transform them back into constituents, or force them to evolve into more nimble and more responsive life-forms for the 21st century. In the long run, you'll be doing them a favor. After all, no one wants to be an idiot.

The next morning, as I was dressing for the day, I received a phone call from Sherry Reson in Marin County. "Are you watching C-SPAN? They're talking about you!" Unfortunately, the hotel's cable TV system didn't include C-SPAN, so I would probably have to wait to see the streaming video in the C-SPAN Web site. It would be several agonizing days before I knew the specifics of what had gone on in Washington, but Art Torres had come through. The American Plan was in the record of the of the Herman-Price Commission.

Herman-Price Commission, October Meeting

Transcript
1 October 2005

MR. TORRES: Diversity has been a very important issue for us and the lack of that diversity in a Presidential nominating process has been very evident to those of us in California. And I appreciate the scenarios that include that kind of diversity that we see within the documents as well. But there's also a group in California of many activists who are concerned. I'm sure they'll raise their voices before the Rules Committee at the appropriate time in terms of their perspective, and that is a Resolution that we will be considering tomorrow in Los Angeles that seriously urges us to consider the American or Graduated Random System which features 10 multi-state primaries evenly spaced over 20 weeks of the approximate length of the traditional Presidential primary schedule. The first primary would take place in a randomly selected group of states whose Congressional Districts total exactly eight with succeeding primaries going progressively larger.

We feel in California that in 2004 election, over $181 million dollars left our state never to come back, and in June—rather in March of 2004 when our primaries were held we were almost irrelevant in a primary nominating process. And I know that each of the members here understands that in other states, New York and others, equally contributed as much and never came back to their home states. We feel that this proposal might very well be seriously considered at the Rules Committee. I know at this point it is a little late in the process to introduce something new but I think that this discussion as a heads-up from California will take place tomorrow and I'm sure there are many people who want to participate there.

But I will, of course, report on our deliberations that take place today to that body tomorrow of about 500 executive board members in Los Angeles. But I wanted to say that the California Young Democrats and the National Young Democrats meeting in San Francisco in August of this year also embrace this proposal and I'm sure Mr. Roosevelt and others, members of the Rules Committee will be hearing from them in the future.

But thank you again for being sensitive to the issue of diversity, especially among Asian, Latino, and African-American voters and to help them become viable and real within the nominating process for the next President of the United States who I in my heart know will be a Democrat.

The CDP Resolutions Committee meeting was scheduled in the early afternoon in Manhattan Beach. Shortly after lunch, Barbara Pyle caught sight of a very influential member of the party standing at the hotel front desk with his luggage beside him, obviously just now checking in. She escorted me over to Bob Mulholland, and introduced me and the American Plan. An hour or so later, our paths crossed again. "I've read this thing over and over, and I still don't understand it. I don't see how it'll help us, and I'm going to stop it." And we walked on down the hall to the Resolutions Committee.

Bob sat in a back row across the room from me, quietly, ready to pounce when the moment came. He was going to have a long wait. The American Plan was near the end of the agenda. In the meantime, we locked eyes with each other repeatedly. His opposition to the American Plan didn't square with the report David and Damian had given of their meeting with Art Torres. Also, apparently something had happened in Washington that morning, although we didn't yet have the details. Wasn't that Torres' doing? Given that Bob worked for Art, just what the hell was going on?

Early in the Resolutions Committee's agenda was a resolution supporting instant runoff voting. At that point, things took an unexpected turn. A senior member of the committee recommended referring the resolution to the Voter Services Committee. His argument was that there were a number of committees devoted to specific classes of issues, and these should handle any resolutions falling within their purviews, whereas the Resolutions Committee was intended as a catchall to handle any oddball resolutions that didn't fit in any of the other committees. The other members of the Resolutions Committee agreed with him, and voted to refer the IRV resolution to the Voter Services Committee. Santa Clara County DCC member Steve Chessin, who was shepherding the IRV resolution through the state party's processes, stormed out of the room in a fury. "This is outrageous!" As I was to learn later, his resolution had been kicked from committee to committee several times.

It was pretty clear that the reason for booting the IRV resolution was going to be applied to the American Plan resolution as well, and we didn't want to wait for then end of the meeting for that to happen. Since the Voter Services Committee was meeting concurrently, David asked to have our resolution moved up as the next item of business and immediately kicked out of the Resolutions Committee in the hope of catching the Voter Services Committee while it was still in session. The Resolutions Committee agreed to that, referred the resolution to the Voter Services Committee, and we were off and running.

Sadly, bursting in on the Voter Services Committee, we discovered that it had already adjourned into its constituent subcommittees. It would not be prepared to take up our resolution until the next Executive Board meeting at the end of January 2006, and consequently, we could not get on the consent calendar for the October 2 general session of the Executive Board. We had just been handed a three-month delay. In contrast, Steve Chessin had somehow managed to move the IRV resolution to the consent calendar.

THE TORRES ADDRESS

Meanwhile, Art Torres was already on an airliner bound for Los Angeles to address the general session of the E-Board the following morning.

What he said took us entirely by surprise. He spoke of having returned from the Herman-Price Commission meeting in Washington, where he had been working to reform the presidential primary system to ensure that in the future Californians would have the opportunity to cast a meaningful vote. My recollection of his words are, "We have a plan in place for 2012, it's called the American Plan, and you'll be voting on it later today."

First of all, the fact that Torres mentioned the American Plan to the E-Board before it would have voted on it, had it been on that day's consent calendar, was a fairly good indication of his support for it. Secondly, he was unaware that we had been booted to the Voter Services Committee and that there would be no vote on the American Plan that day, and given the support Torres had just demonstrated, it was unlikely that Bob Mulholland had had a hand in that maneuver. Third, there was the phrase, "We have a plan in place for 2012." I had never heard the target date of 2012 mentioned until now. I had been thinking in terms of 2008. Why had he said 2012 when the Herman-Price Commission was tasked with recommending changes to the 2008 calendar? One possibility was that the commission was thinking in terms of implementing the American Plan in coordination with the Republican Party, which could not change its presidential nomination rules for 2008, but could for 2012.

On the drive back to the Bay Area, Marilyn reflected on the life of the political activist into which we had recently plunged ourselves: a lot of time on the road, living in hotels, eating and drinking, and trading stories and jokes . . . not an altogether unpleasant existence. A person could get used to it, I agreed. Darius didn't know what he was missing. But I understood perfectly; I had been the same at his age, a shy loner, ill at ease in a crowd of people. I also knew that at my core, I hadn't changed. That same shy loner was still there. I had learned to don a temporary persona of gregariousness. Oh, yes, I greatly enjoyed the party atmosphere, but my persona could not have carried off its performance successfully alone. What I was missing was Marilyn's natural affinity for working the crowd and schmoozing. Our success was due to our ability to work as a team and compensate each other's weaknesses with our own strengths. Still, the weaknesses remained, and one of mine that Marilyn couldn't compensate for was the cumulative effect of overstimulation; there comes a point when I have to get away from the crowd and have quiet time. Some people loathe the long, straight, monotonous drive of I–5 through the San Joaquin Valley; to me, it's the California form of meditation.

NOTES

1. Pearson, Chris. 2005. E-mail, August 17.
2. Phelps, David. 2005. E-mail, August 18.
3. Alden, John. 2005. E-mail, August 24.
4. Phelps, David. 2005. E-mail, August 30.
5. Pearson, Chris. 2005. E-mail, August 26.
6. Gangale, Thomas. 2005. E-mail, September 4.
7. Gangale, Thomas. 2005. E-mail, August 30.
8. Gangale, Thomas. 2005. E-mail, September 1.
9. Pearson, Chris. 2005. E-mail, September 6.
10. Gangale, Thomas. 2005. E-mail, September 3.
11. Carroll, Damian. 2005. E-mail, September 6.
12. Gangale, Thomas. 2005. E-mail, September 8.
13. Curry, Becky. 2005. E-mail, September 7.
14. Phelps, David. 2005. E-mail, September 9.
15. Gangale, Thomas. 2005. E-mail, September 19.
16. Richie, Rob. 2005. E-mail, September 19.

CARRYING CALIFORNIA

ROTATING IN REVERSE

A few days after returning home, we saw the streaming video of the October 1 Herman-Price meeting. There had been no mention of 2012 in the meeting, and on camera, Art Torres had done no more than introduce the American Plan into the record. We inferred that more in-depth discussions must have occurred off camera for him to tell the E-Board that the American Plan was "in place for 2012." Moreover, fitting together other statements in the record indicated that the NASS Rotating Regional Plan had suffered a reverse. Immediately before recognizing Art Torres, commission cochair Alexis Herman reported:

At [the May] meeting we had the staff present a series of working scenarios for the 2008 calendar. Each scenario we discussed in terms of the potential opportunities, challenges, and the political challenges and legal challenges to implement.

We had I think a very spirited discussion at the July meeting on those various proposals. We presented to you at that time a sheet where we asked you actually to rank those various scenarios as we discussed them in the Commission and we committed at that time that in this meeting we would provide the feedback on where we ended up in terms of those scenarios.

The discussion on locating regional primaries was endorsed last week by the Commission on Federal Election Reform headed by Former President Carter and Secretary of State James Baker. It did not rise to a level of prominence, however, as a part of our scenarios.[1]

After Senator Torres introduced the American Plan, commission staffer Phil McNamara gave a detailed ranking of the proposals that the commission had heard in May:

1. Iowa Plus
2. Two Windows
3. Western States
4. Expanding Time (between New Hampshire and the Window)
5. Window No Exceptions
6. Moving Back
7. Five Closest States
8. New Hampshire Plus
9. Rotating Regional Primary Plan
10. Status Quo

That the NASS Rotating Regional Plan "did not rise to a level of prominence" was an understatement, the only option that the commission disliked more was the option of doing nothing at all. In fairness to the NASS plan, however, it must be remembered that the Herman-Price Commission's ranking was in terms of 2008 implementation; the commission had no desire to implement a systematic reform for 2008, and the NASS plan was the only systematic reform on its list. The same forces of timidity that had blocked the American Plan from even being included in commission's proceedings had also blocked the Rotating Regional Plan from further consideration following NASS executive director Leslie Reynolds' presentation at the May meeting.

A week later, I had a second phone conversation with the coauthor of the NASS Rotating Regional Plan.

Conversation with Bill Jones

Memorandum
Thomas Gangale
11 October 2005

He suggested that I contact California Republican Party chairman Duf Sundheim and vice-chairman Ron Nehring. Interestingly, when I related our experience in the California Democratic Party, that we needed to get action at the local level before the state party took an interest, Jones didn't think that would be necessary in the CRP; we can start right at the top. This suggests the possibility that we might get the CRP on board in a couple months, nearly simultaneous with the American Plan resolution going to the CDP E-Board at the end of

January. Still, I would prefer to hedge my bet and contact the San Francisco, Marin and Sonoma central committees. It couldn't hurt.

Jones downplayed the possibility of his taking an active role, although I pointed out that a place at the table in some future venue ought to be reserved for him because of his valuable experience on this issue. Jones preferred to stress the necessity of getting current elected office-holders on board. California secretary of state Bruce McPherson is high on the list, obviously. He also suggested that I contact Rep. Tom Cole of Oklahoma. Jones knew Cole when he was Oklahoma secretary of state. I also note from Cole's biography that he was former Oklahoma governor Frank Keating's chief legislative strategist and liaison to the state's federal delegation. Keating was a member of the Brock Commission.

Jones is concerned that the national Republican Party is going to take its cue from the White House, and of course it was Karl Rove who quashed the Brock Commission report in 2000. Jones said they had the same problem with the Democrats when Bill Clinton was in the White House. He agreed with my observation that whoever is in power is averse to reform because they know how to use the existing system.

Jones is willing to make introductions for me. As with my first conversation with him, he ended with, "Stay on this. Don't give up."

That same day, FairVote's Ryan O'Donnell took a swing at the NASS Rotating Regional Plan, and the Carter-Baker Commission's endorsement of it.

Wrong Answer to Presidential-Primary Problem

Orlando Sentinel
By Ryan O'Donnell
11 October 2005

The day was when presidential contests were decided not by the caucus, but by the cigar. The "smoky backroom deal" was the preferred method long before primaries became the dominant force in picking a party's nominee. Fortunately, political machines and party bosses no longer control who enters the general election. Reforms of the 1970s brought about the demise of this undemocratic end-run around voters, and led to today's system of primaries.

But we still have a scheduling conflict in America. The electoral reform commission headed by Jimmy Carter and James Baker recognized this when its final report called for reform of the primary schedule. Currently, Iowa and New

Hampshire enjoy special first-in-the-nation status, and wield enormous power to influence the outcome. We saw this in 2004, when a nearly defeated Kerry campaign suddenly surged in Iowa, creating unstoppable momentum for the rush of contests to follow.

The Carter-Baker commission proposes "rotating regional primaries." Under their plan, Iowa and New Hampshire still go first. Afterward, four regions of the country hold primaries at one-month intervals from March to June, and take turns being the first region every election.

This would be a positive step. Unfortunately, the plan fails the tests of what a good primary schedule should be.

A good primary schedule does not give a monopoly to a few select states. Carter-Baker gets an F here. The commission wants the regional primaries to begin after Iowa and New Hampshire go first. Because of that politically motivated detail, the plan changes very little. Involving all 50 states is important because America should be fully represented in the decision. As it stands, two small and overwhelmingly white states dominate the process.

A good primary schedule preserves the advantages of starting with small states. Candidates deserve the opportunity for door-to-door politicking, and getting out their message without a king's ransom in campaign funds.

Voters deserve more choices than the megafundraisers who can afford to lavish money early on in big-state primaries. But under Carter-Baker, the most populous states would take turns deciding the nominee. States like New York, California and Texas would squash smaller states in their regions.

A good primary schedule has an extended and set duration. Because two states force the decision so early, the primaries conclude all too often before March. The first "regional primary" would have the same effect. Candidates should get ample public exposure everywhere in the country, and not replace debate with dead air until the general election heats up. Also, with only two months to campaign, it's no wonder many candidates opt out of public financing, putting more influence in the hands of big money.

Without a national plan, states scramble to compete with Iowa. In fact, over the last year, many sought to push their primary dates earlier, in a counterproductive rush to the front. Even so, a recent Democratic commission all but endorsed the strategy of front-loading when it recommended adding more states to the early weeks of the primaries, essentially spawning more Iowas.

What's the solution?

FairVote supports the "American Plan," a variation on the "Delaware Plan" nearly adopted by the Republican convention in 2000, and endorsed by the Young Democrats of America. Like the Carter-Baker regional system, the American Plan creates gaps between clusters of primaries and moves from small to large states. However, it also integrates random order, creating chances for all states to be part of earlier primaries.

Americans know we have an ailing system. What the Carter-Baker Commission, the Democrats and reformers like FairVote disagree on is the prescription. Yet, as we examine what best serves voter choice in this country, let's not go halfway on primaries reform. Let's serve all Americans' interests with the American Plan.

A NEAR MISS

The Fortieth Assembly District Committee adopted the American Plan resolution unanimously on October 9. Despite having stood up the Sonoma County DCC in September, Ray Gallian had prepared the committee enough that with my appearance on October 11 to field some questions, the committee voted on the resolution. I told the FairVote and the LA Boys:

We got a "No" vote.
We also got an abstention. The rest voted "Yea."[2]

We now had five counties and two assembly districts.

Marin County dithered some more. Its Resolutions Committee couldn't seem to report a resolution that had been written for them! Greg Brockbank, who had expressed his support for the American Plan on numerous occasions, advised me that the resolution ought to be on the November agenda.[3] In any case, the relationship with Senator Torres continued to mature, as David Phelps reported to Chris Pearson:

The state party's "Political Director," [Bob] Mullholland remains skeptical of the Plan, and more must be learned about the nature of his relationship to Torres and how that may impact Torres' support.

Torres' support appears to be strong with his comments before the DNC Commission and CDP E-Board, but I have yet to speak with his office directly. Most of my correspondence (with the exception of myself and Damian's direct meeting with Torres) has been done through our Regional Director, John Heaner, who has the Chairman's ear on matters impacting the Los Angeles County region.

Heaner told me that Torres will be speaking in favor of the resolution at the January E-Board meeting. He has also asked Damian and I to assist him in writing a letter to the DNC Commission on his support for the American Plan. We have drafted something that strongly conveys his support for the Plan and urges the current Commission to call for the establishment of a follow-up commission to specifically study long-term systemic change to the presidential primary system beginning in 2012.

The 2012 date originates from the fact that the RNC has already approved their 2008 schedule, which virtually prohibits the DNC from implementing major reforms for that cycle. The DNC can implement changes at any time, whereas the RNC can only make them at nominating national conventions four years prior.

We're hopeful that we can get Torres to insert language calling for the new commission into the DNC Commission's Final Report to be approved at their December meeting. Obviously, this will occur before the California Democratic Party has an opportunity to endorse the resolution, but we believe he will do this anyway. We'll know more once he approves the letter that will go out to Commission members.[4]

Chris came back with news of his own:

I got the chance to chat with [Herman-Price] Commissioner Don Fowler (not to be confused with his son, Donnie). He was intrigued by the plan but felt the political circumstances were against us—because neither party would ever want to snub IA or NH. When I conveyed Brock's lingering passion and wondered if the parties could be joined in their proposal he was still skeptical. Basically he felt relations could be decent but then by July of an election year the desire to work together would dissolve.

I pushed him to see if he thought the commission might recommend another group be convened to look at substantial changes and he thought that sounded reasonable.[5]

My overall impression of the Herman-Price Commission was that it would take on Iowa and New Hampshire, as well as more systematic issues, if the Republicans had a counterpart commission meeting at the same time, deliberating the same issues, and reaching the same conclusions.

The main division in the Price-Herman commission is what to do about Iowa and New Hampshire. The principled stand is that they should not be privileged because we are not the party of privilege. The pragmatic stand is that taking away that privilege hands 11 electoral votes to the Republicans. This points up the need for a bipartisan effort on presidential primary reform. There are huge practical constraints on what a partisan effort can accomplish. A lot of commission members would like to go beyond what they are planning to recommend, but they fear how the GOP might take advantage of that. In the 1 October morning session, the desire for cooperation with the GOP was expressed. I know from reading the 2000 Brock Commission report that they struggled with the same problem. They don't like Iowa and New Hampshire going first either. Believe it or not, they would like to have the first contests elsewhere than those white bread states to test Republican candidates among constituencies of color. But, they fear that unilaterally revoking the Iowa-New Hampshire privilege would hand 11 electoral votes to the Democrats. These two tiny states hold the entire nation hostage by playing one party against the other, and that needs to stop. The only way to end the hostage situation is for both parties to make a joint stand against the hostage-takers.[6]

Chris replied:

Fowler was not reluctant to work with Republicans. He agreed a bipartisan effort is the only way anyone will be willing/able to shift the early role of IA and NH.

I Ie just thinks that even if cooperative efforts move forward the final decision (at least on the GOP side) will be made on the convention floor and any spirit of cooperation is likely to dissolve. The man used to be DNC chair. He clearly grasped all the points you are making. On quick analysis, he likes the plan. He wondered if Congress would have to act because even if the parties adopted the American Plan he points out that NH and IA will likely snub it anyway and hold their primary/caucus as they always do. They don't care if they are stripped of delegates so long as attention/money is showered on them.[7]

My response:

The problem of the GOP having to take the proposal to the convention floor is a good point. If I recall correctly, Bill Brock raised the same point. Two things can mitigate the rise of any last-minute partisan resistance. First of all, if one analyzes the demise of the Delaware Plan in 2000, resistance came from two quarters: populous states opposed it for obvious reasons, and there were those who felt that it was too radical a change for the Republican Party to undertake alone. The American Plan satisfies the concerns of populous states, and in a bipartisan effort to implement it, neither party will be going it alone. Secondly, support for the Delaware Plan was only skin deep. The majority of the Brock Commission liked it, but this support never got to the grassroots. Bill Brock admitted that the failure to communicate the issue to the party rank-and-file was major stumble. With the American Plan, however, we have the beginning of grassroots support, and no matter how many politicians get on board, we must continue the grassroots outreach.

The prospect of Iowa and New Hampshire giving up their delegates in order to keep their first-in-the-nation events as beauty contests is interesting.

That could very well be their decision. I'm not sure it would be consequential, however. It might make them feel good the first time around, but eventually it would be seen as a hollow victory. They would essentially constitute an unauthorized "Round 0" in the American Plan. Iowa and New Hampshire have become so important because of front loading; if you win those first two, you're almost done, because there's no time for anyone to stop your momentum. I would argue that the American greatly reduces the impact of Iowa and New Hampshire even if they decide to remain first. How hard are candidates going to campaign in states that have no delegates at the convention? So, let those delegations push their noses up against the outside windows of the convention halls a few times. Sooner or later they'll decide they're better off inside where the votes are being counted.

I have always thought of federal legislation as the second-best implementation path, and at first I put effort into this in parallel with the party rules implementation path. It was with this in mind that I first approached Rep. Lynn Woolsey two years ago. She was very negative on the idea, and since then I have extracted the historical data that reveals how dismal the efforts in Congress have been over the past 30 years. Actually, I've continued pursuing the federal legislation path, but at a reduced level of effort. In the past few months I've written to Sens. Dianne Feinstein and Barbara Boxer, and Reps. John Conyers, Sander Levin, and Sam Farr. Also, on Bill Jones' advice, I'm in the process of contacting Rep. Tom Cole. A few months back, I began thinking of federal legislation as a follow-up to implementation by party rules in the context of providing federal funding for any additional expenses that states might incur by implementing the American Plan. Such a federal bill could also serve to codify the American Plan as law, thereby bringing Iowa and New Hampshire to heel. With both parties having implemented the American Plan beforehand, federal legislation ought to be a slam dunk, especially if there's money in it for the states.[8]

David zeroed in on the idea of pitching for a new commission that would look beyond 2008 to 2012:

May I suggest that any correspondence sent to the Commission regarding any systemic reform be phrased in a request to establish a follow-up commission, as opposed to a letter focusing on support for the American Plan.

I believe that is the most effective action with regard to the DNC Commission at this point in time.[9]

This made good sense. The Herman-Price Commission only had two months of life remaining to it, and was focused almost exclusively on piddling changes to the calendar for 2008. The best we could hope from it was to plant the seed for a later effort. This was probably even more valuable than obtaining mention of the American Plan in the commission's report. All we really needed was to get into the arena. Once there, we felt that we would prevail over any other plan.[10] The problem, then, was to set up the arena, the venue in which all systematic reform plans would be given serious consideration. What was needed was what the Herman-Price Commission had been billed to be, but wasn't. What was needed was a new commission in the mold of the Brock Commission, and not just one commission, but one in each party. My talk with Representative Tom Cole (R-OK) provided more insight into processes in the Republican Party.

Conversation with Tom Cole

Memorandum
Thomas Gangale
21 October 2005

Rep. Tom Cole was secretary of [secretary of state of Oklahoma and chief of staff for the Brock Commission. [His] boss, Governor Frank Keating, was a member of the commission.

In the course of the conversation, I briefed him on the details of the American Plan, our conversations with former Brock Commission members, and the success of our grassroots effort in California. He was intrigued by my description of the plan as having the strengths of the Delaware Plan and the Rotating Regional Plan and the defects of neither.

Rep. Cole reiterated what Bill Jones and Bill Brock have said about the constraints that the Republican Party has regarding rules changes, i.e., they have to be ratified on the convention floor, and difficulties that such a partisan atmosphere present. The focus is always on winning the next election, rather than on long-term structural changes. Tom Cole's unique insight was this: essentially we have two phases of the project with respect to the Republican Party, and we must deal with a different regime in each phase.

Phase 1 is convincing the Republican leadership of the need to empanel a new commission. Right now the leadership is RNC chairman Ken Mehlman, who takes his orders from the White House, i.e., Karl Rove. Cole agrees with Jones that a grassroots effort is less relevant to the structure of the Republican Party. The more effective approach is to work directly on state party chairs and the two RNC members from each state. I believe that the combination of the California Democratic Party's adoption of the American Plan resolution in January and Bill Jones' influence ought to convince the next California Republican Party chair—presumably the current vice-chair Ron Nehring—of the need to get active on this issue. I asked Tom Cole whether a letter to Ken Mehlman from him and the former Brock commission members would be useful. He said that it would, and he would be happy to see such a letter.

Phase 2 is getting the recommendation of the commission passed on the convention floor. At that point, we are dealing with a new regime, that of the presidential nominee. The convention will do whatever the nominee asks of it. Thus, as we identify potential Republican presidential candidates, we should brief them fully on the American Plan specifically and the presidential primary reform issue generally. We need to get to them well before they get into the thick of fundraising and campaigning. Of course, party insiders such as Tom Cole, former members of the Brock Commission, Ron Nehring, and others could be instrumental in this effort. Additionally, regardless of whether he intends to run, I believe we should approach John McCain because of his track record on campaign finance reform. My guess is that the American Plan would be an easy sell, and his word would carry weight with other reform-minded Republicans. This will help grow a climate of reform in the party in general, tending to condition candidates to the proper orientation on this issue. If McCain turns out to be the nominee, so much the better.

Tom Cole wishes us success, and he looks forward to receiving an information package from me on the American Plan.

The Democratic Central Committee of Marin finally adopted the American Plan resolution at its November meeting. Also joining them in November were the Eighteenth and Thirty-Third AD Committees, and the Orange County DCC. Some, like Madera and Placer, passed it without any of us having set foot in those counties; it had only been necessary to transmit by e-mail the resolution, explanatory material, and a request for a vote of support. With others, such as Los Angeles and Marin, we had to go once to make the pitch, then return for a later vote. People just needed to take some time to get their heads around the problem and our solution. Many times we heard, "I don't understand it." We never heard, "I don't like it." Once they understood it, they liked it, and when the vote came, it was typically close to unanimous or outright unanimous.

Contra Costa County was an exception. One of the people we had met in Manhattan Beach was Nagaraja Rao, chair of the Co-Co DCC. It is interesting that, for all that it sounds entirely unlike an Italian surname, Rao happens to be fairly common in Calabria, my grandfather's region of origin. Certainly far less common in India is Gangale, but it is found there nevertheless, and perhaps it is a variation of the more common Ganguly. So, Nagaraja and I started calling each other "cousin," which has at least a small grain of literal truth, for I have heard it said than no two people alive today are more distant than sixtieth cousins.

Cousin Nagaraja arranged for me to present the American Plan to the Co-Co DCC on November 8. There was nothing particularly unusual about it; I fielded a lot of questions after the presentation as people worked through the set of information in their own ways. Then Cousin Nagaraja called for an end of the Q&A and asked to put the American Plan resolution to a vote. I got worried. A number of the committee members clearly did not want to vote so quickly, but Cousin Nagaraja insisted. The vote was seven to five in favor, but never had the American Plan come so close to losing a vote. I learned an important lesson that night. If a similar situation arose in the future, if I could exert any influence on the process, I would speak out in favor of deferring the vote to the next meeting. There was no point to ramming the American Plan down people's throats when, given time, it sold itself.

America Needs a Fair Presidential Primary Schedule for All States

Manchester Union Leader
By Ryan O'Donnell
29 November 2005

Democrats shouldn't be surprised at a rebuff from New Hampshire as they roll out their plan for an upgraded Presidential primary schedule. The Democratic National Committee Commission on Timing and Scheduling should indeed expect anger to follow such a bold brush off of the state's status.

After all, in Presidential elections, it's every state for itself. We see it during the nomination process, as Iowa and New Hampshire enjoy the power to make or break the contenders, while most other states can do nothing but ratify their decision. We see that dynamic in the fall campaign, as candidates court an ever-smaller club of swing states, leaving the rest in the dust.

Who wants to lose that power?

In the days when political bossism presided over political conventions, there was contempt for listening to the voices of the people in primaries. As Michigan Sen. Arthur Vandenberg famously said while campaigning for the Republican nomination to challenge FDR, "Why should I kill myself to carry Vermont?"

For the Democrats to crowd the early primaries with new states would demote New Hampshire in 2008 to the status Vandenberg disdainfully gave its neighbor Vermont in 1940. All the money, the publicity, the influx of campaign workers, the winter economic boost, and the attention to the issues New Hampshire voters care about would be diminished.

Of course, as a swing state in the general election, New Hampshire would still get some attention. Still, this is the wrong way to reshuffle.

The fact is, Vandenberg had reason to be so disdainful of primaries in his time. Back then, the people were seldom heard when voting for President at the polls.

But the reforms of the 1970s went a long way to smashing the influence of the political machines, and unlike the turn of the previous century, primaries count. Bosses can't go around voters by appointing their own delegates or relying on patronage to line up the votes they need. But even with these changes, the question is, how many primaries count? Unfortunately, not many.

As such, watering down the first-in-the-nation status of New Hampshire is absolutely unfair to New Hampshire voters. Equally, shutting out other states from this immensely important decision is also unfair to voters in the rest of the country. The solution isn't to add more states to the early primary season, but to create a system that gives everyone a fair shot.

A fair primary schedule would preserve the door-to-door retail politicking we see in New Hampshire. This gives voters the chance to get to know the candidates. Doing so also allows candidates to compete without Titanic-sized bank accounts. That means starting out with smaller states and working your way up to more populous ones.

A fair schedule would also incorporate random order, so the same few states don't go first time after time. Larger states should have the chance to go a little earlier as well.

Finally, a fair schedule would have a reasonable and set duration. By setting up clusters of primaries spaced at two-week intervals, we can prevent the process from being over after the first couple of contests. A longer schedule is also an incentive for candidates to take public financing, which is paid out on a monthly basis.

The system just described is the "American Plan," a variation on the "Delaware Plan" nearly adopted by the Republican convention in 2000. The plan was endorsed by the Young Democrats of America as well as FairVote, and is the change that both parties should really be considering.

Everyone should have an equal say in choosing their party's candidate, regardless of where they live. This is an ambitious principle, but also an attainable goal. If we make the right changes, New Hampshire will get a fair say, and so will America.

New Hampshire's Peculiar Institution

Community Newspaper Syndicate
By Thomas Gangale
2 December 2005

Two centuries ago, when southern statesmen wanted to defend the indefensible and mention the unmentionable, they referred to their states' enslavement of African Americans as their "peculiar institution;" peculiar in the sense that it was specific to the economic needs of the agrarian South and to the historical development of its culture. It was perfectly legitimate. After all, slavery had been practiced all over the world at one time or another.

However, in the late 18th and early 19th centuries, moral norms were changing. The Enlightenment had brought forth the concept of human dignity, and the founders of the American republic, being children of that Enlightenment, had brought forth a government dedicated to human equality. In this changing world, any argument in favor of privilege based on history and ancestry was increasingly indefensible.

Today, as a commission of the Democratic National Committee considers making changes to the 2008 presidential nomination calendar, the white homeland of New Hampshire argues for its continued privilege of holding the first presidential primary of the campaign season. It argues for holding the rest of the nation in political second-class status. It clings to this position on the basis of tradition in the face of a changing America, a more diverse America that legitimately calls for opening the political process to broader participation, broader both ethnically and geographically.

As New Hampshire's position becomes more difficult to defend, statements coming out of the Granite State harden. We hear impassioned appeals to its "traditional key role in picking Presidential nominees," and threats to move the state's presidential primary into December 2007 to stay ahead of other states moving their primaries into January 2008. How peculiar that would be! Moreover, former New Hampshire Democratic Party chairman Joseph Keefe has ominously declared that if the DNC commission authorizes other states to leap ahead of the New Hampshire primary, "We will resist that by whatever means necessary."

History records that John C. Calhoun defended South Carolina's peculiar institution with equal fervor, and that tragically, a few years later his state actually did resort to "whatever means necessary."

New Hampshire could spare the nation a looming political war by acknowledging the march of progress and by displaying a generosity of spirit. Its reign as the "first in the nation primary" has an honored place in American history, but it no longer serves a useful purpose. If New Hampshire is prudent, it will abdicate gracefully rather than resist insanely in the last bunker.

Contrast New Hampshire's insistence on perpetuating electoral apartheid with the new vision that California offers the nation. In January 2006, the California Democratic Party is set to endorse a comprehensive plan to reform the presidential nomination process, a plan that is fair to all states. Now known as the American Plan, it spreads the nomination calendar across ten intervals of time and randomly selects the order of the states, so that from one presidential election cycle to the next, any given state would have an opportunity to be earlier or later in the calendar.

Most striking, while New Hampshire insists on remaining first, California relinquishes any claim on ever being first. California realizes that it is too big, that it costs too much money to campaign there, and that the nation is best served by expanding on the concept of "retail politicking" in small, early states. This would allow underfunded grassroots campaigns to score early victories and build momentum going into later, bigger, and more expensive contests. All that California asks for itself is that it have a reasonable opportunity to go early enough in the process to have a meaningful voice in choosing the presidential nominee. California does insist, however, that the calendar be opened to allow small states other than New Hampshire to go first, states more representative of America's diversity.

It is in the nature of the continuing American Revolution that legal and political precedents are only temporary guides for law and governance, serving to give some stability to our institutions until those precedents become outmoded as new societal norms evolve. Our duty, as the inheritors of the American Revolution, is to perpetually strive for a more perfect union, to refine the definition of justice, and to expand the sphere of liberty. It is incumbent on every American generation to bestow on its posterity more than it received from its antecedents. This generation of New Hampshirites can best honor its tradition by passing on that tradition to the other small states.

THE LAST WORD FROM WASHINGTON

October and November had been good months for us. By early December, we had the support of DCCs and ADCs representing 56 percent of California Democrats. It seemed to me that it was within our grasp to return to Manhattan Beach at the end of January 2006 with the support of two-thirds of the party, and I communicated this to Senator Torres.[11] Whatever Bob Mulholland thought of the American Plan, he would have a tough time fighting that level of support.

The DNC Commission of Presidential Nomination Timing and Scheduling, chaired by Alexis Herman and David Price, held its final meeting on December 10.

Herman-Price Commission, December Meeting

Transcript
10 December 2005

MR. TORRES: I wanted to address the section stated "Moving Back the Process in 2012 and Beyond." The American Plan which I had presented before this Commission on two occasions spreads the nomination calendar across ten intervals of time and randomly selects the order of states from one presidential election to the next and any given state would have an opportunity to be earlier or later in the calendar. I would recommend that the DNC Rules and Bylaws Committee consider and review this proposal for the 2012 timing.

CO-CHAIR HERMAN: Is there a second?

VOICE: Second.

CO-CHAIR HERMAN: Discussion?
   (No response.)
CO-CHAIR HERMAN: If there's no discussion, then could you restate? As I look around the room, could you restate the amendment for the record and we will call the question.

MR. TORRES: Yes. I'm merely asking that the DNC Rules and Bylaws Committee review and consider the concept known as the American Plan, which is supported strongly by California. Not that it would put California ahead of any other states because it would be a random plan. But I would just prefer that the Rules Committee consider it for 2012 since I don't have the votes to consider it today.

CO-CHAIR PRICE: Mr. Torres, is it accurate to say that your understanding would be that in the so-called report language, the third component of this report, that somehow that would be incorporated?

MR. TORRES: Yes.

CO-CHAIR PRICE: Fine.

MR. TORRES: To request they review and consider.

CO-CHAIR HERMAN: Consideration of an amendment of the bylaws. Mr. Ickes?

MR. ICKES: Art, could you give a thumbnail about what the American Plan is? It sounds like something on a deli menu.

MR. TORRES: It sounds like what?

CO-CHAIR HERMAN: He says it sounds like a deli menu. I think he's hungry.

MR. TORRES: The American Plan is proposed to spread the calendar of elections across ten intervals of time and randomly selects the order of the states from one presidential cycle to the next. What I'm asking is that there be some consideration and review by the Rules and Bylaws Committee to this proposal for the 2012 consideration, not for 2008.

MR. ROOSEVELT: May I . . .

CO-CHAIR HERMAN: Mr. Roosevelt.

MR. ROOSEVELT: . . . just say that the Rules and Bylaws Committee in my view must consider 2012 because if we are going to have any continuing progress here we have to take a position that the Republicans can possibly sign onto. That has to be done in 2008. Therefore we have to consider 2012 at this point, and the American Plan certainly would be among those considerations in my view, and that's whether it includes lunch or not.

CO-CHAIR HERMAN: Thank you very much. We will now call the question and ask for a show of hands on the amendment to the report document itself proposed by Mr. Torres, that this would be an item of consideration for the Rules and Bylaws Committee in 2012. All those in favor of supporting this amendment, please signify by raising your hands.

   (A show of hands.)

MR. McNAMARA: 25. It's unanimous.

CO-CHAIR HERMAN: It's unanimous.

MR. TORRES: Thank you, Madam Chair.

CO-CHAIR HERMAN: Thank you.

That's it?

That was it. The American Plan was going into the commission's final report as a recommendation for 2012. No debate, no votes against. How could this happen? Either they just didn't care about 2012 or there must have been an awful lot of discussion off camera for so little to be apparent on camera. If the latter were true, Art Torres must have gone to a great many unseen pains to seal the deal so quietly. I reflected on how odd it was, that a man I had spoken to only briefly several months before had accomplished so much of my agenda, and I had hardly any direct evidence of his doing it. What a strange relationship to have with someone. By any usual measure of human relationships, it seemed to be no relationship at all, and yet if one analyzed the results, there was something there. I came to understand that Art Torres was highly accomplished in the art of changing the world quietly. I also began to understand the nature of a type of human relationship that was entirely new to me—the political relationship—a relationship at a distance that had the power to shape the future.

Moving Back the Process in 2012 and Beyond

Report of the Commission on Presidential Nomination Timing and Scheduling
10 December 2005

The Commission is of the view that the entire caucus and primary season occurs far too early, and Commission members expressed considerable frustration that both their pre-window and within-window adjustments were compromised by their inability to adjust the date (February 5) on which the Republican window will open in 2008. As noted above, Republican practice is to approve its rules at the prior national convention. Therefore, the date is set for 2008 and there is no feasible way to change it. But the issue can and must be addressed before 2012.

The Commission believes that early February is far too early to start the caucus/primary season, to say nothing of pre-window contests in January. Now, the early date, plus the powerful impact of Iowa and New Hampshire, plus front-loading within the window, promises to produce a nominee on a date earlier than the first contest used to occur. The Commission has addressed some of these factors, but would move the entire season as much as two months later if it were free to do so.

In considering the options for 2012 the Commission encourages the Party to think boldly, including for example, RBC consideration of the proposal known as the American Plan which would spread the calendar of contests across ten intervals of time and randomly select the order of the states from one presidential election cycle to the next.

There is some precedent for bipartisan consultation on this matter. In its review of the 2004 nominating calendar in the Fall 1999/Spring 2000 called "Beyond 2000," the DNC Rules and Bylaws Committee (RBC) developed a working relationship with the RNC commission headed by Bill Brock (detailed above).

At the time, the Co-Chairs of the RBC had discussions with their Republican counterparts and former DNC Chairman Joe Andrew met with Republican Chairman
Jim Nicholson about the matter. The bipartisan approach to the nominating
calendar reflected the serious commitment by both parties to address concerns
about the schedule.

   The Commission urges Chairman Dean and the DNC to begin a series of
discussions with the RNC as the RNC begins to draft its 2012 rules in anticipation
of the 2008 Convention. Discussion about the Democratic Party's rules for the
next cycle before the current process has even begun will be necessary to attain
what the Commission believes is truly necessary, a bipartisan solution for 2012
and succeeding cycles.

Here was another surprise. As significant as was the inclusion of the American Plan in the report was the exclusion of NASS's Rotating Regional Plan;
it had made an *invited* presentation, whereas there had been no real presentation of the American Plan before the commission. Art Torres had pitched the
American Plan to the commission, but the commission's report had pitched
a shutout to NASS.

I'LL TAKE MANHATTAN BEACH, TAKE 2

One thing I had heard during my brief discussion with staffers for the
CDP's Voter Services Committee on October 2, 2005, was that they didn't
have much experience with handling resolutions. They couldn't remember
the last one that had come their way. This deepened the mystery of why
the Resolutions Committee had booted the American Plan resolution to the
Voter Services Committee. To prepare the Voter Services Committee for its
consideration the American Plan resolution at the January 2006 Executive
Board meeting, I had e-mailed an info package to CDP staffer to Chris
Meyers on October 19 for distribution to members of the committee. I
didn't hear anything back for a couple of months. Finally, on December 14 I
phoned Chris. He informed me that at the January 2006 E-Board meeting,
the committee would form a subcommittee to study the American Plan. The
subcommittee would then report its recommendation to the full committee
at the CDP annual convention in the spring of 2006. I was incredulous, and I
suppose that is putting it mildly. I immediately wrote to Stephen Giangiulio,
one of Art Torres' staffers in San Francisco:

The impact of this additional delay is going to be substantial. . . . The Republican component is especially crucial, for this effort must begin as soon as possible. Any changes recommended by the RNC Rules and Bylaws Committee must be ratified on the convention floor in the summer of 2008. If the RNC is to have a year to study systemic reforms to the presidential nomination process, it would have to form a commission in the summer of 2007. Counting from now, we have approximately 18 months to build support within the Republican Party for forming such a commission. The delay that Chris Myers just outlined cuts our window of opportunity to only 15 months. I don't know that even 18 months is enough time to get the Republicans moving, but it is certainly better than 15 months. . . .

It seems to me that the Voter Services Committee could easily do its work on the American Plan via e-mail and other telecommunications in the next six weeks so that they would be prepared to report to the general session at the next E-Board meeting in January 2006. Is there anything that can be done to expedite this process?[12]

Apparently there was. Within two minutes of the e-mail getting forwarded to Senator Torres, he was on the phone to the CDP staff to straighten things out.[13] In a second phone conversation that afternoon, Chris Meyers assured me that we were back on track for Voter Services Committee action on the American Plan resolution in January. Once again I e-mailed him an info package.

Meanwhile, endorsements continued to roll in during December: the San Joaquin County DCC, Sonoma County Democracy for America, Ventura County DCC, Forty-Third AD Committee, Democrats for Neighborhood Action, and SoCal Grassroots Coordinating Committee. Early in January, the Lake County DCC joined the pack, as did the Santa Barbara DCC with a modified resolution. We now had local party organizations representing 63.5 percent of California Democrats. The goal of getting two-third of the party by the January 28–29, 2006, CDP Executive Board meeting looked very good indeed, and the First AD Committee, Seventy-Second AD Committee, and Inyo County DCC put us over the top.

Still, it was not clear what was going on among the CDP's standing committees. Only three days before the E-Board meeting, CDP staffer Patty Mar informed me that the American Plan resolution was to be included on the agenda for Resolutions Committee. *What?* Art Torres and I had gone to some trouble to ensure that the members of the Voter Services Committee were up to speed on the American Plan resolution and would vote on it that weekend without resorting to forming a subcommittee to study it. Now it was

back with the Resolutions Committee, and all that prep work with the Voter
Services Committee had been for naught?

> We are to be heard only in the Resolutions Committee. I confirmed this with
> Chris Myers. I'm a little concerned over this last minute switch. I had arranged
> to have Chris distribute all of the American Plan literature to the members of the
> Voter Services Committee well in advance of the E Board meeting so that they
> could give the plan due study. This preparation has now been circumvented. Is
> the Resolutions Committee now going to start from scratch, decide that they
> need more time to study the plan, and punt to the next meeting? I have two
> new handouts to give to members of the Resolutions Committee (attached),
> but at this point I don't know if the material I sent to Chris several weeks ago
> has now been forwarded to the members of the Resolutions Committee.[14]

When I e-mailed the American Plan info package to Patty to forward
to the Resolutions Committee, she responded that sometimes sponsors of
resolutions would like to include background material, but because of volume
of material, she did not distribute these to committee members. I was more
than welcome to distribute my materials to the members at the meeting.[15]
So, the scenario being painted was that the Resolutions Committee would
look over my material for a minute or two and then pass judgment on the
American Plan. There was nothing to indicate that the committee had been
prepared on this issue. We could be heading for a disaster.

In the words of Yogi Berra, it was déjà vu all over again. Another E-
Board meeting, and once again, it was in Manhattan Beach. After arriving,
we discovered that as suddenly as the American Plan resolution had been
pulled back by the Resolutions Committee, it was now back in the Voter
Services Committee. Despite feeling a bit of whiplash that was good news.
We agreed that David Phelps would handle the formal presentation before
the committee, and I would assist with the Q&A session. Before we stepped
up to the plate, Damian alerted Art Torres' staffers that we were about to
start, and Torres made an entrance that was entirely inconspicuous except for
the identity of the man who had just made it. David asked from the podium
if Torres wanted to speak, but he declined. His presence had already spoken:
pass this resolution.

And it did pass. As Torres stood up to leave the room, I handed him a signed
copy of the recently published tenth edition of DiClerico and Hammock's
Points of View: Readings in American Government and Politics:

> To Art Torres, a friend and ally.

One of the items that was new to the tenth edition was my chapter, "The Graduated Random Presidential Primary System." A legacy carried forward to that same edition from earlier ones was an article by John F. Kennedy.

Later that day, the general session of the California Democratic Party voted. I had been drawn out of the grand ballroom on some other political matter, and I missed the vote. That was OK. I understood that once again, the world had been changed quietly. We now had the California Democratic Party's official support.

In 2000, lamenting the necessity of California having moved its presidential primary from June to March, while at the same time criticizing the Delaware Plan, which would always put the Golden State in June again, Bill Jones noted in his statement at the end of the Brock Commission report, "Understanding that there is an inherent unfairness in the nation's largest and most populous state always being at the front of the pack, Californians are willing to consider viable proposals that are fair and equitable to each and every state."[16] In adopting the American Plan, California Democrats have declared to the rest of the country, "We don't need to be at the front of the pack, and for the good of the nation, we shouldn't be at the front of the pack. It is sufficient that we have an even chance at being near the front of the pack."

NOTES

1. Democratic National Committee, Commission on Presidential Nomination Timing and Scheduling. 2005. Transcript, October 1; 5. Available from http://a9.g. akamai.net/7/9/8082/v001/democratic1.download.akamai.com/8082/pdfs/2005 1001_commissiontranscript.pdf; accessed December 27, 2005.

2. Gangale, Thomas. 2005. E-mail, October 11.

3. Brockbank, Greg. 2005. E-mail, October 12.

4. Phelps, David. 2005. E-mail, October 17.

5. Pearson, Chris. 2005. E-mail, October 18.

6. Gangale, Thomas. 2005. E-mail, October 18.

7. Pearson, Chris. 2005. E-mail, October 18.

8. Gangale, Thomas. 2005. E-mail, October 18.

9. Phelps, David. 2005. E-mail, October 18.

10 Gangale, Thomas. 2005. E-mail, October 18.

11 Gangale, Thomas. 2005. E-mail, December 6.

12 Gangale, Thomas. 2005. E-mail, December 14.

13 Giangiulio, Stephen. 2005. E-mail, December 14.

14 Gangale, Thomas. 2006. E-mail, January 26.

15 Mar, Patty. 2006. E-mail, January 27.

16 Republican National Committee, Advisory Commission on the Presidential Nominating Process. 2000. *Nominating Future Presidents*, 43. Washington, DC: Republican National Committee. Available from http://www.rnc.org/media/pdfs/brockreport.pdf; accessed February 13, 2003.

PAST PROLOGUE

A MATTER OF TIME

The next several months were fairly quiet ones for the American Plan. I spent the spring writing my master's thesis in international law and doing the coursework for my last class. I graduated from San Francisco State University in May 2006, and I turned my attention to a presentation I was scheduled to make at the International Conference on Environmental Systems in Norfolk, VA, on July 19, along with putting the final touches on the associated paper for journal publication.

On June 12 I received an invitation to present the American Plan at the NASS Summer Conference in Santa Fe, NM, on July 11. This promised to be the toughest room of all, in that I would be presenting to the Rotating Regional Presidential Primary Subcommittee, chaired by Rotating Regional Plan coauthor William Galvin of Massachusetts, and including as its members both Chet Culver of Iowa and Bill Gardner of New Hampshire, neither of whom would take kindly to any mention of deposing their states from their "first in the nation" pedestals. On the other hand, someone on that subcommittee had seen to it that I was invited, so I must have at least one ally. Also, perhaps, the subcommittee, despite its name, saw the handwriting on the wall: the Republicans had passed on the Rotating Regional Plan in favor of the Delaware Plan in 2000, the Democrats had passed on it in favor of the American Plan in 2005. There must be a few former military officers on that subcommittee who remembered that being passed over twice meant you were retired. The Delaware Plan hadn't been heard from since 2000, and no one appeared to take seriously the Carter-Baker Commission's endorsement of the Rotating Regional Plan. So the invitation might well represent a sincere reaching out for a new presidential primary plan for NASS to back, one that the political parties would find palatable enough to implement.

As a run-up to this presentation, I decided to present the American Plan to California Secretary of State Bruce McPherson. There were several reasons for doing this. First, McPherson was not a member of the Rotating Regional Presidential Primary Subcommittee and might not attend its meeting. Secondly, even if he did attend the meeting, I would only be allowed ten minutes to present on a moderately complex idea, whereas if I could get a half hour on McPherson's schedule, I could spend twenty minutes on the presentation and another ten on Q&A. Third, I felt that it was important to court McPherson in the hope of gaining further access to the California Republican Party. It turned out that McPherson's travel plans were in a state of flux, and it looked unlikely that he would arrive in Santa Fe in time for my presentation to the subcommittee; however, his assistant, Geneva Rank, blocked out a half hour for Marilyn Dudley-Rowley and I to brief him on June 27. We were well-received by the Secretary, Undersecretary Bill Wood, and Assistant Secretaries Ashley Giovannettone and Chuck Hahn. They seemed intrigued by the American Plan and they asked excellent questions that displayed a high level of knowledge on the issue of presidential primary reform.

It was a good preparation for the NASS meeting in Santa Fe, and as it turned out, Bruce McPherson attended the subcommittee meeting where I presented the American Plan. The presentation appeared to go well; after all, it was that same one I had given in Sacramento a couple of weeks earlier. Then, immediately after I finished, Eric Clark of Mississippi said, "Well, I still like the Rotating Regional Plan." There were some other remarks that were vaguely along the same lines, but there was no discussion comparing the merits of the two plans, and the remarks appeared to be nothing other than a "not invented here" reflex. The next speaker, Phil McNamara of the Democratic National Committee, seemed to go out his way to contradict me, once by misrepresenting what I had said, then stating a supposed fact that I imagine a lot of the audience knew to be wrong. I was taken aback. I had never seen anyone act that way at the podium. But that was all right; there was a general discussion period scheduled at the end of the session, when I would have my opportunity to respond. Except that that never happened. The presentations ran a bit long, and by the end of the last one most of the subcommittee was in the mood to break early for lunch. On later reflection, however, it probably wasn't necessary to respond to McNamara.

He then told the subcommittee about the Herman-Price Commission's plan to entice back loading by awarding bonus delegates. He admitted that the Republicans had tried the same idea and it had failed, but couldn't recall if that was in 1992 or 1996 (it was in 1996); however, the Democratic attempt will supposedly succeed because they are awarding a higher percentage of bonus delegates. This thesis was falsified by the very next speaker, Mike Mower of Utah, who talked about the Western Regional Primary, and that it is a deliberate exercise in front-loading because these states are tired of being last and being ignored. Then, of course, there's a bill in the California legislature to move its presidential primary to as early as January 2 to ensure that it is first. No one gives a damn how many delegates they get if the race is over by the time they vote.

We had a good side conversation with Pedro Cortes, a short one with Bill Bradbury, and a long one . . . with Bill Gardner. . . . We still don't know who invited us.

So, no, we weren't carried out of the meeting room on their shoulders. David and Damian's initial reaction was that we had suffered a setback, but over lunch they seemed to reconsider. "We're better off than we were yesterday."[1]

Marilyn Dudley-Rowley's "after action report" averred:

> If I were to speculate on who invited us, based on the Secretaries who were present, I would have to say that it was Bill Gardner, with perhaps those whom he is close to, like Pedro Cortes of Pennsylvania. New Hampshire has a vested interest in schmoozing with any reform plan(ners). I understand that they have schmoozed an accommodation with the Rotating Regional Plan. It would be in their interest to schmooze an accommodation with the American Plan. I noticed that Bill somewhat called Phil McNamara down for one of his misfactualizations anviled on Tom when Bill later had the mike.
>
> I think we all agreed that there was a lot of head nodding going on among secretaries, colleagues, and staffs in relation to many of the factual points that Tom mentioned and there was the "ahh" slide that shows how the American Plan fits the 1976 data. [More on the "ahh" slide a little later.]
>
> Secretary Bill Bradbury from Oregon, one of those western states, was really taken with Tom's side conversation with him where Tom mentioned the "Tragedy of the Commons." Bradbury even let out a loud yee-hah on that note.[2] [More on the "tragedy of the commons" a little later.]

The results of any one action are not always immediately apparent. Sometimes two events can be so removed in time from each other, and so many other events have intervened that determining a direct cause and effect is problematic. In any case, on March 27, 2007, nearly nine months after the Santa Fe meeting, Susan Bysiewicz, the Connecticut Secretary of State, announced the moving forward of her state's presidential primary to February 5, 2008, to join with many other states in what was turning out to be a quasinational primary day. The same news release also reported:

> "In the absence of a rational primary process, we are seeing an ad hoc national primary take shape," said Bysiewicz. "Connecticut didn't start this tidal wave but I cannot stand by and allow our voters to become irrelevant. Ultimately, members of both political parties must come together and enact real reform."
>
> Several organizations, including the National Association of Secretaries of State (NASS), and Fair Vote, have authored reform proposals. The so-called Delaware Plan was also considered at the 2000 GOP Convention. . . .
>
> "The front loading of the primary calendar is in no one's best interest," said Bysiewicz. "I am deeply troubled by a process that is getting shorter and more dominated by the candidates with the biggest bank account, not the best ideas."
>
> "I believe that the American Plan presents a better way," continued Bysiewicz. "Candidates will begin in smaller states, which allow for more hands-on campaigning and gives underdog candidates a better chance of having their message heard. A longer process, with more candidates, more ideas, and more involvement from voters will be the result."[3]

We had cracked the solidarity of NASS.

TOO SHORT A SEASON

David Phelps and I met with Art Torres in San Francisco on January 31, 2007, and Damian Carroll participated via telephone from Los Angeles. We came to the meeting with a wish list; Art granted all of them and more. He suggested additional courses of action, and volunteered to do some of them or set them up for us do to. For instance, he suggested that I reserve a room for an hour at the California Democratic Convention in San Diego in April and give a presentation on the American Plan. "That's a great idea, sir," I responded with enthusiasm. "Who should I talk to to make that happen?"

"You're talking to him. *I'll* make it happen."

Driving through Marin County a little while later, David mused on the enormity of what we were trying to accomplish. He had started the grassroots effort less than two years earlier by writing to me after reading my article in *PS: Political Science and Politics.* "We might actually pull this off! Do you realize how big this could be?"

I nodded, "It's like a constitutional amendment, but without having to go through all of the hoops. Of course, this has some hoops of its own to get through. But, yes, the impact of this is going to be in that league. One might think of the American Plan as the Zeroth Amendment." Was it an audacious thing for a few unelected people to attempt, to change the constitution of a government . . . of the people, by the people, and for the people?

A couple of months later, replying to a message from Mark Trezza, chair of the Kings County DCC and an instructor at Fresno City College, I reflected:

> The American Plan is the only [presidential nomination plan] that utilizes both classes of organizational units in the federal legislative branch: the states and the sizes of their House delegations. As you know, the Framers were quite admiring of Newtonian physics and the developing science of engineering, and they delighted in finding ways to apply such interlocking mechanisms in our Constitution. However, no one can think of everything; they could not foresee political parties, much less that political parties would nominate their presidential candidates in a series of state plebiscites, dominated by instantaneous mass media and huge sums of money. As both an engineer and a political scientist, I have tried to "get into the heads" of these Enlightenment thinkers, and to come up with a solution that would have been in their vein of thinking had they been in a position to consider the problem. I don't claim to have thought of everything either, but if I'm lucky, the American Plan is a concept that will serve the nation for a few generations.[4]

If the magnitude of what the American Plan team of David Phelps, Damian Carroll, Marilyn Dudley-Rowley, Rob Richie and his FairVoters, others, and myself, as well as the Rotating Regional Plan and Delaware Plan teams, were attempting to accomplish was huge, so was the problem with which we were struggling. It had been growing worse through communal neglect for decades, at a rate below the stimulus response threshold of most policy makers and opinion leaders, while few raised an alarm over the impending calamity.

The 2008 Presidential Primaries: Another Inconvenient Truth

California Progress Report   *Berkeley Daily Planet*
18 December 2006   **19 December 2006**

Marin Independent Journal
By Thomas Gangale
29 December 2006

The 2006 elections are over, and the 2008 presidential race has begun. Most news coverage will focus on personalities, and once in a while on issues. What will go mostly unreported is the fact that we have a serious structural flaw in the presidential selection process that renders the issues and personalities almost superfluous. The "inconvenient truth" is that the primary/caucus system is an unfolding disaster, a bad process that produces presidential nominees who are less than America's best.

The problem is that every state wants to be first on the calendar. Being first means that all of the candidates desperately want to win your state to claim the mantle as the front-runner. Being later in the season means being ignored by the candidates; by then, one of them has locked up the nomination, and the campaign is already over.

Of course, as states shift their primaries and caucuses earlier in the calendar, Iowa and New Hampshire move their respective caucuses and primary forward to stay ahead of the pack. In 1972, New Hampshire held its primary on March 7. In 2004, the primary was held on January 19.

It's going to get worse before it gets . . . even worse. Earlier this year, when a bill was introduced in the California legislature to move its presidential primary ahead of all other states, to as early as January 2 if necessary, New Hampshire Secretary of State William Gardner threatened to thrust his state's primary into December. The best idea the Democratic Party can come up with to fix the problem only adds to it. In 2008, it is allowing Nevada's caucuses and South Carolina's primary to move near the front of the calendar.

So what? Why should you care when presidential primaries occur, or when the parties' nominees are determined?

In 1976, there were four months of competitive campaigning. The delegates from every state had to be selected before it was determined that Gerald Ford had survived Ronald Reagan's challenge. In 2004, when Dean suspended his campaign, only about one-fifth of the delegates had been selected from a handful of states. To eighty percent of the country, the Kerry nomination was a fait accompli. That's not democracy.

A shorter campaign season also means that any grassroots campaign operating on a shoestring budget is doomed from the start. There is no chance to score a few, early victories in small states where campaigning is inexpensive, leverage these to bring in more media attention and more campaign contributions, and thereby grow the campaign to be competitive in the later, larger, mass-media markets. The real campaign is not about courting votes, it's about counting cash. A Republican National Committee report lamented in May 2000, "It is an indisputable fact that in every nomination campaign since 1980, in both parties, the eventual party nominee was the candidate who had raised the most money by December 31 of the year before the general election." The early primaries dutifully rubber-stamp the decision of the donors. That's not democracy.

So, about a year from now, on December 31, 2007, the presidential nominees of the Democratic and Republican parties will be determined. Just count the money, then indulge in New Year's revelry as you may. The primaries and caucuses that follow will be an empty sham.

The curious thing is that so few have noticed that the real decision has been taken out of the hands of the voters. If, in one quadrennial cycle, was had gone from the campaign calendar of 1972 to that of 2004, we would, as Al Gore's frog, have immediately jumped out of the boiling pot. However, we have sat in that pot for thirty years without noticing that our democracy was slowly being cooked.

And it continues to cook. Since the report of the Herman-Price Commission in December 2005, the flames have grown ever fiercer. As of May 15, 2007, the following states had either moved their presidential nomination events to February 5, 2008, or were considering such a move: Alabama, Arizona, Arkansas, California, Colorado (caucuses), Connecticut, Delaware, Georgia, Illinois, Kansas, Michigan, Missouri, Montana, New Jersey, New Mexico, New York, North Carolina, Oklahoma, Oregon, Pennsylvania, Rhode Island, Tennessee, Texas, and Utah. These states comprise nearly two-thirds of the U.S. population. It's being called Tsunami Tuesday.[5]

On May 3, 2007, Florida took an audacious leap a week ahead of Tsunami Tuesday to January 29, 2008, in defiance of the rules of both national parties, betting that neither would dare not seat the delegation of the fourth most populous state. Florida's move puts its primary on the same day as the South Carolina Democratic primary; the Democratic National Committee, following the recommendations of the Herman-Price Commission, granted South Carolina the special status of moving into the pre-window period, a week behind the New Hampshire's January 22, 2008 primary, but at least a week ahead of any others. With the importance of its primary now swamped by the much more populous Sunshine State, South Carolina is threatening to move a week forward to protect its newly won special status. If South Carolina does move a week forward, however, that will put its primary on the same day as New Hampshire's, and the Granite State will move a week ahead as well. Since in February 2007 the Wyoming Republican Party voted to tie its county conventions to the same date as the New Hampshire primary,[6] these would advance automatically with any change the Granite State might make. The moves by New Hampshire and Wyoming would put them into conflict with the Iowa caucuses, scheduled for January 14, 2008, as of this writing, which would almost certainly move a week forward to January 7, 2008.

It's bad enough as it is, but it might not stop there. There is still plenty of time for other states to move their primaries to January 29, 2008, or even earlier. If Florida can get away with it, why can't others? The anarchic nature of the system should be apparent to everyone at this point. Tom Sansonetti, who pushed for the Wyoming GOP's aggressive stance, believes that the national parties have lost control of the nomination calendar, and he has come to the reluctant conclusion that the only hope is for Congress to step in with legislation.[7] This is a radical departure from the Republican Party's philosophy that the parties ought to have the right to self-regulate free of Congressional interference, and it may be taken as an indicator of a rising level of desperation. Meanwhile, the only legislation introduced in the One Hundred Tenth Congress as of May 31, 2007, is Sander Levin's resurrection of his twenty-year-old Interregional Primary concept, and in the three months since he introduced it he has picked up no cosponsors.

There are those who view these events with hope that we are moving haphazardly toward a *de facto* single-day national primary, which they view as a good thing. It is not. Moreover, even if a single-day national primary were a worthy goal, the way we are going does not lead to it. Absent a decision by national entities—either the parties or Congress—to bring order to chaos, states will continue to go their own way, and always leading this charge will be the Chosen People of Iowa and New Hampshire. But there can be no firsts among equals. The lesson of 2004 is that Howard Dean stumbled in Iowa, fell in New Hampshire, and never got back up, so it is in these states, and possibly also now in Nevada, South Carolina, and Florida that the candidates will spend the most time and money. Per capita, only a pittance will be spent on the February 5 states, for by then the contest will be decided. The two-thirds of the country that votes on that date will have only the appearance of a meaningful choice...if that.

It may be that the flame under the pot is now being turned up so quickly, the changes to the presidential nomination schedule coming so rapidly, that the frogs are starting to jump. In January 2007, I began working with Rob Richie and Bill Brock to produce an op-ed for the former senator's byline. What ended up being published in *Roll Call* on March 6 was quite a bit different than my draft, in which I developed the "tragedy of the commons" concept I had discussed with Oregon Secretary of State, Bill Bradury, in Santa Fe.

The Presidential Primary Calendar: A Tragedy of the Commons

Draft Op-Ed
By Thomas Gangale
12 January 2007

In less than a year, Iowa will kick off the voting for the major parties' presidential nominations. The race may be effectively over long before most states vote.

The problem is that every state wants to be first on the presidential nomination calendar. Being first means that all of the candidates desperately want to win your state to claim the mantle as the front-runner. Being later in the season means being ignored by the candidates; by then, one of them has locked up the nomination, the campaign is over, and your vote is meaningless.

Ironically, as more states have rushed their primaries and caucuses to the front of the calendar, it has resulted in fewer states having meaningful participation in the process. The voters in a few privileged states in the early contests have as many as a dozen candidates from which to choose. For the vast majority of Americans, there is no choice at all . . . until November, and then the choice is between the two major party nominees whom the privileged have chosen for the rest of us.

The presidential nomination calendar is a classic "tragedy of the commons," a phrase popularized by Garrett Hardin in the 1960s. "Picture a pasture open to all. It is to be expected that each herdsman will try to keep as many cattle as possible on the commons. . . . As a rational being, each herdsman seeks to maximize his gain. . . . [H]e asks, 'What is the utility to me of adding one more animal to my herd?' This utility has one negative and one positive component." The positive component is that the herdsman profits from that additional animal; the negative component is the additional grazing of the pasture. "Since, however, the effects of overgrazing are shared by all the herdsmen, the negative utility for any particular decision-making herdsman" is only a fraction of its positive utility. Eventually, the result of these incremental, self-seeking decisions is the ruin of the pasture.

This is exactly what has happened to our presidential nomination process over the past several decades. Each state has sought to maximize its own advantage, to the detriment of the nation as a whole. They have overgrazed the commons of the calendar, and the American voter lives in electoral starvation.

The solution to this tragedy of the calendar is the same as for the overgrazed pasture; the interested parties must cooperate in the common interest, and institute a system of managing the commons in a rational manner for the benefit of all. The best way to accomplish this is through a coordinated change to the rules and bylaws of the two major political parties. Both are aware of the problem, and since each has made attempts to solve the problem on its own, sometimes actually exacerbating the problem, both parties are also aware that they must cooperate to solve the problem.

What is lacking is the political will to do so, and the media and civic organizations bear some responsibility for this. Cooperation does not come naturally to the parties, and cooperation entails political risks. The media and the public must signal to the parties that cooperation is worth the risk. There must be a vigorous public discussion on solving this tragedy of the commons.

The Democratic National Committee and the Republican National Committee are waiting to hear from you.

Nation's Presidential Primary Calendar Is a Political Tragedy

Roll Call
By Bill Brock
6 March 2007

In less than a year, Iowa will kick off the voting for the major parties' presidential nominations. A month later, the race may be effectively over—long before most states vote. As a result we have almost unwittingly allowed the evolution of a system for nominating our next president that leaves most Americans out of the process, emphasizing money, surface appearances and media appeal over careful analysis. This fact reflects a dangerous lapse on the part of both national political parties.

The problem is that every state wants to be first on the presidential nomination calendar. Why not? Being first means that all of the candidates desperately want to win your state to claim the mantle as the front-runner. That not only gives your state a great deal of free media attention, but a lot of cash as reporters and camera operators join candidates, staff and countless volunteers rushing back and forth in their desperate quest for that critical "one more vote." Being later in the season (which now may effectively mean having your primary or caucus anytime after February) means being ignored by the candidates, for by then, one of them has locked up the nomination, the campaign is over and your vote is meaningless.

Ironically, voters in these few privileged states in the early contests will have as many as a dozen candidates from which to choose. For the rest of us, for the vast majority of Americans, there will be no choice at all ... until November, when the choice is solely between the two major party nominees whom the privileged have chosen for the rest of us.

The refusal to address this inexcusable situation is but a reflection of the fact that too many political "leaders" these days are not willing to lead on matters that require the taking of risk. It is no challenge to act on "easy" or "popular" matters, for one can do so by simply taking advantage of one's position as a member of the majority party. Republicans did so in the past six years, Democrats will do so in the next two.

Taking action on hard matters, on the other hand, can happen only when there is bipartisan determination to do so. That requires members in both parties to lay aside partisan differences, cross the political aisle and work with their counterparts to craft a solution in the national, as opposed to their parochial, interest. That the two national parties remain unable or unwilling to prevent our steady slide into this dangerously unrepresentative "devil take the hindmost" presidential nomination system is shameful.

A coordinated change to the rules and bylaws of the two major political parties is thus essential. Admittedly, cooperation does not come naturally to the parties, and yes, cooperation entails political risks. Yet six years ago, virtually every former chairman of the Republican National Committee worked as part of a national commission of political leaders to address this need. We crafted something we called the Delaware plan, which would revamp the schedule to have small states vote first, then gradually larger states, but with the most delegates awarded in the final set of primaries to give big states a central role as well. More time for thoughtful consideration by all voters, more opportunity for lesser-known candidates to establish their credentials, more one-on-one contact, less emphasis on big money at the outset, less danger of denying the later states a voice—all this and more, not a bad combination.

Importantly, many thoughtful Democratic leaders were very much involved in working alongside us. The effort collapsed when I was unable to put the matter to the 2000 Republican National Convention—for reasons largely unrelated to the subject at hand. Now the California Democratic Party has embraced the American plan, a proposal with a similar goal that regularly changes the order of primaries and gives large-population states a shot at an earlier primary. In sum, the subject is not yet dead, but it clearly remains on life support.

I still like the Delaware plan as being the most equitable to all states, and the one that gives all our citizens a full voice in the selection of our political leaders. Yet almost any rational proposal would result in a much better balance than today's increasingly broken system, one that will within the next 12 months disenfranchise the majority of the American people from the nominations process of both major parties. Inexcusable? Yes, absolutely.

The bottom line: Continued inaction is unworthy of this nation, much less of our two great parties.

In the spring of 2007, a number of prominent bullfrogs took up the chorus. George F. Will wrote on March 15:

> The parties could create less helter-skelter processes. One proposed plan would divide the nation into four regions voting at monthly intervals, with the order of voting rotated every four years. Another plan, which would not provoke the Almighty, would preserve Iowa and New Hampshire's solitary grandeur as places where the least well-known and well-funded candidates find the lowest barriers to entry into contention. Then voting would occur over 10 two-week intervals, with the largest states coming last, or in some randomized or rotating clusters.[8]

David S. Broder, a long-time critic of the process, wrote on May 10, 2007, a week after Florida announced its move:

> The mandate for the next pair of national party chairmen should be to agree on a sensible national agenda for the primaries—either a rotating regional system that gives all states a turn at being early or a plan that allows a random mix of states to vote, but only on dates fixed in advance by the parties, and separated at intervals that allow voters to consider seriously their choices.[9]

Hendrik Hertzberg's device of discussing the presidential nomination calendar in terms of the small "c" constitution of the United States neatly captured the scope of the issue in his April 16, 2007 article in the *New Yorker:*

> Over the past few months, the constitution of the United States has been quietly amended. We're not talking here about the written, capital-"C" Constitution, which can't be changed on the sly, but about the constitution broadly understood: the rules and procedures by which our government is constituted. A lot of that constitution is outside the Constitution, notably when it comes to elections. The framers' document makes no mention of parties, primaries, or nominating conventions—understandably, as they hadn't been invented yet. Article II, Section 1, which is about "chusing the President," has plenty to say about electors' meeting "in their respective States," and making "a List of all the Persons voted for," and signing, certifying, and sealing their Lists before sending them on to "the Seat of the Government." But it says nothing about political campaigns, political parties, or nominating conventions—let alone about sound bites, thirty-second spots, bundled contributions, or independent expenditures, any one of which has more effect on who gets "chusen" than all the signing, sealing, and certifying on earth. . . .
>
> This year's informal constitutional amendment is a radical revision of the political calendar. For several election cycles, states have been pushing, more

or less politely, toward the front of the primary-season queue. This time, all semblance of good manners has been abandoned. We've stampeded ourselves over a cliff into a yearlong primary campaign climaxing next February 5th, when as many as twenty-two states, representing sixty per cent of the nation's population and a like proportion of the two parties' Convention delegates, will hold their primaries all at once. . . .

The closest anyone has come to cutting the Gordian knot of the primaries was a little-known effort in 2000. A group of Republican grandees led by Bill Brock, a former senator from Tennessee and national party chairman, spent months hammering out what was dubbed the Delaware Plan, which, beginning in 2004, would have mandated four sets of primaries, a month apart, beginning with the small states (twelve of them, including New Hampshire) and ending with the largest (which would pick a majority of the total delegates). . . . Various other ideas—revolving regional primaries, for example, or randomly chosen primaries at two-week intervals—continue to float around. Eventually, though, Congress will probably have to take the lead in sorting out the mess.[10]

Significantly, each of these articles is mentioned the American Plan in concept if not by name. We had become a subject of national conversation. The *Philadelphia Inquirer*, which had published my first op-ed in 1999, focused on the American Plan to the exclusion of all others in its March 18, 2007, editorial:

One reform proposal gaining favor is the "America Plan," which has the goal of creating a nominating process that is more competitive over a longer period of time. . . .

By focusing at the start on states with smaller populations and smaller media markets, candidates with less money might not be forced out of the race early. A shorter interval between the last primary and the party conventions would help to maintain voter interest in the campaign.

For a rational system such as the American Plan to be in place for 2012, the national parties should approve it at their 2008 conventions. Congress would then need to approve legislation formalizing the new system. A rare moment such as now, with no incumbent president or vice president running for office, is the best possible time for reform of a dumb system.[11]

ALL OUR YESTERDAYS

Speaking on the advantages of the Delaware Plan, former chairman of the RNC Rules Committee, Tom Sansonetti, declared that letting the smallest states begin the contest "allows a grassroots campaign to catch fire. The Jimmy Carter example in '76, the Gary Hart example from '84, the Eugene McCarthy example for that matter in 1968."[12] The fact that the chairman of a Republican committee would refer to the campaigns of three Democrats eloquently bespeaks the bipartisan reach of this issue. Not to be overlooked, however, is George McGovern's prairie progressive populist victory over party insiders in 1972, the large measure of success with which Ronald Reagan challenged Gerald Ford in 1976, and his Western conservative populist victory over Republican apparatchik George Bush in 1980. Moreover, an interesting question is, if the American Plan had been in place in those years, would it have been conducive to the candidacies of Eugene McCarthy, George McGovern, Jimmy Carter, Ronald Reagan, or Gary Hart?

Let us embark on a voyage through time. First of all, let us look ahead to the 2008 caucus and primary schedule that is taking shape (see Figure 14.1). On February 5, 2008, about two-thirds of the delegates to both national conventions will be selected. The total movement in the schedule versus the previous election cycle is unprecedented in history.

Now let us travel back through the past, stopping at each presidential election year. Figures 14.2 through Figures 14.8 carry us through the years, and we can see that with the exception of 1992, in every case the schedule has been more front-loaded than in the preceding cycle. The year 1992 marked a momentary retreat from the front-loading of 1998; however the advent of Super Tuesday in 1988 marked an unprecedented surge in front-loading, and 1992's slight pullback war far from being a return to the 1984 schedule.

Figure 14.9 compares the Democratic and Republican delegate selection schedules for national conventions in 1976 with the American Plan schedule. This is the "ahh" slide to which Marilyn Dudley-Rowley referred in regard to the July 2006 presentation to NASS in Santa Fe. The fidelity with which the American Plan reproduces the schedule profiles for 1976 is nothing short of startling. The time-phasing of delegate selection processes for 1960 through 1972 was no great departure from the 1976 schedule, and so those years also track very well with the American Plan profile. We can answer the question definitively: could a Eugene McCarthy or a Jimmy Carter have made a successful run under an American Plan schedule, and could a Ronald Reagan have challenged the sitting president from his party? Actually . . . *they did!* And, it is the same schedule by which Robert Kennedy would have won the Democratic nomination.

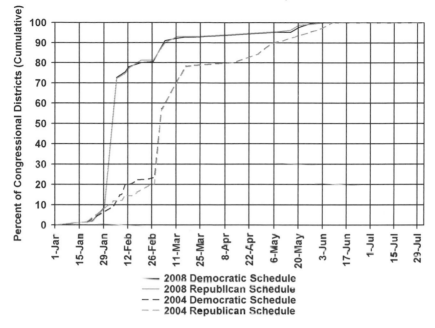

Figure 14.1: 2004 and 2008 schedules compared. *Source:* NASS.

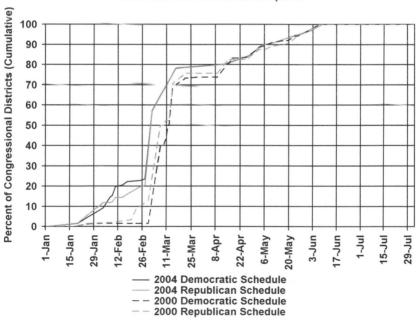

Figure 14.2: 2000 and 2004 schedules compared. *Source:* Appleman 2000.

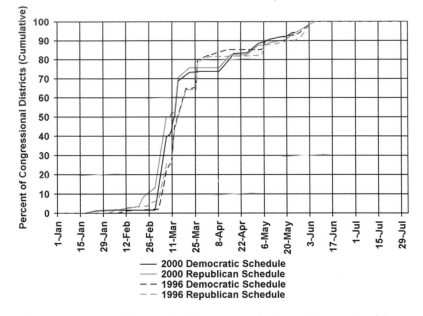

Figure 14.3: 1996 and 2000 schedules compared. *Source: Congressional Quarterly* 1996; Appleman 2000.

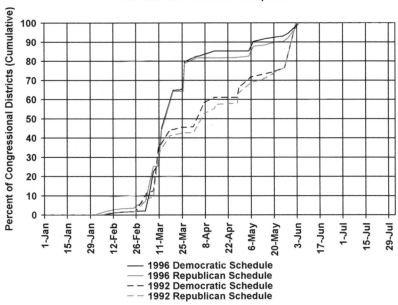

Figure 14.4: 1992 and 1996 schedules compared. *Sources: Congressional Quarterly* 1992a, 1992b, 1992c, 1992d, 1996.

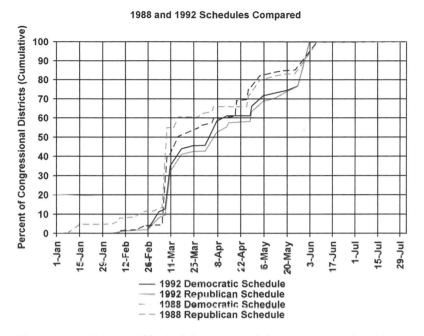

Figure 14.5: 1988 and 1992 schedules compared. *Sources: Congressional Quarterly* 1988a, 1988b, 1988c, 1992a, 1992b, 1992c, 1992d.

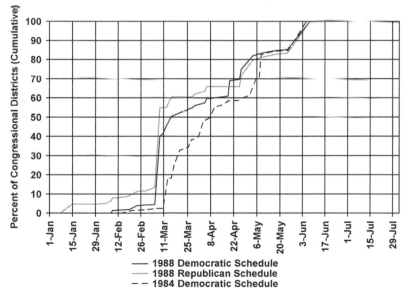

Figure 14.6: 1984 and 1988 schedules compared. *Sources: Congressional Quarterly* 1984a, 1984b, 1988a, 1988b, 1988c.

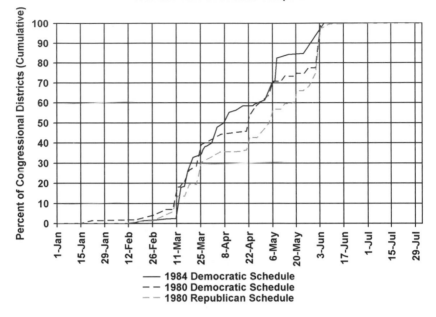

Figure 14.7: 1980 and 1984 schedules compared. *Sources: Congressional Quarterly* 1980a, 1980b, 1980c, 1980d, 1984a, 1984b.

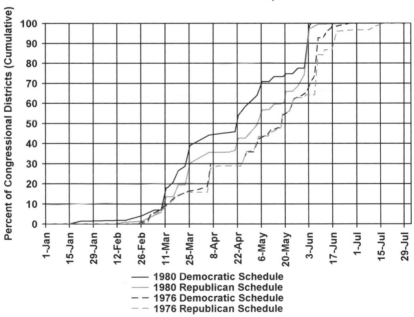

Figure 14.8: 1976 and 1980 schedules compared. *Sources: Congressional Quarterly* 1976a, 1976b, 1976c, 1980a, 1980b, 1980c, 1980d.

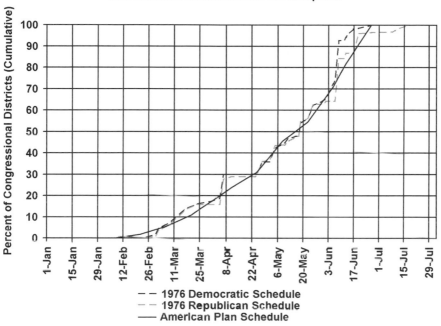

Figure 14.9: 1976 schedule and American plan compared. *Sources: Congressional Quarterly* 1976a, 1976b, 1976c.

THE VOYAGE HOME

We began our exploration of the presidential nomination process in 1968, with Eugene McCarthy's near-upset in New Hampshire, the assassination of Robert Kennedy in Los Angeles, and the riot outside the Democratic National Convention in Chicago, and it seems that we have made a round trip, for to 1968 we have returned, holding up as examples of insurgent campaigns Bobby Kennedy and Gene McCarthy. Rage—over the nomination of Hubert Humphrey without ever facing the voters, over the unending grief of an unwinnable war, over hopes murdered by assassins' bullets— touched off the riot and fanned its flames. Out of the ashes arose a resolve to reform the presidential nomination process, and to give that process to the people. The whole world was watching. For a few short years, those reforms made possible outsider candidacies such as George McGovern, Jimmy Carter, Ronald Reagan, and Gary Hart. In his nomination acceptance speech at the 1972 Democratic National Convention in Miami, Senator McGovern exhorted, "Come home, America." Now, after our travels through time, the way home is clear, home to that era of reform, when America had a deliberative process for choosing its presidential nominees and did not rush to judgment based on slickly packaged sound bites and infomercial blitzes. The American Plan can bring America home; it can bring the nomination of its presidents home to its people—where it belongs.

However, while such a structural reform is necessary, it is not sufficient for restoring American democracy. We must be mindful that every home needs a homemaker, thus bringing America home will require every American to be a homemaker of democracy. It is no easy occupation; there is mind-numbing drudgery, there are thankless tasks. There are also the rewards of accomplishment, but they are almost never immediate and they are the resultants of a thousand disparate acts. We are the parents of democracy although we grew up as its children, for the American Revolution renews itself with each generation. But the process of renewal can be discordant, and its outcome dysfunctional, when we don't recognize our parental role or take our responsibilities seriously. Today we see all around us the havoc that our neglect has wrought. I regret that I have come to realize this rather late in life, but having realized at last, I have tried to tell what I have learned and what I hope is a way toward putting our house in order. If you think otherwise, that's good; grab a broom and push your own ideas for all they're worth. It's your house, too, and democracy is everyone's child.

NOTES

1. Gangale, Thomas. 2006. E-mail, July 11.
2. Dudley-Rowley, Marilyn. 2006. E-mail, July 11.
3. Bysiewicz, Susan. 2007. "Bysiewicz Stands Up for Connecticut Voters—Proposes Feb. 5th Presidential Primary Day: Sec. of the State Says Current Primary Process is 'Broken,' Calls for Reform." News release, March 27. Available from http://www.sots.ct.gov/releases/2007/03-27-07PrimaryDateMoves.pdf; accessed April 6, 2007.
4. Gangale, Thomas. 2007. E-mail, March 20.
5. Todd, Chuck. 2007. "Will Tsunami Tuesday Be an Afterthought?" MSNBC.com, May 10. Available from http://www.msnbc.msn.com/id/18593870/; accessed May 30, 2007.
6. Barron, Joan. 2007. "Wyo GOP Wants Early 2008 Presidential Pick." *Casper Star-Tribune*, February 6. Available from http://www.casperstartribune.net/articles/2007/02/06/news/wyoming/7de7f01615c29bd48725727a000b91a2.txt; accessed February 6, 2007.
7. Gangale, Thomas. 2007. E-mail, January 18.

8. Will, George F. 2007. "Why This Primary Push?" *Washington Post*, March 15. Available from http://www.washingtonpost.com/wp-dyn/content/article/2007/03/14/AR2007031402176.html; accessed March 18, 2007.

9. Broder, David S. 2007. "No Way to Choose a President." *Washington Post*, May 10. Available from http://www.washingtonpost.com/wp-dyn/content/article/2007/05/09/AR2007050902445.html; accessed May 10, 2007.

10. Hertzberg, Hendrik. 2007 "Pileup." *New Yorker*, April 16. Available from http://www.newyorker.com/talk/comment/2007/04/16/070416taco_talk_hertzberg; accessed April 14, 2007.

11. *Philadelphia Inquirer*, 2007. "Move the Vote Forward: Of Primary Concern in PA." March 18. Available from http://www.philly.com/inquirer/opinion/20070318_Editorial___Move_the_Vote_Forward.html; accessed March 18, 2007.

12. University of Virginia, Center for Governmental Studies. 2001. *Report of the National Symposium on Presidential Selection*, 18. Charlottesville: University of Virginia. Available from http://www.centerforpolitics.org/reform/nssreport_entire.pdf; accessed January 4, 2003.

APPENDIX 1: MODEL STATE BILL FOR IMPLEMENTING THE GRADUATED RANDOM PRESIDENTIAL PRIMARY SYSTEM

A BILL

To provide for primary elections and caucuses for selection of delegates to political party Presidential nominating conventions.

SECTION 1. SHORT TITLE.

This Act may be cited as the "Graduated Random Presidential Primary Act of ___."

SECTION 2. FINDINGS AND DECLARATION.

The people of the state of ___ acting through their elected legislative representation find and declare that:

(a) The quadrennial election of the President and Vice President of the United States is among the most important civic acts of the voters of the State of ___.

(b) The Process leading to the nomination of candidates for President and Vice President of the United States should be as open and participatory as possible.

(c) It will enhance voter participation, strengthen the political process and protect the rights of all states and their citizens to have a coordinated, orderly and defined electoral schedule.

(d) The State of ___ will participate in a graduated random presidential primary system as defined herein.

SECTION 3. DEFINITIONS.

In this Act:

(1) DISTRICT—The term "district" means-
   1. Each district having representation in the House of Representatives.
   2. The District of Columbia, the Commonwealth of Puerto Rico, and the Territories of American Samoa, Guam, and the Virgin Islands shall each count as one district for the purposes of this Act.
(2) ELECTION YEAR—The term 'election year' means a year during which a Presidential election is to be held.
(3) NATIONAL COMMITTEE—The term 'national committee' means the organization which, by virtue of the bylaws of a political party, is responsible for the day-to-day operation of such political party at the national level, as determined by the Federal Election Commission.
(4) OTHER JURISDICTION—The term 'other jurisdiction' means District of Columbia, the Commonwealth of Puerto Rico, and the Territories of American Samoa, Guam, and the Virgin Islands.
(5) POLITICAL PARTY—The term 'political party' means an association, committee, or organization which-
   1. Nominates a candidate for election to any Federal office whose name appears on the election ballot as the candidate of such association, committee, or organization; and
   2. Won electoral votes in the preceding Presidential election.
(6) PRIMARY—The term 'primary' means an official primary election conducted or sanctioned by the State of ___ held in any year that is evenly divisible by the number four at which delegations to a national Presidential nominating convention of a political party are to be chosen.
(7) STATE COMMITTEE—The term "State committee" means the organization which, by virtue of the bylaws of a political party, is responsible for the day-to-day operation of such political party at the level of the State or other jurisdiction, as determined by the Federal Election Commission.
(8) STATE LAW—The term 'State law' means the law of a State, the District of Columbia, the Commonwealth of Puerto Rico, or the Territories of American Samoa, Guam, and the Virgin Islands.

SECTION 4. SELECTION OF DELEGATES TO CONVENTIONS.

The delegates to each national convention for the nomination of candidates of a political party for the offices of President and Vice President shall be selected by primary election, as provided by State law. Such State law shall conform to the requirements of the national committee and the national nominating convention of the political party involved.

SECTION 5. SCHEDULE.

(a) PARTICIPATION IN THE NATIONAL SCHEDULE—Notwithstanding any other provision of the law to the contrary, the State of ___, consistent with its decision to participate in the Graduated Random Presidential Primary System, as defined in this section, shall hold its presidential primary not sooner than the first Tuesday of the interval assigned to the State of ___ by the National Association of Secretaries of State, but in no case later than the last Tuesday of the interval assigned, according to the system defined in this section.

(b) DEFINITION OF DELEGATE SELECTION INTERVALS AND STATE ELIGIBILITY—The schedule for the selection of delegates shall consist of ten consecutive intervals of time, defined as follows—

    (1) The duration of Interval 1 shall be 14 days. During Interval 1, delegates shall be chosen from randomly assigned States and other jurisdictions whose aggregate number of districts is 8.

    (2) The duration of Interval 2 shall be 14 days. During Interval 2, delegates shall be chosen from randomly assigned States and other jurisdictions whose aggregate number of districts is 16.

    (3) The duration of Interval 3 shall be 21 days. During Interval 3, delegates shall be chosen from randomly assigned States and other jurisdictions whose aggregate number of districts is 24.

    (4) The duration of Interval 4 shall be 14 days. During Interval 4, delegates shall be chosen from randomly assigned States and other jurisdictions whose aggregate number of districts is 56.

    (5) The duration of Interval 5 shall be 14 days. During Interval 5, delegates shall be chosen from randomly assigned States and other jurisdictions whose aggregate number of districts is 32.

    (6) The duration of Interval 6 shall be 14 days. During Interval 6, delegates shall be chosen from randomly assigned States and other jurisdictions whose aggregate number of districts is 64.

    (7) The duration of Interval 7 shall be 14 days. During Interval 7, delegates shall be chosen from randomly assigned States and other jurisdictions whose aggregate number of districts is 40.

    (8) The duration of Interval 8 shall be 14 days. During Interval 8, delegates shall be chosen from randomly assigned States and other jurisdictions whose aggregate number of districts is 72.

    (9) The duration of Interval 9 shall be 7 days. During Interval 9, delegates shall be chosen from randomly assigned States and other jurisdictions whose aggregate number of districts is 48.

    (10) The duration of Interval 10 shall be 14 days. During Interval 10, delegates shall be chosen from randomly assigned States and other jurisdictions whose aggregate number of districts is 80.

(c) The tenth and last interval shall end on the last Saturday of June in a year in which Electors shall be chosen for President and Vice-President.

(d) The National Association of Secretaries of State shall administer the random process by which States and other jurisdictions are assigned to delegate selection intervals.

SECTION 6. VOTING AT NATIONAL PARTY CONVENTIONS BY STATE DELEGATES.

(a) PROPORTIONAL REPRESENTATION—The [appropriate State committee] shall establish a procedure for the apportionment of delegates to the national Presidential nominating convention of each political party, in which the results of the State primary are used to allocate members of the State delegation or Congressional district delegation (or combination thereof) to the national convention, to Presidential candidates based on the proportion of the vote for all of the candidates received in the primary in the State or other jurisdiction.

(b) SELECTION OF DELEGATES-

    (1) SUBMISSION OF NAMES—Not later than the date on which a candidate is certified on the ballot for the State of ___, such candidate shall submit to the [appropriate State committee], in priority order, a list of names of individuals proposed by the candidate to serve as delegates for such candidate.

    (2) SELECTION—Delegates apportioned to represent a candidate pursuant to the procedure established under subsection (a) shall be selected according to the list submitted by the candidate pursuant to paragraph (1).

(c) VOTING AT THE NATIONAL CONVENTIONS—Each delegate to a national convention who is required to vote for the winner of the State primary under the system established under subsection (a) shall so vote for at least 2 ballots at the national convention, unless released by the winner of the State primary to which such delegate's vote is pledged.

APPENDIX 2: THE GRADUATED RANDOM PRESIDENTIAL PRIMARY AND CAUCUS ACT

A BILL

To provide for primary elections and caucuses for selection of delegates to political party Presidential nominating conventions.

Be it enacted by the Senate and House of Representatives of the United States of America in Congress assembled,

SECTION 1. SHORT TITLE.

This Act may be cited as the Graduated Random Presidential Primary and Caucus Act of____.

SECTION 2. DEFINITIONS.

In this Act:

(1) CAUCUS—The term "caucus" means any convention, meeting, or series of meetings held for the selection of delegates to a national Presidential nominating convention of a political party.

(2) DISTRICT—The term "district" means—

    (A) Each district having representation in the House of Representatives.

    (B) The District of Columbia, the Commonwealth of Puerto Rico, and the Territories of American Samoa, Guam, and the Virgin Islands shall each count as one district for the purposes of this Act.

(3) ELECTION YEAR. The term "election year" means a year during which a Presidential election is to be held.

(4) NATIONAL COMMITTEE—The term "national committee" means the organization which, by virtue of the bylaws of a political party, is responsible for the day-to-day operation of such political party at the national level, as determined by the Federal Election Commission.

(5) OTHER JURISDICTION—The term "other jurisdiction" means District of Columbia, the Commonwealth of Puerto Rico, and the Territories of American Samoa, Guam, and the Virgin Islands.

(6) POLITICAL PARTY—The term "political party" means an association, committee, or organization which—

(A) Nominates a candidate for election to any Federal office whose name appears on the election ballot as the candidate of such association, committee, or organization; and

(B) Won electoral votes in the preceding Presidential election.

(7) PRIMARY—The term "primary" means a primary election held for the selection of delegates to a national Presidential nominating convention of a political party, but does not include a caucus, convention, or other indirect means of selection.

(8) STATE COMMITTEE. The term "State committee" means the organization which, by virtue of the bylaws of a political party, is responsible for the day-to-day operation of such political party at the level of the State or other jurisdiction, as determined by the Federal Election Commission.

(9) STATE LAW—The term "State law" means the law of a State, the District of Columbia, the Commonwealth of Puerto Rico, or the Territories of American Samoa, Guam, and the Virgin Islands.

SECTION 3. SELECTION OF DELEGATES TO CONVENTIONS.

The delegates to each national convention for the nomination of candidates of a political party for the offices of President and Vice President shall be selected by primary election or by caucus, as provided by State law. Such State law shall conform to the requirements of the national committee and the national nominating convention of the political party involved.

SECTION 4. SCHEDULE.

(a) DEFINITION OF DELEGATE SELECTION INTERVALS AND STATE ELIGIBILITY—The schedule for the selection of delegates shall consist of ten consecutive intervals of time, defined as follows—

(1) The duration of Interval 1 shall be 14 days. During Interval 1, delegates shall be chosen from randomly assigned States and other jurisdictions whose aggregate number of districts is 8.

(2) The duration of Interval 2 shall be 14 days. During Interval 2, delegates shall be chosen from randomly assigned States and other jurisdictions whose aggregate number of districts is 16.

(3) The duration of Interval 3 shall be 21 days. During Interval 3, delegates shall be chosen from randomly assigned States and other jurisdictions whose aggregate number of districts is 24.

(4) The duration of Interval 4 shall be 14 days. During Interval 4, delegates shall be chosen from randomly assigned States and other jurisdictions whose aggregate number of districts is 56.

(5) The duration of Interval 5 shall be 14 days. During Interval 5, delegates shall be chosen from randomly assigned States and other jurisdictions whose aggregate number of districts is 32.

(6) The duration of Interval 6 shall be 14 days. During Interval 6, delegates shall be chosen from randomly assigned States and other jurisdictions whose aggregate number of districts is 64.

(7) The duration of Interval 7 shall be 14 days. During Interval 7, delegates shall be chosen from randomly assigned States and other jurisdictions whose aggregate number of districts is 40.

(8) The duration of Interval 8 shall be 14 days. During Interval 8, delegates shall be chosen from randomly assigned States and other jurisdictions whose aggregate number of districts is 72.

(9) The duration of Interval 9 shall be 7 days. During Interval 9, delegates shall be chosen from randomly assigned States and other jurisdictions whose aggregate number of districts is 48.

(10) The duration of Interval 10 shall be 14 days. During Interval 10, delegates shall be chosen from randomly assigned States and other jurisdictions whose aggregate number of districts is 80.

(b) The tenth and last interval shall end on the last Saturday of June in a year in which Electors shall be chosen for President and Vice-President.

(c) Each State or other jurisdiction shall choose delegates on a day, determined by each State or other jurisdiction, which day shall be within the assigned interval, but which shall not be required to be the same day throughout all of the States and other jurisdictions assigned to the specified interval.

(d) The Federal Election Commission shall administer the random process by which States and other jurisdictions are assigned to delegate selection intervals.

SECTION 5. QUALIFICATION FOR BALLOT.

(a) CERTIFICATION BY FEDERAL ELECTION COMMISSION—The Federal Election Commission shall certify to the States and other

jurisdictions the names of all seriously considered candidates of each political party—

(1) For the first primary in the election year, not later than 6 weeks before
such primary; and

(2) In the subsequent primaries in the election year, not later than one
week after the preceding primary in such election year.

(b) STATE PRIMARY BALLOTS—Each State or other jurisdiction shall include on its primary ballot—

(1) The names certified by the Federal Election Commission; and

(2) Any other names determined by the appropriate State committee.

SECTION 6. VOTING AT NATIONAL PARTY CONVENTIONS BY STATE DELEGATES.

(a) PROPORTIONAL REPRESENTATION—Each State committee shall
establish a procedure for the apportionment of delegates to the national
Presidential nominating convention of each political party, in which the
results of the State primary are used to allocate members of the State
delegation or Congressional district delegation (or combination thereof) to
the national convention, to Presidential candidates based on the proportion
of the vote for all of the candidates received in the primary in the State or
other jurisdiction.

(b) SELECTION OF DELEGATES—

(1) SUBMISSION OF NAMES—Not later than the date on which a
candidate is certified on the ballot for a State or other jurisdiction,
such candidate shall submit to the State committee, in priority order,
a list of names of individuals proposed by the candidate to serve as
delegates for such candidate.

(2) SELECTION—Delegates apportioned to represent a candidate pursuant to the procedure established under subsection (a) shall be selected
according to the list submitted by the candidate pursuant to paragraph
(1).

(c) VOTING AT THE NATIONAL CONVENTIONS—Each delegate to
a national convention who is required to vote for the winner of the State
primary under the system established under subsection (a) shall so vote for
at least 2 ballots at the national convention, unless released by the winner
of the State primary to which such delegate's vote is pledged.

SECTION 7. OPTIONAL STATE CAUCUS TO SELECT DELEGATES.

(a) ELECTION—Instead of, or in addition to, holding the primary required
under section 6, a State or other jurisdiction may elect to select delegates

to a national Presidential nominating convention of a political party in accordance with this section, through a caucus held by any political party which has the authority to nominate a candidate.

(b) SCHEDULE—A State or other jurisdiction that makes an election under subsection (a) shall ensure that the caucus does not commence earlier than the date such State or other jurisdiction otherwise would be required to hold a primary under section 4.

(c) QUALIFICATION FOR BALLOT—A State committee of a political party that holds a caucus shall certify and include candidates in the same manner provided under section 5.

(d) VOTING AT NATIONAL PARTY CONVENTIONS BY STATE DELEGATES—Each State committee shall establish a procedure for the apportionment of delegates to the national Presidential nominating convention of each political party, in which the results of the State caucus are used to allocate members of the State delegation or Congressional district delegation (or combination thereof) to the national convention, to Presidential candidates based on the proportion of the vote for all of the candidates received in the primary in the State or other jurisdiction.

SECTION 8. ENFORCEMENT.

The Attorney General may bring a civil action in any appropriate United States district court for such declaratory or injunctive relief as may be necessary to carry out this Act.

SECTION 9. REGULATIONS.

The Federal Election Commission shall prescribe such regulations as may be necessary to carry out this Act.

SECTION 10. EFFECTIVE DATE.

This Act shall apply with respect to Presidential elections taking place more than 2 years after the date of the enactment of this Act.

INDEX

About the Author

THOMAS GANGALE is the author of the American Plan for reforming the presidential nomination process, which is gaining support within the National Association of Secretaries of State and the national and state committees of both parties and on the editorial pages of national newspapers, including *The New York Times*.